State and Local
Government

State and Local Government

The Political Economy of Reform

Edited by
Alan K. Campbell
and
Roy W. Bahl

THE FREE PRESS

A Division of Macmillan Publishing Co., Inc.
NEW YORK

Collier Macmillan Publishers
LONDON

The Free Press
A Division of Macmillan Publishing Co., Inc.
866 Third Avenue, New York, N.Y. 10022

Collier Macmillan Canada, Ltd.

Library of Congress Catalog Card Number: 75–43361

Printed in the United States of America

printing number

1 2 3 4 5 6 7 8 9 10

Library of Congress Cataloging in Publication Data
Main entry under title:

State and local governments.

  Includes bibliographical references and index.
  1. Local government--United States--Addresses, essays,
lectures. 2. Municipal services--United States--Ad-
dresses, essays, lectures. 3. State governments--Ad-
dresses, essays, lectures. I. Campbell, Alan K.
II. Bahl, Roy W.
JS323.S78   352.073   75-43361
ISBN 0-02-905180-0

Contents

List of Contributors

Roy Bahl is Professor of Economics and Director, Metropolitan Studies Program, The Maxwell School, Syracuse University.

Norman Beckman is the Acting Director of the Congressional Research Service, Library of Congress.

Guthrie Birkhead is Professor of Political Science and Associate Dean, The Maxwell School, Syracuse University.

Jesse Burkhead is Professor of Economics, The Maxwell School, Syracuse University.

Ruth Bosek is Research Associate, Advisory Commission on Intergovernmental Relations.

John Callahan is Director, Legislator's Education-Action Project, National Conference of State Legislatures.

Alan K. Campbell is Professor of Political Science and Dean, The Maxwell School, Syracuse University.

Young Hyo Cho is Professor of Urban Studies, Center for Urban Studies, University of Akron.

Robert Firestine is Associate Professor of Political Economy, University of Texas at Dallas.

Dennis A. Gilbert is Assistant Professor of Political Science, University of Louisville.

Michael Kirst is Associate Professor of Education and Business Administration, School of Education, Stanford University.

Robert Lineberry is Associate Professor of Political Science and Urban Affairs, Northwestern University.

Vincent Marando is Director of Graduate Studies, Institute for Urban Studies, University of Maryland.

Robert Merriam is Chairman of the Advisory Commission on Intergovernmental Relations.

Jerry Miner is Professor of Economics and Chairman, Department of Economics, The Maxwell School, Syracuse University.

Seymour Sacks is Professor of Economics, The Maxwell School, Syracuse University.

Walter Vogt is Lecturer in Economics, San Diego State University.

Michael Wasylenko is Assistant Professor in Urban and Regional Planning, University of Wisconsin at Madison.

William Wilken is Research Director, Legislator's Education-Action Project, National Conference of State Legislatures.

Joseph Zimmerman is Professor of Political Science, State University of New York at Albany.

Preface

The Maxwell School of Citizenship and Public Affairs of Syracuse University noted its Fiftieth Anniversary in 1973-74 by sponsoring a variety of lectures, symposia and conferences. The Metropolitan Studies Program, one of the school's largest and strongest units, sponsored a conference devoted to the history, politics and economics of state and local government reform and reorganization. These essays and commentaries are a product of that conference, although most of the essays underwent substantial revision and editing following the conference.

Several of the essays are products of research done over the past decade and a half by the faculty and graduate student staff of the Metropolitan Studies Program, while others are by scholars from across the country, many of them former Maxwell School graduate students who have devoted their scholarly activities to trying to understand the processes and results of state and local government reform and reorganization.

The editors of this volume believe that the essays taken together present a useful description and an appropriate framework for analyzing subnational governmental restructuring. If the volume breaks new ground, it relates to the emphasis on determining the results of governmental reorganization rather than the normal tendency of most such literature to either champion reform or make the case for reform through deductive reasoning.

As would be expected from a product of the Maxwell School's Metropolitan Studies Program, there is considerable emphasis on the relationship between state and local governmental reorganization and urbanization and metropolitanization. The movement and sorting out of people and economic activities caused by these phenomena are a fundamental cause and condition of the reforms and reorganization which have occurred or are being advocated.

That such change will continue is practically guaranteed by the fiscal and economic base problems of most of the country's large central cities, particularly those in the Northeastern and North Central parts of the nation. Although there are some aspects of the New York City problem which result from the unique characteristics of that city, the underlying economic base difficulties are shared by a great many other cities. For many there is no solution short of fundamental restructuring. Although the kind of restructuring—transfer of functions, redrawing of boundaries, or new types and increased amounts of intergovernmental aid—will differ from place to place, change will occur.

As these essays demonstrate, the form the restructuring takes will have differential impacts on the efficiency and the equity of the resulting system. Restructuring does make a difference, and it is an important obligation of social science scholars to determine the character and consequences of those differences. We hope and believe this volume makes a contribution to understanding those differences. Hopefully too, the techniques employed here for investigating them will be found useful as further research is undertaken.

This volume is the result of the efforts of many people, but most appreciation is due the contributors. They responded willingly and promptly to editorial suggestions and made every effort to fit their pieces to the general framework of presentation imposed by the editors. The secretarial and administrative staffs of both the Maxwell School Dean's office and the Metropolitan Studies Program put in long hours in preparing the manuscript. They have our thanks.

Criticism of the volume's coverage and themes should be directed at the editors.

Alan K. Campbell
Roy W. Bahl

State and Local
Government

1. Municipal Reform Revisited: The 1970s Compared with the 1920s

Alan K. Campbell and
Guthrie S. Birkhead

A municipal reform is some measure designed to improve city government for the welfare of the entire population. Whether every reform measure does actually tend to better conditions is a question which cannot be answered in advance and upon which there may always be differences of opinion.

William Anderson, 1925

Any balanced critique of 50 years of local government reform in the United States should begin by noting that a great deal has been accomplished in that time if the aims of the reformers are the measures of success. The short, secret ballot, the direct primary, the council-manager plan, administrative reorganization, and other devices have been widely adopted. Many reforms espoused today have been on the market since at least the 1920s; others are of more recent vintage. Perhaps more noteworthy, however, is an increased complexity in the rationale for reform. Elimination of corruption, reduction in the role of political parties, and greater efficiency and economy remain as goals of reform. Nevertheless, they probably carry less weight than do concern for greater effectiveness in the delivery of services, more interpersonal and interjurisdictional equity in the quantity and quality of services provided, more equitable tax systems, and bureaucracies more in tune with the service needs of divergent client groups.

These changes have led to different structural and procedural prescriptions, sometimes in conflict with those prescribed by the earlier reformers. "Responsiveness" now competes with centralized hierarchical authority as a desired goal. So, also, effectiveness vies with efficiency, client empathy with professionalism, tax base adequacy with home rule, "neighborhood" (formerly ward) with at-

1

large, city-wide representation. The clear and fairly consistent goals of reformers of the 1920s are alive but often conflict with newer goals. The neatness and internal consistency of the reform package of the 1920s has been reduced. And yet Professor Anderson's second sentence may be repeated: one simply doesn't know if reform produces the intended results or not.

Reform, at base, involves questions of value. Norms underlie it, in greater or lesser proportion according to the spokesman. Muckrakers at the turn of the century were outraged by bosses and by corruption. "Too many governments," although not the central issue of that period, was perceived by a few reformers in the 1920s as a bad condition. Inefficient and undemocratic local government was a prime concern of academicians and good government-philes alongside these first two targets. Furthermore, the "disparities" or mismatch between needs and resources among parts of the metropolis became the central moral dilemma for reformers of the late sixties. Yet one person's evil may be another's good. The machine was resurrected and deified beginning with Robert Merton in the 1950s, and even the disparities are apparently a benefice in the minds of advocates of public choice.

The outrage at the disparities in today's metropolitan areas, as well as concern about other facets of substate government which are less than ideal today, is perhaps shared by a minority of Americans. This paper is an attempt to place the present conditions in a 50-year perspective. Municipal reform has never been a strong national movement, but instead has been a series of state and local campaigns. Thus attempts to generalize about it are risky. The twenties are as good a base decade as any to start with, since the total of state and local campaigns was probably greater then than ever before. The National Municipal League was vending its wares, and bureaus of municipal research were at work in many of the larger cities. Academic political scientists were speaking out more strongly than today in support of the philosophy of reform.

THE TWENTIES

The twenties of the flappers and speakeasies were carefree, and the national ethos was perhaps materialistic. In that materialism they resembled at least the early seventies. The reaction to Teapot Dome was a yawn from coast to coast. Whether the impact of Watergate will be more lasting remains to be seen.[1] Yet the twenties were also an uneasy era. The Wall Street bombing ushered them in and the Great Depression ushered them out. Bossism was alive in many cities. Tammany was the favorite example, but only one of many. For a long time the reformers had been worried about local corruption. Lincoln Steffens pinned down what he believed to be its cause to an audience in Los Angeles:

"Oh, I think I see," I said. "You want to fix the fault at the very start of things. Maybe we can, Bishop. Most people, you know, say it was Adam. But

Adam, you remember, he said that it was Eve, the woman; she did it. And Eve said, no, no, it wasn't she; it was the serpent. And that's where you clergy have stuck ever since. You blame that serpent, Satan. Now I come and I am trying to show you that it was, it is, the apple."[2]

Steffens's comment reflects a common criticism of governmental reformers, particularly from the political left. They suggest that no amount of changing governmental structure will alter who benefits from the American governmental system because of the elitist control of that system. They argue that only fundamental changes in the economic and social system will cause any basic alteration of who gets what out of the system. Reform and reorganization are seen as a rearranging of the chairs on the Titanic. Despite this criticism, reformers and reorganizers continue to try to alter the system in order to make it more equitable and more democratic.

Inefficiency and amateurism in administration were a second target. Bosses thrived on inefficiency, but that condition seemed to characterize nonbossed governments also. The economy and efficiency drive was to wax strong in the twenties and peak in the thirties. Administrative concepts developed at the local level were applied to the national government by the Brownlow Committee in the thirties and the Hoover Commissions in the forties and fifties.[3] At the local level the major resource for reform was the research bureaus and their studies, beginning with the New York Bureau founded in 1906.

Finally, the tilting with bossism was based on what progressives felt was a democratic goal. Richard S. Childs, a leading reformer of the twenties, was to reminisce much later:

Our objective is not good government exactly but democratic government. . . . We cannot devise a system of government that will automatically produce good administration but we can . . . identify systems which will almost inevitably be democratic. And if we achieve a practical working of the democratic process, the self-interest of the voters can be appealed to for correction of lapses in performance, and sensitive responsiveness of the mechanism will facilitate the ability of such self-interest to prevail.[4]

Recent historians have often neglected this theme of reformers or have dismissed it as mere rhetoric. One caricature of their criticism is that municipal reform was a conspiracy on the part of WASPs and businessmen to combat the ethnics crowding into the big cities of the Northeast. In many cities reformers were upset at the prospect of the leaders of the immigrant hordes sitting in city hall, but the blanket indictment is doubtless untrue. The secret ballot and the short ballot headed the list of reform devices and were destined to work in a basically democratic manner, even if one is not so sure of nonpartisanship or the direct primary. Voting is a recourse available, at least in theory, to the unwashed as well as the washed. A strong executive may respond as readily to the masses as to the elite.

Nevertheless some of the more thoughtful reformers knew that the results of reform were not readily identifiable. There was some talk of "before and after" studies, but research tools were relatively undeveloped for such purposes.[5] Many observers thought that the movement had already produced good results, while others were less certain. Chester C. Maxey wrote in the *National Municipal Review*, "Extravagant claims of efficiency and economy subsequent to political unification have been made everywhere, but are exceedingly difficult to pin down to hard facts."[6]

Reformers therefore perceived crises or problems, and the answers they provided were first of all mechanical in nature—gimmicks? The antidotes for bossism and for inefficiency were the council-manager plan, the merit system, a neat hierarchical structure with responsibility pinpointed. If these could be installed, then the recommended follow-up strategy was twofold: elect *good men* to office (here the WASPishness of reformers was showing), and organize a research bureau to serve as a gadfly.

This diagnosis of the maladies of the local intrajurisdictional system and the prescriptions for its cure had been developing since at least the 1870s. A new ingredient, however, was added in the twenties. The 1920 census documented for scholars and other reformers what only a few of them had suspected before that time. That census delineated 29 "metropolitan districts" which included cities of 200,000 or more population, as well as 29 other "districts" with cities over 100,000 and including the suburban territory within 10 miles of their limits. Since 1910 the suburbs in these 58 areas had been growing faster than the central cities. In the 58 "districts" lived 28.6 percent of the total U.S. population. More important, the increase in the total U.S. population had been only 14.9 percent in the previous decade as compared with 26.4 percent in the 58 districts.[7]

With these data, the academics found a new justification for reform. Maxey wrote, "The great problems which demand governmental action in metropolitan communities—public health, recreation, public utilities, crime, and the like—hold political boundaries in contempt."[8] Harvard's W. B. Munro wrote in his college textbook, "Out of all this is sure to rise, in due course, some movement for unification, complete or partial, such as will ensure the broad treatment of metropolitan problems by a centralized authority."[9] Out there in the real world, a few campaigns were mounted to establish metropolitan government, as in Pittsburgh–Allegheny County and Oakland–San Mateo. The syndrome of "too many governments" had been identified and the battle against it begun.

By the end of the decade, the National Municipal League Committee on Metropolitan Government had fully developed the motif of metropolitan governmental integration:

> This integration must be so effected as to foster the development of a vigorous metropolitan consciousness in the entire area, promote proper standards of service throughout, preserve and cultivate a healthy consciousness of locality in the constituent parts, and secure a proper treatment of purely local, as distinguished from metropolitan affairs.[10]

A sense of the interrelatedness of governments and problems was emerging, and it was to eventuate in the next decade with the federal government hesitantly and often inconsistently entering on the side of the reformers. The new concern of the thirties and subsequent decades, with time out for World War II, was to be the entire federal system, and the weapon was to be the functional program with its grants and standards. Adequacy of services, rather than rationality of structures, was to become the central concern of federal politicians and bureaucrats.

THE SEVENTIES

In the 1970s the United States had more than double the 1920 population—two-thirds of it metropolitan—and was a much more affluent country. Not yet adjusted psychologically to the atomic age or space age, it reeled under the impact of Vietnam, Watergate, and then the energy shortage, inflation and recession. In this perspective, it is hard to understand how the municipal reform movement could have survived. We are told Americans have a greater sense of efficacy with regard to local government than with regard to other levels of government. Still, the level of local or metropolitan governmental visibility is rarely high. One plausible explanation for the snail's pace at which people think metropolitan reform has moved is this: maybe in a world where all else changes so rapidly, people want to keep local government as it is—cozy, sprawling, small, large, friendly, impersonal.

But the reformers have survived, with changes. The same local elites still, as in the twenties, take the lead in individual city, county, or metropolitan reform campaigns; probably a little of the evangelistic fervor of earlier reformers is missing. Nor does it seem that opponents have changed—the "ins" (officeholders and related interest groups) still oppose reforms most devoutly. In several cases they have been joined by the black leadership in opposing metro ideas. This tendency for black opposition is not unlike the attachment of European ethnic groups to central city political machines during the 1920s. Politics, sports, and entertainment have been about the only avenues of improved mobility for these groups.

Reform, on the other hand, is stronger and better organized nationally than in the twenties. The National Municipal League is a constant resource for local reformers with a much wider range of interests: election laws, campaign finance, legislative reapportionment, and the role of state government. Business organizations, especially the Committee for Economic Development, are more deeply in the campaign for local governmental reform than ever before. National organizations of state and local officials are more reform-oriented than would be suspected if the attitudes of their members toward reform of their own jurisdictions were taken as a guide. The International City Management Association, the National Association of Counties, the National League of Cities, and the National Conference of Mayors strongly support many of the intrajurisdictional reforms suggested in the 1920s. They shy away from reorganizations that would impact on current boundaries, but their role in championing federal aid programs has become increasingly significant.[11] Probably without the support of these organizations, revenue sharing would have had a much more difficult time in Congress.

In the national government over 1,000 grant programs had been set up by 1973, and these programmatic influences had profound impacts on the substate level of government, impacts which are not yet well understood. One hypothesizes that federal action has strengthened existing local systems and their fragmentation more often than it has produced changes perceived as constructive by reformers. One prominent example illustrates the conflicting methods:

> Twenty-four federal programs enacted between 1961 and 1972 embodied a regional approach in the form of requirements and incentives for multicounty comprehensive or functional planning, grant-in-aid review and administrative districting. Nineteen of these had regional institution-building components, and ten gave preference to single-purpose organizations designed for a specific program.[12]

In Washington the brightest spot for reformers was the Advisory Commission on Intergovernmental Relations, and in its publications a broadened array of devices and substantive programs, emphasizing the metropolitan and regional levels, was enjoying a renaissance.

In universities, the ranks of reformers by 1970 had been deserted by most political scientists, but, on the other hand, economists and sociologists were much more visible and vocal on the subject of reforming substate governments. This situation is attributable in part to the increasing complexity and sophistication of research methods since the 1920s and in part to the changing and reinterpreted targets of reform. The most useful contribution to the debate about reorganization and reform has come from the economist. The application of the tools of economics to the measurement of changes produced by reorganization has brought a tighter and more precise framework to the analysis. Although output measurement is difficult, and perhaps in some cases impossible, the questions that the economists ask about reform sharpen the issues and the arguments.

To be sure, many of the old evils of local government are still being perceived by reform-oriented locals: official corruption, inefficiency, and high taxes often are featured in local headlines in the seventies. Bossism, as a viable issue, is pretty well gone, but has been replaced, for at least some of the more radical critics of local government left over from the late sixties, by elitism or "the system." More importantly, concern about poverty, mainly in central cities, and about disparities in service levels among parts of the metropolitan area motivates the compelling drive for equity in service levels and income distribution. And this is, of course, the issue with which the present generation of scholars has identified its own special urge for substate reform—as part, however, of more general reform of the entire federal system.

The primary emphasis in the 1920s and 1930s was on the internal structure of urban governments; the emphasis in the 1960s and 1970s has been on the jurisdictional scope of such governments. The concern with the misfit between the economically and socially interrelated areas (called metropolitan) and the governmental jurisdictions overlying them had its origin in the 1920s, but it came into full flower in the 1950s and 1960s. Nor was this surprising, as the suburban movement forecast by the 1920 census was dramatically slowed by the depression of the 1930s and by World War II.

As if to make up for lost time, the exodus from the central cities to the suburbs in the 1950s and 1960s was a genuine explosion. While people from the countryside moved into the cities, the middle- and upper-income population of those cities gathered their belongings and moved outside the city limits. The motivations for this latter move were undoubtedly mixed, but survey evidence verifies that detached houses, green lawns, and better schools lured many. Whether it was the pull to these suburban attractions or the push from the condition of the cities remains a debated issue. Whatever the motivation, the movement of people and of economic activity is now well understood.

The call for reform of the local government system was reinforced by this movement of people and economic activity. The logic was simple and was that of the twenties: as the metropolitan area was economically and socially interrelated, it seemed to follow that the governance system should reflect this interdependence. The specific response was to suggest a metropolitan-wide jurisdiction. Annexation had become an unusable tool in most parts of the country, and county government was deemed inadequate, so the suggestion was often for a new government, not simply to expand city boundaries or to join city and county. In the few cases where consolidations occurred (Nashville-Davidson and Jacksonville-Duval, for examples), the resulting government had more functions and was more tightly organized than the county government before reorganization.

It is important to note that the reform emphasis in the 1950s and 1960s on adequate jurisdictional scope represented a substantial shift from the concern in the 1920s and 1930s with the internal structure of urban governments. The earlier emphasis on "boss politics" and on the need for greater professionalism was virtually ignored in the local campaigns to establish some form of metropolitan-wide government. Many critics of recent efforts argue as if the justifications for metropolitan reform were the same as those offered for the internal structural reforms of the 1920s. For instance, "economy and efficiency" are still invoked in reform campaigns, but rarely has corruption or inefficiency been seen as the chief motivation for establishing a broader jurisdiction.

Using the 1920s justification for reform as a measure against which to judge the success of recent efforts has produced a debate that often is irrelevant to what the newer metropolitan reformers believe to be the central issue: the mismatch between boundaries and socioeconomic patterns. These "hard-headed" political scientists argue that the current governmental system is a product of unmanageable political forces and will always serve those with political power. Often this group of self-proclaimed "scientists" maintains that the student of governmental and political phenomena should restrict his analysis to explanations rather than to prescriptions for change.

Public Choice

Another group of critics maintains that the present system of local governments provides opportunities for citizens to vote with their feet. Deriving their political logic from the economic analysis of Tiebout, Buchanan, and others of the "public choice" school, they say that people can select a residence in that government jurisdiction where the combined services and costs best suit their preference patterns.[13]

Public choice advocates argue that the nearer the public sector can approach the alternatives permitted by the private market, the better. This private market analogy is, of course, appropriate if the public sector is simply perceived as a set of services citizens may purchase on the basis of their ability to pay. They adopt the view that the public sector has the same purposes as the private sector.

Public choice advocates use the concept of economic rather than technical efficiency to attempt to relate choice of public services to personal preferences. Accordingly, consumers of public services should be able to select public services as they select private services, thereby maximizing the utility of the goods and services. As preference patterns differ from individual to individual, the logical outcome would be a government for every individual or a common government for individuals who have exactly the same preference patterns. Obviously, this theoretical construct for determining the best governmental system omits any role for government in overcoming jurisdictional externalities or any role for using government services to redistribute income. This difference comprises the heart of the argument between public choice advocates, who defend the fragmented governmental system, and reformers, who believe government has a role to play in overcoming externalities and in redistributing income. Public choice advocates argue, "If ample fragmentation of authority and overlapping jurisdictions exist, sufficient competition may be engendered to stimulate a more responsive and efficient public economy in metropolitan areas."[14]

The argument that the public choice model cannot relate services to needs easily, if at all, is summarized by the proposition that such use of the local public sector to offset disparities is totally inappropriate, and other solutions for the problem must be found. Bish and Ostrom argue that

> the cost of voting with their feet, for example, may be too great for many poor people. The cost of making their demands known to city hall may also

be too high for them to pay. They may have little option but to bear the burden of poverty until alternative structures can be devised both to facilitate a redistribution of income and to provide governmental units that are more responsive to the demands of the poor.[15]

As Scott has said, "Some will remain behind"; the poor will remain in the central city and its old neighborhoods.[16] To a reformer, of course, such a posture is morally indefensible.

Although the public choice advocates do not suggest a system to increase equity, they provide an explanation for the difficulty in accomplishing metropolitan reform. Since such reforms might result in a redistribution of resources and services, persons satisfied with their current situations, already having voted with their feet, will oppose the reforms. The history of the failure of metropolitan reorganization amply demonstrates the satisfaction with the current system most people within metropolitan areas feel.

What these public choice people are up to is a confusion between a metaphor—a technique of analysis—and a prescription. To compare a metropolitan area and governmental services there with a market place is an interesting and useful tool, providing manifold insights. To say that the metropolitan area ought to be retained in its present situation to provide a means of citizen choice in residential location is a mistaken use of such a metaphor.

If technical rather than economic efficiency is used as the criterion for determining optimum jurisdiction size, the choice would depend on the character of the service being provided. The public sector is a "multi-industry" system, and the optimum administrative area in efficiency terms, obviously, will vary for each "industry." It follows, therefore, that the appropriate jurisdictional size would be different for each service or activity of government. Fragmentation would be on functional lines, as to some degree it now is, rather than geographic, which it also now is.

Unequal Service Levels

Consolidated government or area-wide jurisdiction does not, of course, guarantee equity in the provision of services to all parts of a single jurisdiction. Numerous studies have documented the higher level of certain services provided within large cities to middle- and higher-income communities, as compared with services provided to the low-income portions of the same cities. Further, it is quite possible that the particular services provided do not reflect the needs and aspirations of all parts of a community, even though there may be equity in distribution.

This lack of a fit between services provided and services needed characterized many large city governments in the middle and late 1960s and led to the demand for decentralization, with an increase in community or neighborhood control. Decentralization demands were normally related to the provision of education services, but they gradually spread to include other services. Experiments with different modes of decentralization, from little city halls to actual control by neighborhoods of parts of some services such as education, are going on in dozens of localities today. The justification for these decentralization demands usually stems from perception of a lack of responsiveness on the part of the central city government.

This lack, indeed is frequently attributed to the professionalization of the bureaucracy. It is argued that such professionalization is in reality institutionalization of middle-class values and, therefore, the resulting services do not match the communities to which the services are provided. This body of opposition, this logic, has most directly attacked the efficiency goals that have lingered from the 1920s. The emphasis of that reform rationale on professionalism, on at-large elections, and on getting "politics" out of local government is believed by many critics to have made the governmental system unresponsive in adjusting services to the taste of recipients. Election by wards and a revival of some patronage have recently appeared among the demands of these reformers.

Such efforts to overcome the inequities in service delivery have undoubtedly produced an adjustment in services in some cities. In many cities today more resources are devoted to education in low-income areas than in other parts of the city. Further, federal antipoverty efforts often have concentrated resources in these areas of cities.

The institutional response, however, has been slow, and it is interesting to note the argument that this is a fortunate situation for people in the low-income areas. If, indeed, decentralization and community control were carried to the logical conclusion of neighborhoods becoming dependent upon their own resources, the disparities in resource bases that now exist in all metropolitan areas would be greatly increased. In fact, it has been argued,

> . . . the larger the political subdivision, the more likely will its disadvantaged, minority blacks, ethnic as well as economic receive a fair shake. When racial stand-patters barricaded themselves behind state's rights, liberals successfully relied on more inclusive, more progressive federal powers. Where municipalities have refused to better themselves in order to meet the needs of topsy growing megalopolises, liberals have championed more inclusive, more progressive metropolitan government. [Recently], however, compassionate liberals . . . have U-turned. They it is who are pushing decentralization in education and community control of socio-political institutions.[17]

Too Many Substate Units

While reorganization theorists argue among themselves about the best forms of local government, changes go on continually in the number and nature of substate governments. Since 1942 the Bureau of the Census has documented the sharply decreasing total of such governments. One notes in passing that the greatest factor there was school district consolidation—a highly successful reform movement that has been, at best, remotely related to the municipal reform movement. Important to the school consolidation movement was the role of state governments. As has been explained,

> The states did bring about the reorganization of school districts through the use of the carrot of state aid. Obviously, they could move in the same direction relative to general local governments. The likelihood of their doing so, however, is reduced by the greater stakes which political parties have in local governments than they had in school districts. Jobs, contracts, and elective offices at the local level are important to the continued viability of the parties and to the extent reorganization threatens this relationship, it will be opposed.[18]

In several Canadian provinces, the provincial governments have acted firmly to change local boundaries, create metropolitan and regional governments, and revamp provincial-local fiscal systems.[19]

If "too many governments" was news until the early sixties, too many substate districts became a focus in the late sixties and early seventies. If the number of quasi-governmental and administrative areas or districts were counted, it would surely be in the thousands and might even approach the total of 78,218 governments listed by the census in 1972. Only when one includes with the total governments the total of other substate districts does the real complexity of the system become apparent.

Try to visualize a continuum with the regular local governments, as defined for census purposes, at the right extreme: municipalities, towns, counties, special districts, and general metropolitan governments. At the left extreme think of the more or less purely administrative areas for state government purposes. In between lies this congeries of substate districts. If placed on the continuum, those to the right would have some of the characteristics of governments, such as the Minneapolis-St. Paul Metropolitan Commission or many quasi-independent public corporations. To the left would lie entities with more of a federal or state administrative character—A-95 agencies or regional transportation agencies— still, however, with formal provision for access to decision making by local governments, interest groups, or individuals. The new "multijurisdiction areas," clearly intended to be under "local policy control," are of this nature.[20] A move to the left is toward broader area coverage, larger constituencies, and closer state or federal initiatives from higher in the federal system. A move to the right is toward local autonomy, more attention to access and representation, and smaller constituencies. Here are reflected past reform initiatives from leverage points low in the federal system.

This condition worries many reform types today, including particularly the Advisory Commission on Intergovernmental Relations (ACIR). A-95 arrangements thus far have not been effective, even as a review process for project applications. Since the first issuance of U.S. Office of Management and Budget

Circular A-95 in 1968, the state governments have been encouraged to attain coterminality of all their administrative areas. Forty states are said to be working at this today, but the going is slow.[21] Neither states nor the federal government has been able to adopt a consistent approach to the impact that they would like to have on local government organization. Block grants and revenue sharing tend to strengthen the fragmented system, while demands for regional planning and for clearance of local grant requests by a regional body will have the opposite impact. In general, it can be demonstrated that the federal thrust has created a large number of regional jurisdictions, some of them functional, some of them general, but has simultaneously often provided the hard cash necessary for otherwide economically nonviable jurisdictions to survive.

WHAT DIFFERENCE DOES IT MAKE?

Despite all the efforts for urban reform and all the debate about it, the basic question of "What difference does it make?" remains unanswered as it did in the 1920s. The goals of reform, then as now, are ill-defined and frequently contradictory. Is it "good," "democratic," "effective," "equitable," "efficient," or "responsive" government that is sought at the local level? One frequently hears that the goal of municipal reformers today is "equity" as compared with the "efficiency" of four decades ago. But the truth is that there is little understanding of the ends.

The 1970s may see a major effort to develop the tools to deal with the question of what difference it may make. It appears that, in bits and pieces, the effort has begun. But careful definition and widespread agreement on the terms must be the first or at least an early step. "Efficient," "effective," "equitable," and "responsive" must all gain clearer meaning and more common understanding if they are to become operational terms. Economists are leading the way.

Probably the most progress has been made in clarifying the concept of efficiency, since it was the center of attention during the early reform movement, and more recently economists have used the concept intensively. Distinguishing between economic and technical efficiency is the first step. Developing "output" measures is perhaps the second, and recent work on productivity demonstrates how difficult that is. Efforts in this direction, however, by some cities and states, the federal government, and the Urban Institute seem to us to point in the right direction.[22]

"Effectiveness," a word intended to avoid the narrowness of "economy and efficiency," is much more tentatively defined and understood. It aims to relate outputs or "impacts" to agency goals. Effectiveness represents the effort to bring together efficiency and *quality*, with possibly equal emphasis on quality and costs. Impact or "outcome" of a program is more nebulous still. It must take account of public perceptions of the service and thus hinges on interrelatedness and feedback. Impact and "responsiveness" are extraordinarily hard to disentangle.

"Responsiveness" supposedly would relate service delivery to what people or consumers, in fact, want or demand. Some fairly good work is now being done in the attempt to measure attitudes about services, primarily by the Urban Institute.[23] If so-called objective measures of service outputs are ultimately developed, it will be interesting and useful to contrast these objective outputs with the effect they have on consumer attitudes (subjective outcomes).

Finally, "equity" is most popular today, as supposedly an appropriate measure or goal for the delivery of services at the local level—delivery by all governments. The intention of this concept seems clear: services should be directly related to "needs." Simple equality in the sense of the same amount for everyone is not the goal; rather, the relating of quality and quantity of services to need is the intent. The concept is closely allied with current economics usage of efficiency, as related to demand. But how needs are identified or measured also remains problematic. There is a long history of discussion and disagreement on this subject, and the debate continues today.

The whole effort, of course, depends on our ability to measure input, process, and output variables with precision. Despite all the attention being given these subjects today, whether such measurement can be accomplished remains an open question. That is just about where we were in the 1920s, except that the issues seem to be better understood today.

NOTES

1. David H. Bennett, *From Teapot Dome to Watergate* (Maxwell School, Syracuse University, May 1974).

2. *Autobiography* (New York: Harcourt, Brace, 1931), p. 574.

3. Frederick C. Mosher, ed., *American Public Administration: Past, Present, Future* (University of Alabama Press, 1975).

4. *Civic Victories* (New York: Harper, 1952), p. xvii.

5. What was apparently the first dissertation at the Maxwell School of Syracuse University was written by Clarence Ridley in 1927 and later published with the coauthorship of Herbert Simon as *Measuring Municipal Government* (Washington: International City Managers' Association, 1943).

6. *National Municipal Review*, XI (August 1922), pp. 229 ff.

7. U.S. Bureau of the Census, vol. 1, *Population, 1920* (Washington, 1921). See especially pp. 62 ff. and tables 40 and 41.

8. *National Municipal Review, loc. cit.*

9. *Municipal Government and Administration* (New York: Macmillan, 1923), p. 437.

10. *The Government of Metropolitan Areas in the United States* (New York: National Municipal League, 1930), p. 41. Compare the recommendations by the Committee for Economic Development in *Reshaping Metropolitan Areas* (New York: Committee for Economic Development, 1970).

11. Donald H. Haider, *When Governments Come to Washington: Governors, Mayors and Intergovernmental Lobbying* (New York: Free Press, 1973).

12. David B. Walker and Carl W. Stenberg, "A Substate Districting Strategy," *National Civic Review,* 63 (January 1974), p. 5.

13. Charles M. Tiebout, "A Pure Theory of Local Expenditures," *Journal of Political Economy,* October 1956, pp. 416–24; James M. Buchanan, "Federalism and Fiscal Equity," *American Economic Review,* September 1950, pp. 583–99; and James M. Buchanan and Gordon Tullock, *The Calculus of Consent* (Ann Arbor: University of Michigan, 1962.)

14. Robert L. Bish and Vincent Ostrom, *Understanding Urban Government: Metropolitan Reform Reconsidered* (Washington: American Enterprise Institute for Policy Research, 1973).

15. *Ibid.,* p. 31. A logical extension of public choice arguments brings one to the idea of breaking large central cities into smaller governments. This is the reform proposal of Committee for Economic Development, *op. cit.,* which based it on other logic, however. Public choice advocates are less clear on the need for a second tier of government in metropolitan areas.

16. Anthony Scott, "The Economic Goals of Federal Finance," *Public Finance,* 3 (1964), p. 268. See also Jesse Burkhead and Jerry Miner, *Public Expenditure* (Chicago and New York: Aldine-Atherton, 1971), chap. 8.

17. Nathan Perlmutter, "We Don't Help Blacks by Hurting Whites," *New York Times Magazine,* Oct. 6, 1968, p. 31.

18. Alan K. Campbell and Jesse Burkhead, "Public Policy for Urban America," in Harvey S. Perloff and Lowdon Wingo, Jr., eds., *Issues in Urban Economics* (Baltimore: Johns Hopkins Press, 1968), p. 585.

19. See U.S. Advisory Commission on Intergovernmental Relations, *Substate Regionalism and the Federal System* vol. V, *A Look to the North: Canadian Regional Experience,* G. S. Birkhead, ed. (Washington, 1974). See also Nova Scotia, Royal Commission on Education, Public Services and Provincial-Municipal Relations, *Report* (Halifax, 1974).

20. Melvin Mogulof, "Federally Encouraged Multi-Jurisdictional Agencies in Three Metropolitan Areas" chap. 5, in U.S. Advisory Commission on Intergovernmental Relations, *op. cit.,* vol. II, *Regional Governance: Promise and Performance* (Washington, 1973).

21. Walker and Stenberg, *op. cit.*

22. For description of some of the work on public sector productivity, see Urban Institute and International City Management Association, *Measuring the Effectiveness of Basic Municipal Services: Initial Report* (Washington: Urban Institute, 1974); *The National Science Foundation Proceedings of*

the First Symposium on Rann: Research Applied to National Needs, Section on Public Sector Productivity (Washington, 1973) pp. 139–172; and the special issue of *Public Administration Review,* November-December 1972, Chester A. Newland, symposium ed.

23. Urban Institute, *op. cit.,* pp. 99–112.

Comment: It Is Better to Have Reformed and Lost than Never to Have Reformed at All—or Is It?

Robert L. Lineberry

Campbell and Birkhead have said it well, but they have not said it all. The continuities between the metropolitan reformers of the 1920s and the reformers of the 1970s are striking indeed, especially if, as they say, one employs as referent the aims of the reformers themselves. The underlying faith in the efficacy of structural reform has not abated. The eternal concern for the public-regarding goal of the "community as a whole," its poor who cannot vote with their feet and its rich who can, remains. The concentration on too many governments, what has become in modern parlance too many "substate districts," continues.

The existence of 80,000 units of local government, perhaps doubled by the number of quasi-governmental units, still boggles one's conception of symmetry, if not efficiency. Yet part of the issue today, as Campbell and Birkhead rightly argue, turns upon the issue of "reform for what?" Complex values like efficiency, equity, equality, and economy are supported by every reformer, at least until they have to be defined, or worse, until they have to be traded off. It is also a part of the reform tradition to cling to goals more as matters of doctrinal piety than as consequences of hard analysis.

What Campbell and Birkhead do not pay sufficient attention to, it seems to me, is an increasing challenge to the reformers' ability to meet their own goals. There are at least two sources to this challenge, only one of which Campbell and Birkhead acknowledge, let alone examine. The first is a growing recognition by both citizen activists and some political scientists that the institutions of the reform movement entail negative externalities. This is a manifestation of the Bobbie Burns rule of policy impact analysis, *i.e.*, that the best-laid schemes of mice, men, and reformers "gang aft agley."

Reforms which have weakened the office of mayor, strengthened the hands of sinecured bureaucrats, overshadowed elected officials with city managers, and eliminated parties through the nonpartisan ballot, have all served to make the city—in Theodore Lowi's words—"well run but badly governed." The at-large elections of the reform movement have reduced the neighborhood base of local government and badly damaged minority representation on governing bodies. Consequently, there stands emergent a new breed of "reformers of the reforms." In countless cities these forces have battled against the structural reforms of the twenties, even while they paradoxically have articulated the selfsame virtues of democracy, responsiveness, and accountability.

16

Granted that Campbell and Birkhead confine their attention to a single aspect of the reform package—the demand for reorganized governmental structure in the metropolis—there is a parallel counterforce operating to challenge the policy impact of metropolitan reorganization. These changes have exacted a heavy cost in representation of central city blacks, and minority spokesmen have become as chary of reform as suburbanites. And possibly with good reason. In Jacksonville, where city-county consolidation became reality, the strength of black voting blocks was cut exactly by half—from 40 percent of the old city of Jacksonville to 20 percent of the new consolidated government. Perhaps, the black critic might suggest, it is no coincidence that the principal geographic locale for metropolitan reorganization has been the American South.[1]

If the first challenge to the reform ethic today is essentially political, the second is so far mostly an abstract and intellectual one. This comes from the "public choice and collective goods" scholars. These writers make a virtue out of necessity and defend governmental fragmentation because it maximizes citizen choice and facilitates economy of scale.[2] Arguing that reform of metropolitan governance is wrong (that's for sure), Bish and Ostrom contend that

> People have long recognized that it is possible for a 'remedy' to be worse than a 'disease.' Perhaps it is time to consider the possibility that the prevailing metropolitan reform orthodoxy has led us to rely upon remedies which are aggravating the situation they are designed to correct.[3]

The multiplicity of urban governments, they contend, offers more effective citizen demand processing because

> Citizen demands can be more precisely indicated in smaller rather than larger political units, and in political units undertaking fewer rather than more numerous public functions. . . . When neighborhood conditions and people's preferences vary substantially . . . information about these variations is apt to be lost if people have recourse only to a single large unit of government.[4]

It is at these choice theorists that Campbell and Birkhead draw their deadliest aim. Most, but not quite all, of their criticism is well targeted. To Campbell and Birkhead, choice theorists confuse the metaphor of multiple governments as a marketplace with a prescription. It is also a profoundly conservative metaphor, implicitly defending the vast discrepancies in resource bases and service outputs so dramatically highlighted by the *Serrano* and *Rodriguez* challenges.

Most social scientists had assumed that belief in the moral imperative of the free marketplace had been long dead and buried. But it now reappears clad in all the emperor's new clothes and applied to the problem of metropolitan governance. These free marketers have critiqued more effectively the reformers of the twenties with their efficiency hangups than the reformers of the seventies, who are more concerned with economic inequalities exacerbated by metropolitan fragmentation.

As with the free market of yore, so it is with the "metropolitan services marketplace" of the choice theorists: consumer choice reigns supreme, so long as you can afford it. Bish and Ostrum, the leading exponents of the marketplace model, grant only (in a passage quoted by Campbell and Birkhead) that the poor "may have little option but to bear the burden of their poverty until alternative structures can be devised. . . ."[5] This inattention to frictions in the free market is a far more hostile stance toward the plight of the poor than that of Professor Friedman, the modern godfather of the free market, who has at least demonstrated an unwavering commitment to a negative income tax to soften the realities of the free market.

There are, however, two analytic perspectives from the public choice theorists which reformers would be wise to explore. The first is their contention that the appropriate strategy is to *work from functions performed to institutional arrangements rather than the other way around.* If choice theorists are fixated on the metaphor of the mythical marketplace, the reformers remain transfixed by the goal of structural symmetry. Some years ago, the Advisory Commission on Intergovernmental Relations made a halting effort to "assign" functions to the "appropriate" jurisdiction whether area-wide or local: fire protection should go here, pollution control there, etc. Unfortunately, the effort was bereft of both analytic and empirical evidence. Assuming that we do not take the present institutional structures as givens—and neither the reformers nor the choice theorists claim to—then both camps could agree upon the virtue of research on the consequences of different-sized units for packaging public services.[6]

The second perspective of the choice theorists is even more compelling. They argue that *institutional arrangements cannot be analyzed apart from their externalities and tradeoffs.* These are issues the reformers have rarely faced. Crucial today, for example, is an implicit tradeoff for central city blacks between an expanded metropolitan tax base deriving from governmental reorganization and a diminution of their political control over policies.

How much power should blacks be asked to trade off for how much improvement in their economic base? Gains in equity may only be won, perhaps, at the cost of political responsiveness. Improvements in responsiveness may cost something in terms of economic equality. And all these choices entail externalities which reformers have mostly ignored. Reformers have too long assumed that multiple, even contradictory goals can be achieved simultaneously. They cannot. And this argument is entirely consistent with Campbell and Birkhead's belief that reformers need to settle the question of "reform for what?"

Perhaps the key difference between the reformers of the twenties and those of the seventies is a certain self-consciousness. The latter both know more and need to know more, for they are confronting more realistically the oldest issue since Madison: how shall a people organize their government so as to maximize their choices among contending values?

NOTES

1. See, for evidence, the paper by Vincent Marando in the present volume. See also my article "Reforming Metropolitan Governance: Requiem or Reality," *Georgetown Law Journal,* 58 (March-May 1970), pp. 675–718.

2. The seminal paper on the metropolitan marketplace model is C. M. Tiebout, "A Pure Theory of Local Expenditures," *Journal of Political Economy,* 64 (October 1956), pp. 416–24. The best contemporary statements are Vincent Ostrum, *The Intellectual Crisis in American Public Administration* (University, Ala.: University of Alabama Press, 1973), and Robert L. Bish and Vincent Ostrum, *Understanding Urban Government: Metropolitan Reform Reconsidered* (Washington: American Enterprise Institute for Public Policy Research, 1973).

3. Bish and Ostrum, *op. cit.,* p. 5.

4. *Ibid.,* pp. 24 and 26.

5. *Ibid.,* p. 31. In fairness to Bish and Ostrum, it must be pointed out that Campbell and Birkhead fail to quote the last sentence of the Bish-Ostrum paragraph on the poor: "The poor are most in need of neighborhood governments in which the costs of articulating demands can be kept to a minimum." If so, however, the poor at the moment would appear to have the worst of all possible worlds in the central cities, caught in the largest governments (which Bish and Ostrum deplore) with the weakest resource bases.

6. In terms of research on the consequences of different jurisdictional arrangements for urban service delivery, the choice theorists unquestionably have the lead. See, *e.g.,* Elinor Ostrum and Gordon Whitaker, "Does Local Community Control of Police Make a Difference? Some Preliminary Findings," *American Journal of Political Science,* 17 (February 1973), pp. 48–76.

Comment: Evaluating Municipal Reform: The 1970s Compared to the 1920s

William H. Wilken

I must agree with Campbell and Birkhead's main point that there has been much more debate about the proper course of municipal reform than research about its consequences. I have reservations, however, about two related views: one, their explicit claim that we know little more about the effects of municipal reform today than we did 50 years ago; the other, their implicit judgment that more and better information about the results of municipal reform would be useful to the improvement of urban government.

Clearly, a great deal is known about the effects of municipal reform on its historically oldest targets—corruption, inefficiency, and bossism. Especially since the mid-1950s researchers have demonstrated conclusively that the attack on these targets has been basically successful, but at the cost of ancillary outcomes of questionable value. We know, for example, that the adoption of at-large elections has undercut the ward politics basis of bossism quite effectively, but at the cost of limiting the access of minorities to the political process.[1] Similarly, we know that the proliferation of professionalized civil service has reduced municipal corruption and inefficiency, but not without frequently hamstringing the effectiveness of municipal executives. I could cite other examples, but it would belabor the point.

If Campbell and Birkhead's complaint about inadequate research on the outcomes of municipal reform is addressed to the literature that examines the effects of city-county consolidations and related types of government reform, then I must express greater sympathy for their view. Until quite recently, very few researchers had attempted to distinguish between the manifest purposes of metropolitan government reorganization and its true effects. Substantial studies under the aegis of the Advisory Commission on Intergovernmental Relations, the National Academy of Public Administration, and other organizations however, now are beginning to delineate these outcomes.

As I point out in a recent monograph,[2] there is more and more evidence that metropolitan reorganization can yield political and administrative changes that are dear to most champions of reform: most notably, greater effectiveness and efficiency in service delivery; increased fiscal equity; and expanded citizen access to the political process and its benefits. These gains, however, appear to fall considerably short of the benefits that one might expect from the rhetoric of reform's most enthusiastic proponents.

From the experience of Toronto, Miami, Nashville, Jacksonville, Indianapolis, and a few other metropolitan areas, it would seem that greater effectiveness of

20

service delivery is the only promise of reorganization that is fulfilled on a relatively consistent and widespread basis. This, however, is not to suggest that greater effectiveness is universal. For the most part, increased effectiveness is limited to functions related to physical development and so-called hardware services, occurring much less extensively in functions pertaining to human development and "software" services. Equally important, stepped-up effectiveness seems to be much more common in the delivery of services received by the residents of rapidly growing suburbs than by the inhabitants of declining inner city areas.[3]

Compared to the gains of reorganization in the area of government effectiveness, the benefits in the area of efficiency not only seem somewhat more sporadic but also are not as well documented. If in a somewhat impressionistic fashion, some research suggests that reorganization can result in greater service output at less resource cost when it is used to abolish instances of gross service duplication. Whether it can capture the legendary economies of large-scale service delivery, however, remains open to lively debate. And perhaps most important, there is almost no reliable evidence on the capacity of reorganization to produce government that is able to provide a closer match between the outputs that it supplies and the outputs that citizens prefer.

Like the effects of metropolitan reorganization on efficiency, the consequences of reorganization on fiscal equity seem to be positive, but not definitively so. Existing research indicates that the capacity of reorganization to achieve more equal treatment of similarly situated citizens, as well as to discriminate in its dealings with unequally situated citizens, is not linked to any simple structural formula, but to unspecified combinations of at least three factors. These include the commitment of state government to the idea of equity; the nature of the channels for greater equity created by reorganization; and the willingness of citizens to exploit these channels—a factor which often seems quite strongly conditioned by the character of existing political leadership.

Perhaps the least certain outcome of metropolitan reorganization is its impact on citizen access to the political process and its rewards. It appears, for example, that blacks hold more elected offices and public jobs after reorganization than before. Yet it is difficult to conclude that blacks have gained this access because of reorganization itself or, even more important, that blacks or any other groups feel that they have more access. Available data are simply too weak.

As I indicated earlier, I have reservations not only about Campbell and Birkhead's assessment of municipal reform research but also about their apparent conclusion that more research about its outcomes would be useful to the improvement of urban government. My reservations about the utility of additional research, however, are not based on doubts about its absolute value, but on misgivings about its relative value. Clearly the absolute value of more study would be hard to dispute. At the very least it not only would enable us to design reform plans that would be more effective but also would allow us to develop a better understanding of what urban governments can and cannot accomplish.

Yet, in the final analysis, I am inclined to believe that additional research on the outcomes of municipal reform is less likely to contribute to the improvement of urban government than research in other areas—and for the following reasons:

First, it is almost impossible to implement any significant municipal reform plan without the support of local voters, and I see little evidence that they are about to reverse their traditional opposition to major changes in the status quo. Indeed, I think it is just as likely that local voters will grow more intransigent now that there is evidence that the courts may use steps toward metropolitan government, for delivering municipal services, specifically excluding public education, as a pretext for ordering school busing for racial balance on a metropolitan basis.

Second, and relatedly, I see increasing evidence that it may be much more politically feasible to attack the problems that hobble urban government at the state level rather that at the local level through the vehicle of municipal reform. Traditionally, of course, most states have been reluctant to address themselves to urban problems. In recent years, however, at least three factors—legislative reapportionment, court decisions, and local fiscal pressure—have encouraged state legislatures to significantly revise their attitudes, especially toward two of these problems—school finance disparities and property tax burdens. Since 1970, for example, state legislatures have exhibited an unusual willingness to give significant recognition to the unusual educational burdens of urban areas. Moreover, some legislatures have given serious consideration to property tax relief like that of Vermont, which provides benefits not just for low-income homeowners but also for the low-income renters who concentrate in urban areas. To be sure, it might be argued that many state legislatures will be unwilling to extend their interest in urban problems other than in the areas of education and property taxation. Yet even if this speculation proves correct, what it fails to recognize is the possibility of attacking many urban problems indirectly through the kind of fiscal relief and redistribution that could accrue from well-researched school finance and property tax legislation.

Third, and finally, I suspect that the growing concern for the value of equity in government raises fundamental questions about the appropriateness of municipal reform as a vehicle for improving the quality of local government and urban life, and for the following reasons. To begin with, almost all research on municipal reform indicates that it has not been able to deal very effectively with the most important equity issues, i.e., issues involving the redistribution of income and control over social access.

Additionally, I think there is strong evidence that most equity issues will prove much more amenable to solution at the national level than at the local level. As is well known, metropolitan areas tend to vary greatly in the economic resources that could be brought to bear in addressing equity issues; thus, while reform may increase the potential for greater equity within any metropolitan area, it does not address the equally important issue of equity among metropolitan areas—a perennial issue in almost every state that is dominated by a single economic capital. Equally important, every metropolitan area in the country faces the same political handicap in attempting to cope with equity issues; namely, none is large enough to control powerful economic interests aggregated at a national level. Hence, somewhat like Lowi, I see no reason to expect that reformed metropolitan government could deal with equity issues any more effectively than present state governments.

In sum, then, I view additional research on municipal reform as both needed and potentially useful. Yet, unlike Campbell and Birkhead, I think we know much more about the effects of municipal reform today than we did 50 years ago. Moreover, I think we must be relatively skeptical about the eventual utility of municipal reform, however well researched.

NOTES

1. James Q. Wilson, *City Politics* (New York: Vintage Books; 1963), chaps. 7 and 11.
2. "Successful Centralizing Reorganizations" in Charles R. Warren and Thomas P. Murphy, eds., *Organizing Public Services in Metropolitan America* (Lexington, Mass.: Lexington Books, 1971).
3. *Ibid.*, and "The Impact of Centralization on Effectiveness Economy, and Efficiency" chap. 6, "The Impact of Centralization on Access and Equity" chap. 7.

2. The Politics of Metropolitan Reform

Vincent L. Marando

The dominant theme of the reform literature on local governmental organization in metropolitan areas is the need for increased political integration. The arguments advanced in favor of political integration are variations on the theme that local governments can be more effectively reorganized. The basic rationale is either that there are too many local governments, that local governments do not have the resources or capacity to meet the demands of their residents, or that the geographic limits of local government do not "fit" the major problems of modern-day urban areas. Although there is no consensus and there is often disagreement, there is awareness among students of governmental organization that the status quo is inadequate and that some form of reorganization is necessary to achieve a greater degree of political integration.

The reasons advanced for achieving increased political integration range widely. Some observers feel that there are too many local governments that overlap and that fewer are needed. Others contend that the problem is not the number of local governments, but the lack of coordination among them in dealing with area-wide concerns.[1] Still others insist that the major problems of local governments are evidenced by their lack of resources and/or the basic character of their populations, *i.e.*, the predominantly poor and minority status of central city residents.

Like the perspectives on the problem, the proposals for reorganization to achieve increased political integration in metropolitan areas, vary. Among the major reorganizations proposed are consolidation of existing local governments into fewer units; the expansion of existing local governmental boundaries to encompass larger proportions of the urban area; the realignment of local governments into two tiers, each responsible for differing functions; the creation of regional mechanisms, such as councils of governments (COGs), which leave local governments relatively undisturbed but increase their capacity to deal with area-wide problems.

24

There is some question as to the relative merits and need for reorganization of local governments in metropolitan areas. Whether the structure of local government actually causes or is merely one symptom of urban problems is still open to debate.[2] Assuming that there is a need for local governmental reorganization, there is the important question of political acceptance. For any change in local governmental organization to be adopted it must be politically acceptable. Some forms of reorganization are politically more difficult to achieve than others. This fact permeates any discussion or decision concerning options to reorganize local governments in metropolitan areas. Consolidation of local governments into fewer units is extremely difficult, whereas the functional cooperation among local governments or the creation of a regional mechanism may be less difficult. Putting aside the issue of the relationship between local governmental structure and the resolution of urban problems the question to be considered here is political acceptability.

The purpose of this paper is to examine the political factors that affect reorganization of government in metropolitan areas and to discuss the nature of the political processes by which metropolitan reform occurs. The extent of political acceptance and processes leading to acceptance will be examined by focusing upon three types of reorganization: city-county consolidation,[3] annexation, and COGs. These three forms were selected because they represent a broad range of political acceptability. They will be examined to highlight various political process characteristics of reorganization.

I contend that metropolitan reorganizations are influenced as much by political factors as by their substantive objectives. It will be argued that political attachments to existing local governments, together with the requirement of voter approval in public referenda, severely limit politically feasible reorganizations. These politically based reorganization obstacles have fueled greater interest in less than metropolitan-wide reorganizations (annexation), which do not threaten existing local governments and require no public referenda (COGs). This analysis of reform efforts suggests that more state involvement will be required if many metropolitan-wide reorganizations are to be accomplished.

CITY-COUNTY CONSOLIDATION

Attempts and Adoptions

Table 2-1 provides a summary of the referenda outcomes of 47 reorganization efforts from 1945 to 1974.[4] Most obvious from Table 2-1 is that all reorganization adoptions occurred in single-county metropolitan areas. There is only one case where multicounty metropolitan reorganization has come before the public for voter approval. That is the St. Louis city–St. Louis County case,

TABLE 2-1. *Rate of Voter Support for Local Government Reorganization in 47 Referenda, 1945–74*

Year	Reorganization Referendum	Reorganization Support (%)	
		Success	*Defeat*
1949	Baton Rouge–East Baton Rouge Parish, La.	51.1	
1952	Hampton–Elizabeth County, Va.	88.7	
1953	Miami–Dade County, Fla.		49.2
1957	Miami–Dade County, Fla.	51.0	
	Newport News–Warwick, Va.[1]	66.9	
1958	Nashville–Davidson County, Tenn.		47.3
1959	Albuquerque–Bernalillo County, N.M.		30.0
	Knoxville–Knox County, Tenn.		16.7
	Cleveland–Cuyahoga County, Ohio		44.8
	St. Louis–St. Louis County, Mo.		27.5
1960	Macon–Bibb County, Ga.		35.8
1961	Durham–Durham County, N.C.		22.3
	Richmond–Henrico County, Va.		54.0[2]
1962	Columbus–Muscogee County, Ga.		42.1
	Memphis–Shelby County, Tenn.		36.8
	Nashville–Davidson County, Tenn.	56.8	
	South Norfolk–Norfolk County, Va.	66.0	
	Virginia Beach–Princess Anne County, Va.	81.9	
	St. Louis–St. Louis County, Mo.		40.1[3]
1964	Chattanooga–Hamilton County, Tenn.		19.2
1967	Jacksonville–Duval County, Fla.	64.7	
	Tampa–Hillsborough County, Fla.		28.4
1969	Athens–Clarke County, Ga.		48.0
	Brunswick–Glynn County, Ga.		29.6
	Carson City–Ormsby County, Nev.	65.1	
	Roanoke–Roanoke County, Va.		66.4[2]
	Winchester city–Frederick County, Va.		31.9
1970	Charlottesville–Albemarle County, Va.		28.1
	Columbus–Muscogee County, Ga.	80.7	
	Chattanooga–Hamilton County, Tenn.		48.0
	Tampa–Hillsborough County, Fla.		42.0
	Pensacola–Escambia County, Fla.		42.0
1971	Augusta–Richmond County, Ga.		41.5
	Charlotte–Mecklenburg County, N.C.		30.5
	Tallahassee–Leon County, Fla.		41.0
1972	Athens–Clarke County, Ga.		48.3
	Macon–Bibb County, Ga.		39.6
	Suffork–Nansemond County, Va.[1]	75.7	
	Fort Pierce–St. Lucy, Fla.		36.5
	Lexington–Fayette County, Ky.	69.4	
	Tampa–Hillsbrough County, Fla.		42.0
1973	Columbia–Richland County, S.C.		45.9
	Savannah–Chatham County, Ga.		58.3[2]
	Tallahassee–Leon County, Fla.		45.9

TABLE 2-1 *continued*

Year	Reorganization Referendum	Reorganization Support (%)	
		Success	*Defeat*
1974	Augusta–Richmond County, Ga.		51.5[2]
	Portland–Multnomah County, Ore.		27.5
	Durham–Durham County, N.C.		32.1
Total Outcome (Numbers)		12	35
Local Reorganizations Attempted		47	

[1] Warwick, Va., was a city at the time of the referendum. It had incorporated in 1952; but it was included in this analysis because of its suburban and rural character (in 1958) and because it was Warwick County just six years prior to the referendum. A similar situation of city-county consolidation preceded the consolidation of Suffolk and Nansemond County.

[2] The type of majority requirement is vital in consolidation referenda. In these four instances city-county consolidation was not possible despite the majority voting percentage in its support. In all of these attempts, the "double majority requirement," which stipulates separate approval by city voters and county voters, resulted in defeat, since a majority of county voter support was not achieved.

[3] St. Louis–St. Louis County portions of the 1962 statewide referendum are reported in this table.

where the city has been legally separated from the county. However, even in the St. Louis area the total metropolitan area was not included in the reorganization.

Reorganization referenda generally fail, and there are usually three rejections for every voter acceptance. The data in Table 2-1 also indicate no discernible trends with regard to reorganization successes by year(s) or state(s). Reorganization is just as likely to fail, or pass, today as was the case three decades ago. Detailed analysis of the Cleveland area indicates that over a 28-year period involving 10 separate reorganization referenda, there was no overall trend in favor of metropolitan reform.[5]

The 12 voter-approved reorganizations of local governments have occurred in seven states. Most of the states where major reorganization has occurred have been in the South, and it is in this region that most reorganization efforts have been attempted. Thus reorganization attempts and success have been a Southern regional phenomenon.

In particular, 5 of the 12 reorganization successes have occurred in the Commonwealth of Virginia. An explanation here rests with the particular characteristics of that state's law, which grants all first-class cities a status independent of counties.[6] Also, the small size of the Virginia metropolitan areas involved leads to less complex local governmental situations and a higher probability of reorganization support.

Table 2-1 also illustrates that reorganization was not successful in large metropolitan areas, those with a population of more than 1 million. In Cleveland

and St. Louis, the two largest metropolitan areas to attempt major reorganization, the proposals were defeated. Voter support for reorganization in the Cleveland metropolitan area was 44.8 percent, while the 1962 St. Louis consolidation was defeated in a statewide referendum by over 70 percent of the electorate. Voters in Dade County (Miami) accepted reorganization by a 51 percent majority. At the time of the 1957 reorganization acceptance, Dade County did not have a million population.

The major implication of the data in Table 2-1 is the difficulty of attaining voter acceptance of governmental reorganization. The statement by Victor Jones that "since 1898 there has been no thorough-going integration of local government in the larger metropolitan areas" is nearly as correct today as when it was written in 1942.[7] Only Nashville, Tennessee, and Dade County (Miami, Florida) stand as exceptions to this statement. And if a large metropolitan area is taken to mean more than 1 million persons, there are no exceptions to the statement.

Reorganization has been a continuous concern in many areas, resulting in several public referenda on reorganization in the same area. Multiple attempts in a single area do not imply eventual reorganization success. Cleveland, Ohio, and St. Louis, Missouri, have had long histories of governmental reform. However, neither metropolitan area has had a voter-approved reorganization.

REFORM INITIATION

Community Problems That Led to Reform Consideration

The community problems that stimulated most governmental reform efforts were of a noncrisis nature. The problems that confronted metropolitan areas and that led to consideration could be considered inconvenient or, at most, serious. In the "inconvenient problem" category are duplication of functions, too many administrative agencies, and a lack of long-range planning. The serious problems include lack of adequate water and sewer facilities, inequitable city-county tax bases, blight and congestion, and air and water pollution.

Whether problems are critical, are serious, or merely cause inconveniences is a matter of values and depends upon who is doing the classifying. Generally, middle-class citizens, in conjunction with governmental "experts," identify and articulate the problems confronting the area. The ideal of a more efficient and economical method of governmental performance underlay the identification of many specific problems. The problems identified were, in most cases, abstract in nature (lack of a comprehensive governmental control), reform-oriented (duplication of functions), or determined to exist by an "expert's" definition (lack of a comprehensive metropolitan growth plan). The basis of determining the communities' problems and the nature of their seriousness were judged according to normative and value-based ideals as to what the community "ought" to be like, rather than based upon what the populace needed and wanted.

York Willbern succinctly summarized the point when he stated that "when surveyors of public opinion actually go from door to door, as has been done in some of the best-financed of metropolitan surveys, asking people what they consider to be crucial problems of metropolitan life, the answers have been surprising. Most people questioned were not particularly worried or unhappy about anything in their environment."[8]

The experience of Jacksonville–Duval County appears to be the only exception to the lack of a perceived crisis. In Jacksonville, widespread public concern over criminal indictments of governmental officials and the disaccreditation of public schools created a crisis in the minds of many citizens. A grass-roots recognition of severe urban problems in all cases but this one did not provide the stimulus for seeking governmental reform. The problems were defined by a narrow segment of the population that felt it was representative and qualified to speak in behalf of the total community. Although recognition and articulation of "problems" has been sufficient to initiate reform, it has not necessarily led to public acceptance of reorganization.

Establishment of a Reorganization Study/Charter Commission

Initial interest in local governmental reorganization usually begins with a variety of private, civic, and community groups rather than with local governmental officials. The academic community, Chambers of Commerce, Leagues of Women Voters, and metropolitan newspapers are four sources that have led the initiation of local governmental reorganization.[9]

Initiation of reorganization is rarely publicly opposed. There is little public debate or full discussion on the issue of whether a community should involve itself in local governmental reorganization. The pattern is that a group, such as those mentioned above, supports reorganization and initiates a movement to have the issue become public and this ultimately results in referenda. The opposition arises much later in the reorganization process, but by the time of the reorganization referenda, there are clearly identifiable groups that oppose reform.

Following the initiating group's display of interest, the next step in the process is the establishment of a study/charter commission. The primary means of establishing a commission is adoption by referendum. State legislation may be necessary to permit the local area to have a referendum on the question. Voter interest is usually high enough to endorse such an investigation, and very few study-charter commission referenda are defeated. However, voter support in approving a reorganization study does not necessarily indicate that the same level of support to implement the reorganization will be guaranteed in the final referendum.

Available data indicate that the average voter support for establishment of the reorganization study/charter commission is 72.6 percent, while the average voter support for reorganization of local government is 46.8 percent. Thus the establishment of a study/charter commission and acceptance of governmental reorganization are separate issues in the voters' minds.

Reorganization Study and Reform Proposals

The study of reorganization and reform proposals have sprung from several similar sources, depending upon the community and its reform experience. The supporters of the establishment of a commission have included interest groups, such as the Chamber of Commerce, which view governmental reorganization as having healthy economic implications. Professional politicians who are not on friendly terms with the dominant local political coalition also support reorganization study. These local officials may include members of the minority party or the mayor whose core city is prohibited from expansion by a county controlled politically by a different group. In the South, where a reform proposal legally must come before the state legislature, members of the local delegation to the legislature initiate reform study. Also included as study supporters are intellectuals who feel that they have no access to the current organization of the polity.[10] In St. Louis, political scientists from two local universities were actively involved in the metropolitan survey and reform proposals. Final groups involved in reorganization study might be classified generally as governmental reformers or citizens interested in good government. These would include members of Citizens' Leagues and Good Government Councils, Bureaus of Research, and the League of Women Voters.[11]

A study group, which is also usually enpowered to draft a charter, is created by governmental action. Local governmental bodies generally finance the commission, although contributions from national and local foundations have supported reform study/charter groups. For example, the St. Louis Metropolitan Survey was financed to the amount of $300,000 by the Ford Foundation and the McDonnell Aircraft Corporation Charitable Trust.

Once created, the study/charter commissions engage in study that vary extensively in cost, time to complete the study, and the extent of investigation. The purpose of all government reorganization studies is to identify the problems confronting the metropolitan area, evaluate governmental performance (particularly costs), and suggest alternatives that will alleviate the problems and make the operation of local government more effective, efficient, and economical by some form of reorganization.

The quality and type of reorganization study do not appear to be a critical factor in determining the passage or failure of the reform proposal by the electorate or, where applicable, the state legislature. The voters rejected reform in St. Louis, Missouri, and Charlotte, North Carolina. Yet the studies conducted in these two areas are among the best of metropolitan surveys.

The study of reorganization is both a necessary and ritualistic component in the process of reform. Politically, it seems that reorganization cannot proceed without a study that appears scientific in its analysis and unbiased in its recommendation. The reorganization case studies reflect some dispute as to whether the reorganization proposal itself is crucial to the support of reorganization. However, most case studies conclude that the quality of the study itself appears to hold little weight with the public. In most cases, very few voters were familiar with the details of a reorganization study. The public is not actively involved in or aware of the development of the study or final reform proposal adopted by the study/charter commission.

REORGANIZATION CAMPAIGNS

Voter turnout in most reorganization referenda is small. An ACIR report states that typically only one in four eligible voters participates in reorganization elections.[12] It is not surprising that local governmental reorganizations, which normally are not grass-roots movements, result in low voter turnouts. There is evidence to indicate that a substantial proportion of the public belong to no formal organization, exclusive of church-related groups and labor unions, and these organizations are generally not active in reorganization efforts.[13] If the public as a whole is uninterested in reorganization and few people belong to formal groups, how can they be reached concerning the merits of reorganization?

The typical local governmental reorganization campaign is mass-media-based. This approach normally combines professional public relations assistance with mass communications coverage via newspapers, radio, television, and billboards. As might be expected, since so few citizens belong to civic-oriented groups, the communication reorganization information to formal organizations have not been notably successful. Debates and speeches concerning reorganization made to civic groups and reliance upon the mass media influence very few people.

Having no party organization, supporters of reorganization can reach voters only through the mass media. However, voting studies indicate the limitations of the mass media on elections, particularly during the often brief period devoted to reorganization campaigns. The media simply cannot fulfill the primary role of activating mass support for reorganization.

In reorganization campaigns, various community groups surface both in support of and in opposition to reform. Most campaigns are organized around loose coalitions of groups. Both the pro and anti groups collect contributions to purchase newspaper and billboard space as well as television and radio air time. In addition, written material in the form of "fact" pamphlets are mailed to residents. The "ever-ready" speakers bureau is evident in most reform campaigns.

Political party leaders and elected local officials are generally not intensely involved in their support of reform. Even public officials who support reform usually do not become active campaigners. Group opposition to reorganization is often lacking during the beginning of a campaign, but usually surfaces during the middle and final stages of a reorganization effort. Groups and individuals who have remained silent concerning a reform issue become increasingly vocal as a campaign gets under full swing. The opposition groups often claim that they are in favor of reorganization but insist that the proposed charter is not the best means to implement reform.

Reorganization campaigns are not similar to the campaigns of political candidates for the office of mayor or congressman. Close competition for office often forces political candidates to develop well-organized campaigns in order to win the election. Reorganization campaigns rely heavily on the "logic" inherent in reorganization and very little on the organizational requisites of contacting and mobilizing voters.

Since many reform commissions' findings are relatively complex, symbolism is used to activate support. For example, in St. Louis two issues—appointed rather than elected officials, and increased taxes—were expounded effectively by those opposed to the reorganization. The proposed charter had nothing to do with these issues. In fact, there probably would be more appointed officials and increased taxes with or without reorganization. The opposition, however, was able to link the two issues with the charter. The questions of local control and increased costs became the symbolic cries of the opposition and were important in the defeat of the reorganization plan. In other words, the opposition forces were able to exploit the black community's fears that it would be unable to capture political control of the city, and the fears of the whites who saw rising taxes as a threat to their socioeconomic status. In most cases, the strengths and weaknesses of the complex reorganization issues are reduced to simplistic and often erroneous slogans that are used by groups for and against governmental change.

Even a well-organized campaign, however, may not be sufficient to win the voter. Frequently, political observers have felt that the stronger and more localized a "get out the vote" effort, the greater the possibility for success. The referenda efforts in Winchester city-Frederick County, Virginia (1969), and Augusta-Richmond County, Georgia (1971), undermine this belief. In the Virginia referendum, a 61 percent voter turnout produced a substantial rejection of consolidation, while 59.5 percent of the Augusta-Richmond County, Georgia, voters overwhelmingly defeated the effort there. In the latter example, strong anticonsolidation sentiments existed from a number of sources—city and county employees, city blacks, the sheriff and his 100 employees. Motivated by different reasons, these groups did not combine to conduct a coordinated anticonsolidation campaign, but their individualized efforts did help to stimulate high voter turnout and substantial negative voting. In contrast, the 1974 Augusta-Richmond County turnout was 37 percent, which resulted in a majority vote (Table 1). In Portland-Multnomah County, Oregon, a 51 percent turnout rate resulted in a 72.5 percent rejection of consolidation.

VOTER RESPONSE IN REORGANIZATION REFERENDA

Voter Turnout

The rate of voter turnout in consolidation referenda appears to make little difference in the level of voter support or in the passage or rejection of reorganization proposals.[14] This assessment concerning the effect of high voter turnout levels are at odds with the observations made by the ACIR in its voter study.[15]

High levels of voter support for reorganization have existed where voter turnout has been low. For example, in the 1970 Columbus-Muscogee County, Georgia, referendum 29 percent of the voters turned out, and over 80 percent of them supported consolidation. Governmental reorganization passed in Dade County (Miami) with only 26 percent of the voters participating. Reorganizations have passed and failed when voting turnout has been both light and heavy. Voter rejection of reorganization has occurred when 22 percent of the voters turned out (Albuquerque-Bernalillo County, New Mexico, 1959), 30 percent turned out (St. Louis-St. Louis County, 1959), and 61 percent turned out (Winchester city-Frederick County, Virginia, 1969).

The fact that voter turnout does not influence support of reorganization implies certain campaign strategies that may be pursued. Campaign efforts probably should not be aimed at the public in general, but rather at select groups and districts where potential support is believed to exist. For example, getting out the right vote (middle-income residents, professionals) appears to be more important than attempting to get a large turnout. It is other factors, in conjunction with voter turnout rates, that influence reorganization acceptance; voter turnout alone seems to make little difference.

City versus County Vote

Voting turnout by central city and the county area outside the city provides some interesting contrasts. County residents tend to turn out in higher percentages than do city residents; in no reorganization area did the city have a higher voter turnout than the county.[16] Moreover, the differences in the levels of city and county voter participation are substantial, with an average 16 percent higher voting participation in the county. Not only do county residents turn out in higher percentages, but they oppose reorganization to a greater extent than do city residents. The data in Table 2-2 illustrate the greater negative response of county voters than city voters toward reorganization. In 16 of the 17 reorganization referenda reported in Table 2-2, county voters exhibited more opposi-

TABLE 2-2. *Levels of City and County Voting Opposition in 17 Consolidations*

| Year | Reorganization Referendum | Percent Levels of Opposition | | Difference in Favor of County |
		City	*County*	
1959	Knoxville–Knox County Tenn.	50.8	63.4	12.6
	St. Louis–St. Louis County, Mo.	66.0	75.0	9.0
	Cleveland–Cuyahoga County, Ohio	55.5	53.2	-2.2
1961	Richmond–Henrico County, Va.	30.8	60.6	29.8
1962	Columbus–Muscogee County, Ga.	52.0	74.5	22.5
1964	Chattanooga–Hamilton County, Tenn.	81.3	83.3	2.0
1969	Athens–Clarke County, Ga.	40.2	70.7	30.5
	Brunswick–Glynn County, Ga.	62.7	78.1	15.4
1970	Columbus–Muscogee County, Ga.	18.3	62.1	41.8
1971	Augusta–Richmond County, Ga.	50.3	64.9	14.6
	Charlotte–Mecklenburg County, N.C.	56.9	88.1	31.2
1972	Athens–Clarke County, Ga.	47.6	58.1	10.5
	Suffolk–Nansemond County, Va.	15.6	27.6	12.0
1973	Columbia–Chatham County, S.C.	41.2	65.6	24.4
	Savannah–Chatham County, Ga.	25.4	67.7	42.3
1974	Augusta–Richmond County, Ga.	37.7	55.1	17.4
	Portland–Multnomah, Ore.	67.8	83.9	76.1
Averages		47.6	66.8	19.4

Note: The reorganization data presented in this table represent all available information from nationally published materials.

tion to reorganization than did city voters. Only in Cleveland did non-central city voters narrowly give greater support to reorganization.

The difference in the average opposition to reorganization between the city and the county residents is more than 19 percent. In the "average" reorganization effort county voters manifest greater voter opposition (as high as 42 percent) than do city residents. An extreme example is Portland-Multnomah, Oregon, where county residents voted against consolidation by more than six to one.

Reorganization: Unique Community Conditions

In several cases conditions unique to specific reorganization effects appear to be the most important in influencing the final outcome or reorganization efforts. The local government conditions of Jacksonville-Duval County, Florida, fit well into this "unique" category. The criminal indictments and the disaccreditation of schools provided a solid foundation for consolidation success in that area. Without these types of unique and critically important reorganization preconditions, the creation of an acceptable charter and the campaign efforts will probably not be sufficient to achieve city-county consolidation.

Voting support for consolidation was aided in the Columbus-Muscogee County, Georgia, 1970 consolidation referendum by the fact that more than 95 percent of the participating county-wide voters were city residents. This condition resulted from the city's aggressive annexation policy following the first defeat in 1962 of city-county consolidation. In 1970, most of the voters in Muscogee County were already residents of the city of Columbus. Furthermore, Columbus-Muscogee County seemed programmed for consolidation success by the requirement of a "double county" majority. This type of majority requires both city and county-wide voter approval. In other words, the votes of the city residents are counted twice—once in the city balloting and again in the county-wide tabulations—as city residents are also county residents. Consolidation would have been rejected in Columbus-Muscogee County if separate city and county majority approvals (the "double majority" requirement) had been required. The county residents, as small a proportion as they were (less than 5 percent of total voters), voted firmly against consolidation and could have determined the fate of local government under different election requirement circumstances.

The Nashville-Davidson County, Tennessee, 1958 and 1962 consolidation referenda are interesting in terms of unique conditions. The use of the "green sticker" tax on all automobiles using city streets, the aggressive role of the mayor, and the open debate between the two major city newspapers on the consolidation issues all combined to make the 1962 consolidation referendum substantially different from the one held in 1958.[17] Hence the 1962 referendum generated much more interest and more intense voter involvement.

In another "unique" situation, mass-media campaign techniques have been credited with the passage of at least one governmental reorganization—Miami-Dade County, Florida.[18] The explanation in this instance rests with the uniquely transient nature of the area residents. Most residents, particularly those living in suburban areas, had lived in Miami less than two decades. These conditions stimulated citizen dependence on mass-media communication for information due to weak community attachments and low participation in primary associations. Thus the mass media in Miami had a much greater impact upon voter support than has been true in other consolidation attempts. In addition, only a "single county-wide majority" was necessary to achieve reorganization there.

To separate precisely the "unique" circumstances from conditions generally associated with reorganization support is a difficult task.[19] Reorganization support is influenced by many factors that are intertwined in complex processes, and any attempt to examine the specific influences of the interdependent factors must be viewed with appropriate caution. It appears that "unique" factors are uniformly positive in their relationship to acceptance of reorganization support, and it is these factors that appear to be a necessary component in any success.[20] Unique conditions alone, however, may not be sufficient for achieving reorganization success.

ANNEXATION: "PIECEMEAL" METROPOLITAN REORGANIZATION

Annexation is currently not considered a significant form of governmental reorganization. Annexation has been described as a limited reorganization solution, both because of the rather stringent requirements established by most states and because of the general absence of unincorporated land adjacent to major cities.[21] As one author states, annexation is more likely to be advantageous to smaller municipalities than larger ones.[22] It is this paper's contention that annexation has not been adequately examined as a serious reorganization option, in that it is not seen as a comprehensive reorganization solution (less than the entire metropolitan affected, *i.e.,* a piecemeal solution) and in that annexation has come to be identified as a viable method of reorganization only in the smaller metropolitan areas of the South and West. Preliminary analysis indicates that these assessments of annexation are not accurate. In the aggregate, annexations have affected more people and greater area than any other form of governmental reorganization. Without annexation there would have been practically no population growth in the nation's 243 central cities between 1960 and 1970. Approximately 98 percent of all central city growth (4 million) was accomplished by annexation.

The extent of annexation varies by region of the country. In Figure 1, city population increases through annexation from 1960 to 1970 are contrasted by region. Annexation has occurred extensively throughout the United States with the exception of the Northeast. In the Northeast, the gain from annexation has been negligible—30,000 for the entire nine-state region. In the North Central region, a gain of more than a million through annexation was sufficient to overcome a large population decrease within central cities. In the West, a gain of 800,000 persons in central cities accounted for almost half of their total growth, while in the South, the annexation of almost 2 million people accounted for five-sixths of total central city growth. In sum, Figure 1 indicates that annexation is extensively used in metropolitan areas throughout the nation, excluding the Northeast.

The extent of annexation also varies by size of metropolitan area, as shown in Figure 2. Cities in the small metropolitan areas of less than 100,000 and cities in the largest areas of 3 million and more did not extensively annex. However, within the wide range of middle-sized metropolitan areas (100,000 to 3 million) over 3½ million urban residents were annexed to cities. Annexation has been

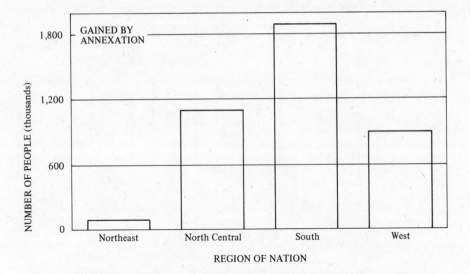

Figure 1. **Increase in Population of Central Cities by Region, 1960–70**

widely used in the large, if not in the largest, metropolitan areas. Contrary to expectation, annexation is not extensively utilized in small metropolitan areas.

Within metropolitan areas annexation of population varies by type of city. Approximately two-thirds of all central cities and about half of the noncentral cities annexed populations between 1960 and 1970. Table 2-3 indicates that annexation is frequently used by noncentral cities. Metropolitan noncentral cities, often suburbs, are less enclosed by local governments and are more likely to be adjoined by unincorporated land. In fact, a large proportion of growth in metropolitan areas is occurring in unincorporated areas surrounding noncentral cities, particularly in the South. These unincorporated areas, often with high growth rates, are being politically reorganized through annexation into suburban cities

TABLE 2-3. *Cities Annexing or Not Annexing, 1960–70, by Metropolitan and Nonmetropolitan Location in 1970*

| | Metropolitan | | | | Nonmetropolitan | |
| | Central City | | Other | | | |
Cities, 1960–70*	Number	Percent	Number	Percent	Number	Percent
Annexing	209	68.1	488	52.5	513	76.7
Not Annexing	98	31.9	442	47.5	156	23.3
Total	307	100.0	930	100.0	669	100.0

*Includes all incorporated cities of 10,000 or more population in 1970 that were 2,500 or more in 1960 and were identified in the 1960 census.

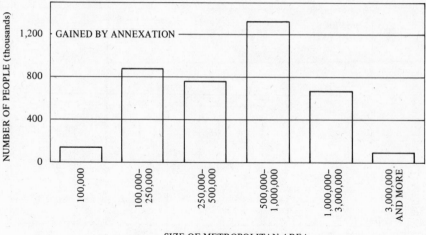

SIZE OF METROPOLITAN AREA

Figure 2. Increase in Population of Central Cities by Size of Metropolitan Area, 1960–70

—not central cities. Annexation to suburban cities may be indicative of an emerging form of metropolitan reorganization.

Observations on the Politics of Annexation

Compared to city-county consolidation, annexation within metropolitan areas is politically feasible and widely used—excluding the Northeast—and probably will continue to be a major form of reorganization. It is in the suburban areas that most metropolitan growth is occurring, and it is the suburban cities, in comparison with central cities, that are more likely to be surrounded by unincorporated areas. The full range and impact of annexation in metropolitan areas have not been adequately documented or assessed. It is likely in many metropolitan areas that through annexation suburban cities will come to rival the central city in size and population. At the minimum, annexation may be a means by which suburbs can expand to provide viable governance for increasing proportions of metropolitan areas.

Legislation concerning annexation varies a great deal, from permissive requirements (*e.g.*, municipal and judicial determinations) to legal requirements that hinder annexation (*e.g.*, voter approval in both annexed and annexing areas.) Whether state legislation facilitates annexation or not, legislation exists in most states that spells out annexation procedures. State annexation legislation routinizes and regularizes the annexation procedure. Although variation exists, annexations in most states are determined at one level of government, usually the local level, by those governments and populations affected by annexation. State governments normally do not involve themselves with local annexation activities.

In contrast to annexation, most states do not have constitutional or statutory requirements concerning other forms of governmental reorganization, such as city-county consolidations or a two-tiered metropolitan government. These forms of metropolitan reorganization often must be resolved, either separately or simultaneously, at the local and the state levels. Most metropolitan reorganization, in effect, is determined and shaped by the political processes at two levels of government. Metropolitan reorganization proposals—such as city-county consolidations—are drafted at the local level and additionally must be submitted to state legislatures as local bills. Thus political considerations and compromises concerning these forms of reorganization are shaped in two political arenas that may have differing constituencies that manifest conflicting interests. Political adoption of reorganization is more difficult to achieve when two sets of political processes (state and local) are required, in contrast to reorganization that is shaped at one level. Obviously, state legislation establishing clear, permissive requirements would facilitate such metropolitan reorganizations as city-county consolidation.

Annexation is a nonideological method of metropolitan reorganization. There are a multitude of reasons and objectives motivating city annexation attempts— increasing a city's tax base by acquiring industrial areas; obtaining open land; extending liquor ordinances to formerly unincorporated areas; or obtaining a "desired" mix of social and racial residents. The range of reasons could be extended to include all objectives that local governments are established to achieve. Annexation is not a reflection of a middle-class, public administration ethic, which stresses area-wide government as a means of bringing more rationality to the governance of metropolitan areas.

Annexations are a response to real problems—not the imagined needs of a metropolitan area shaped by a middle-class bias for efficiency, economy, and rationality. One only has to examine city-county consolidation efforts to assess their ideological middle-class bias.[23]

In sum, annexation is politically feasible and is an extremely flexible method of reorganization; it can closely follow the desires of various interests that can be brought together in the "political marketplace." In most annexations there is a common interest among the parties (those annexing and those being annexed), each having relatively clear and immediate reorganization interests. Of course, this piecemeal approach to metropolitan reorganization carries some implications for area-wide governmental coordination. Nevertheless, the extent to which annexation fits the political marketplace and accounts for expanding a city's territorial control within metropolitan areas needs closer examination. The extensive reliance upon annexation in many metropolitan areas throughout a large portion of the nation should stimulate research not only because annexation is a politically feasible method of reorganizing general local government but also to assess if annexation can be adapted to the broader range of metropolitan-wide governance concerns.

COUNCILS OF GOVERNMENTS: AN ADD-ON METHOD OF REORGANIZATION

Councils of governments (COGs) are the most politically feasible form of area-wide metropolitan reorganization. The number of COGs has dramatically increased from a handful in the 1950s to their current existence in virtually all the nation's metropolitan areas. This increase in the number of COGs has primarily been responsive to federal legislation which emphasized metropolitan-wide decision-making requirements. Specifically, several federal aid programs required that funding depend upon the creation of metropolitan-wide mechanism, usually a COG.[24]

Rather than take the creation of a COG as evidence of metropolitan reorganization, one should realize that the real politics of metropolitan reorganization occurs after a COG has been established. Beyond the documentation of the existence of a COG, few data have been collected on the types of problems that they are equipped to handle or do handle. In addition, only speculation and isolated examples of specific COGs are available to determine whether COGs are evolving into governmental mechanisms that approximate an authoritative government.

After its creation, a COG must function in metropolitan areas where human differentiation exists spatially. The fact that people in metropolitan areas, especially suburbs, live in homogeneous communities and protect many of their values through local governmental structures affects COGs as well as other metropolitan reorganization mechanisms. This spatial differentiation and the variations in life styles give parameters to the COG's activities as a metropolitan governing mechanism. Federal support aside, it is the life-style implications of the COG's potential power that shapes the politics of metropolitan reorganization.

Thus COGs tend to engage in only those policy areas that do not affect the life styles of metropolitan residents. COGs engage in programs like sewage and solid waste, data processing and collection, transportation planning, and a myriad of activities of technical assistance to local governments but avoid programs with social implications. Few COGs undertake programs dealing with public or subsidized housing, zoning, urban renewal, or enforcement of open occupancy ordinances.

Table 2-4 lists governmental functions and services which COGs have the general authority to provide, whether provided or not. In Table 2-4 the services and functions are classified as to whether their provision would generate poten-

TABLE 2-4. *Social Implications and Conflict Potential of Functions and Services Provided by COGs*

Service or Function	Social Implications	Core City–Suburb and Suburb–Suburb Conflict Potential
Sewer Planning	None	Low
Water Planning	None	Low
Sewage and Solid Waste	None	Low
Data Collection	None	Low
Transportation Planning	None	Low
Comprehensive Land-Use Planning	None	Low
Open Space Planning	None	Low
Air and Water Pollution Control	None[1]	Low
Communications	None	Low
Flood Control	None	Low
Economic Development	None	Low
Codes and Licensing	None	Low
Libraries	None	Low
Fire Protection Programs	None	Low
Law Enforcement	Certain phases—yes[2]	Certain phases high
Recreation	Certain phases—yes[2]	Certain phases high
Education	Certain phases—yes[2]	Certain phases high
Health	Certain phases—yes[2]	Certain phases high
Zoning	Yes	High
Subsidized Housing	Yes[3]	High
Public Housing	Yes	High
Urban Renewal	Yes	High
Community Action	Yes	High
Senior Citizens Programs	Yes	High
Open Occupancy	Yes	High
Juvenile Delinquency	Yes	High
Noise Control Program	None	High

[1]This table views social implications and conflict in a short-range time perspective (five years). It is conceivable that issues such as air and water pollution control may produce a high amount of conflict among local governments in years to come.

[2]Certain phases of law enforcement have a social implication, such as police investigations and patrol services, whereas police communications systems and training academics have no social implications. The same can be said for recreation, education, and health.

[3]Examples of subsidized housing would be singlefamily housing (Sec. 235) and Multifamily housing (Sec. 236) programs of the federal government.

tial conflict among member governments of COGs. Conflict lines are assumed to exist if life styles are likely to be threatened by programmatic action by the COG. Programs with social implications would probably create conflict between central city and suburbs, and among suburbs with varying life-style orientations.[25] It is assumed that COGs would provide few services that carry with them a high potential for conflict among the various units of local government within metropolitan areas. However, a few COGs have engaged in policy activities that have strong social implications, and the discussion will now turn to the political processes involved in these cases.

COGs and Lower-Income Housing Dispersal

The dispersal of lower-income housing on a metropolitan-wide basis is a governmental activity that generates a great deal of conflict within and among local governments. Several COG s have considered, and a few COGs have adopted, a plan that allocates lower-income housing throughout metropolitan areas (a "fair share" plan). Such a plan is based on the principle that all localities assume a "fair share" of the metropolitan areas's lower-income housing. The critical distinguishing feature of a COG's fair share plan is that it allocates lower-income housing *among* local jurisdictions and on a *metropolitan-wide basis*.

As of January 1974, five councils of governments of the approximate 243 that exist nationwide had adopted a fair share plan.[26] An additional 25 COGs are in some stage of developing a fair share plan. Of the five COGs, only the Miami Valley Regional Planning Commission (MVRPC) of the Dayton, Ohio metropolitan area has had a fair share plan long enough to get an indication of its impact. Since September 1970, when MVRPC adopted the nation's first fair share plan, more than half of the metropolitan areas's lower-income housing has been built in the suburbs. Prior to the fair share plan, approximately 90 percent of the metropolitan area's lower-income housing units were built in the central city of Dayton. Of the proposed lower-income housing yet to be built, 27 percent will be built in the city of Dayton and 73 percent in suburban and outlying areas.

The experience of one COG on the issue of locating lower-income housing is certainly not representative of what will occur throughout the nation's metropolitan areas. Nor is there any evidence that Dayton's fair share planning efforts will be adopted by COGs throughout the country. Although Dayton's experience does indicate that a COG can successfully deal with an important metropolitan problem that contains a high degree of potential conflict among the local units of government, it has not demonstrated what will occur in other areas.

Fair share planning has acted as a catalyst in restructuring the metropolitan planning and decision-making process. The politics involved in this form of metropolitan reform are primarily administrative in nature. No public referenda are required to adopt a fair share plan. That is, urban planning administrators shaped and sought adaption of fair share planning by the governing body of the COG. It was through administration processes that fair share plans gained support and were presented to COGs for adoption.

Fair share planning provides a vehicle for urban planners, at both metropolitan and federal levels, to address a generic problem: the relative weakness of planning as compared with decision making in metropolitan areas. Urban planners share common concerns about the strengthening of the planning process as well as the allocation of lower-income housing on a metropolitan-wide basis. The planners' concern for allocating lower-income housing on a metropolitan-wide basis is an objective that fits their goal of strengthening the planning process. The result was the development of a COG that functioned on a high-conflict issue as if it were an authoritative metropolitan government.

Through complex and sophisticated political processes—primarily administrative in nature—urban planners at various levels of government participated in a symbiotic form of metropolitan reform. The planning officials from the different levels of government each had something to gain and needed to rely upon each other. The COG planners had the capacity and authority to develop fair share plans, and HUD planning officials controlled funding and lent legitimacy to fair share planning. This mutually dependent relationship thrusted COGs into an extremely strong role as the official reviewer (A-95 review), influencing where lower-income housing was to be located within metropolitan areas.[27] It is the COGs' review power over requests for federal support which is the determining factor. In this capacity COGs participate, quite forcefully, in the decision-making process. Although COGs do not solely determine where lower-income housing is to be located, they utilize their fair share plans to gain an authoritative role in directing federal funds to support area-wide policy. Although fair share planning is atypical of general COG activities, it illustrates that COGs may be able to play a more significant role in the future in metropolitan governance.

SUMMARY OBSERVATIONS

This paper has offered the perspective that the politics of metropolitan reorganization differs according to the specific reform under consideration. The three types of reorganization—city-county consolidation, annexation, and councils of governments—are adopted through political processes that are shaped by various legal constraints, group support and opposition, and a multitude of other factors. The adoption of a city-county consolidation is politically much more difficult to achieve than either annexation or the establishment of a COG. Yet city-county consolidation is thought to represent more of a comprehensive metropolitan reorganization than either of the other two reforms. The political feasibility and the comprehensiveness of reorganization are interrelated, yet represent two dimensions of reform that are separate objects of analysis to urban scholars.

In terms of political feasibility, there has been a wide variation in the adoption of metropolitan reorganizations. With few exceptions most successful city-county consolidations have occurred in small and middle-sized (less than a million population) Southern metropolitan areas. The impact of social differentiation and racial factors (both white and black resistance) between city and suburb appears to be having an increasingly negative influence upon the adoption of city-county consolidation. The establishment of a city-county consolidation involving voter acceptance through a referendum presents an unusually difficult political barrier to adoption. The wide reliance upon annexation in metropolitan areas throughout the United States—with the exception of the Northeast—is testimony to its political feasibility. Annexations are often characterized by negotiation between a municipality and a specific population to be annexed. If a referendum is required, it does not apply to the entire metropolitan area, but is territorially limited to those affected by the annexation. Political feasibility is the trademark of the COG, as evidenced by its establishment in virtually all metropolitan areas. The politics of COGs occur after their formation and are primarily administrative in character. Yet COGs are not really new governmental structures. With few exceptions COGs do not engage in the formulation of metropolitan-wide policies that significantly alter existing social and economic functions or redistribute tax resources among existing localities.

The discussion presented in this paper suggests that where voter acceptance is required, the selection of metropolitan areas in which reorganization is to be implemented is more important than the reform process itself. The requirement of voter acceptance not only represents a barrier to reorganization but also predetermines the outcome. This is not to suggest that factors involved in the reform process (*e.g.,* type of proposal, group involvement, type of reform campaign) are not important, but the process is quite limited in its effect upon reorganization adoption. A metropolitan area includes environmental and political system conditions that have an immeasurable impact upon the probability of local acceptance of governmental reorganization.

Recognizing the political constraints accompanying voter acceptance, several factors have consistently been found to be related to reorganization outcomes. Of course, exceptions exist to every generalization concerning factors affecting support of reorganization.[28] However, I contend that the generalizations may apply to all but a few of the United States' urban areas. It is the exceptional urban area that is blessed with unique circumstances that culminate in successful local governmental reorganization. These unique situational factors are a necessary condition for adopting reorganization; however, they may not be sufficient for achieving consolidation. Without a genuine crisis or unique circumstances, the probability of achieving a successful reorganization through city-county consolidation is extremely low.

In all but a few metropolitan areas the following political process conditions exist. First, city-county governmental reorganization is not usually a grass-roots movement. It springs forth from the desires of only an interested few—namely, civic groups, academics, and community business leaders. Hence reorganization campaign efforts have great difficulty in reaching large numbers of people when the issue is not one of widespread public concern. Scott Greer's observations about the St. Louis plan are applicable to reorganizations in general. Greer says, "Seldom have so many business men, lawyers, elected officials, politicians, administrators, and League ladies taken public stands on abstract and difficult issues. Seldom have so few worked so hard and succeeded in confusing so many."[29] Furthermore, the problems facing urban areas have not been severe enough to indicate that reorganization is an obvious course of action, and neither scholars nor the public is convinced that reorganization would make a significant difference in resolving the major problems in urban areas.

Second, it appears that the benefits of a reorganized government are either too abstract or too long-range for the more finite interests of the typical voter, who is not interested in the possibility of additional services regardless of how "fair" the price, and yet efficiency, economy, equity, and better quality of services for less money are the prime reasons given for reorganization. Reforms, based upon such rationales as community control of community functions, and the achievement of more equitable distribution of tax burdens and improved services may be too abstract for the common voter. Apparently these reasons are not enough to convince a majority of voters that reorganization should be accepted. Without real and immediate problems, reorganization will remain an abstraction to most voters, and voter support will be difficult to achieve.

Furthermore, many people are not being reached through the usual mass-media campaign strategy that is employed in most reorganization efforts. Local governmental reorganization campaigns are run differently than campaigns for major political offices. A more traditional campaign approach, similar to the methods employed by competitive political candidates, would be more effective in gaining voter support. As one study indicates, the most important factor in determining the direction of the vote is the mobilization of political support or opposition.[30] No metropolitan reorganization can pass over the active opposition of the political parties, nor is reorganization likely to pass without active partisan support.[31] There is much information available on how to get an individual elected to office, which could be applied to reorganization campaigns in order to understand voting behavior and campaign techniques needed to obtain support for reorganization.

Voter approval appears to be the most restrictive political requirement affecting the adoption of metropolitan reorganization, especially where majority approval is required in each political subdivision affected. In large metropolitan areas, which are characterized by many political subdivisions, particularly the specialized homogeneous suburban communities, reorganization requiring voter approval is extremely difficult. Metropolitan reorganization requiring voter approval has not been achieved in any area of more than 1 million population during the twentieth century. Where reorganization has occurred in large metropolitan areas, it has been achieved without local referenda. In addition to the creation of COGs, reorganizations without referenda have been achieved by state legislative action in Denver, Colorado, Indianapolis, Indiana, and Minneapolis-St. Paul, Minnesota.

Metropolitan reorganization alters and threatens many established and emerging interests. Foremost among concerned subpopulations in metropolitan areas are central city blacks and suburban whites. For example, metropolitan reorganization in the form of a city-county consolidation carries negatively perceived consequences, such as higher taxes and less access to and/or control of government, which restrict the formation of local policies to meet the needs of subpopulations in metropolitan areas. Can observers concerned with the politics of metropolitan reorganization expect reform through referenda when reform threatens the utilization of local governments to achieve the valued interests of metropolitan subpopulations?

Metropolitan reform is an issue that resembles in important ways the civil rights and state legislative reapportionment issues of the 1950s and 1960s. It was not reasonable to expect Southern states and communities to adopt civil rights legislation through local elections. Likewise, state legislative reapportionment was not achieved within the legislative bodies that were to be affected. In both cases, change was effected by the issue being resolved by a separate political body at another level of government. These three types of issues all directly and profoundly affect the interests of those involved. It is appropriate that political scientists reexamine metropolitan reform to assess more accurately the dynamics of change that accompany an issue that affects locals interests and values. Without unduly straining the parallels among the issues, the data presented in this paper indicate that metropolitan reorganization, if left to voter approval, is not likely to be adopted at the local level.

Metropolitan reorganization is most likely to be achieved at the state government level—utilizing some form of local representation. As state government assumes an increasingly greater concern with metropolitan governmental organization, the states' influence and involvement will expand. As states increase their activities in metropolitan reorganization, they will be returning to their former role of direct involvement in it. Between 1805 and 1907, all metropolitan reorganizations were mandated by state legislatures—without local referenda.[32] The difference now is that subsequent to reapportionment urban interests, which are proportionately represented in state legislatures, will prevent nonurban domination of metropolitan reform.

Where and how states are to involve themselves more directly in metropolitan reorganization is an open question, and the answer, in all probability, will vary across the nation. Although states have always had varying degrees of legislative requirements for reorganization, they create new arenas for achieving metropolitan governmental reorganization. These new arenas may be special committees of the legislature, the executive department, specific reorganization commissions, or judicial bodies.

Scholars concerned with the political processes of metropolitan reorganization can refocus on the politics of creating new arenas for establishing metropolitan re-organization at the state level. A new arena at the state level is certainly no panacea for metropolitan problems. In fact there can be too much state involvement. In addition, the record is not clear as to the exact effects of reorganized metropolitan government upon solving urban problems. Whether the reorganized areas of Jacksonville and Miami, Florida, are more effective than nonreorganized areas has not been adequately assessed. In addition, analysis is needed which examines the differences between reorganizations adopted through state action (*e.g.,* Indianapolis and Minneapolis-St. Paul) and those adopted through local referenda (*e.g.,* Miami and Nashville).

The creation of new arenas for metropolitan reorganization at the state level would increase the probability of reform and allow a broader perspective on urban problem resolution, which could carry with it a set of criteria based upon multigovernmental objectives and allow regional norms to be more fully aired. The various local interests can be represented, so that the necessary compromises could be based upon a more accurate understanding of the interdependencies of subpopulation interests within metropolitan areas. In addition, local politics, which tend to be based upon personalities and symbolic arguments, would be tempered with the more "objective" and less intense state-level perspective.

In conclusion, political factors are the major obstacles to governmental re-organization in metropolitan areas, and these factors are particularly evident in metropolitan reorganization based upon voter approval. An increased state role, in the form of a new arena, reformulates the issue of metropolitan reorganization and provides a new paradigm for analysis and reform.

NOTES

1. D. R. Grant, "Urban Needs and State Response: Local Government Reorga-nization," in A. K. Campbell, ed., *The States and the Urban Crisis* (Engle-wood Cliffs, N. J.: Prentice-Hall, 1970, pp. 59–84.

2. E. Banfield, *The Unheavenly City* (Boston: Little, Brown, 1970).

3. "City-county consolidation" is used in this paper as a generic term that re-fers to reorganization based upon two levels of local governmental authority and service delivery. Most consolidations leave current municipalities intact, as well as establishing differential service districts for urban and rural areas. Thus they come to resemble the federated form of reorganization of Miami-Dade County. More importantly, the major observations of the political processes offered in this paper apply to both city-county consolidation and the federated form of metropolitan reorganizations.

4. Excluded in this listing are all "borough type" consolidations, which are common in the state of Alaska. Two considerations seem to justify these omissions: (1) the borough consolidations have occurred in very small areas; and (2) the areas consolidated in Alaska are atypical of the urban-suburban

patterns of life styles in the other areas that have attempted local governmental reorganization.

5. R. A. Watson and J. H. Romani, "Metropolitan Government for Metropolitan Cleveland: An Analysis of the Voting Record," *Midwest Journal of Political Science,* November 1961, p. 372.

6. C. W. Bain, *Annexation in Virginia* (Charlottesville: University of Virginia Press, 1966).

7. V. Jones, *Metropolitan Government* (Chicago: University of Chicago Press, 1970), pp. 55-8.

8. Y. Willbern, *The Withering Away of the City* (Bloomington: Indiana University Press, 1963), p. 95.

9. J. C. Bollens and H. J. Schmandt, *The Metropolis* (New York: Harper & Row, 1965), pp. 498-9.

10. S. Greer, *Metropolitics: A Study of Political Culture* (New York: Wiley, 1963), p. 22.

11. *Ibid.*

12. Advisory Commission on Intergovernmental Relations, *Factors Affecting Voter Reactions to Governmental Reorganization in Metropolitan Areas* (Washington: Government Printing Office, 1961).

13. A. H. Hawley and B. G. Zimmer, *The Metropolitan Community* (Beverly Hills, Sage Publications, 1970).

14. A simple correlation coefficient of -.31 was found to exist between voter turnout and voter support. The computation of this simple correlation coefficient is based on data for 11 consolidation referenda. These data represent all available information from nationally published source materials. In addition all data on voting are reported in terms of support for reorganization as opposed to the acceptance or rejection of reorganization. The number of adoptions is so small as to severely limit analysis based on reorganization adoption or rejection.

15. Advisory Commission on Intergovernmental Relations, *op. cit.*

16. This observation is based upon city-county voting data from six reorganization attempts. Data from these six areas represent all available data from nationally published source material.

17. Bollens and Schmandt, *op. cit.,* pp. 510-2.

18. E. Sofen, *Miami Metropolitan Experiment* (Bloomington: Indiana University Press, 1963), p. 76.

19. V. L. Marando, "Voting in City-County Consolidation Referenda," *Western Political Quarterly,* 26 (March 1973), pp. 90-6.

20. T. M. Scott, "Metropolitan Governmental Proposals," *Western Political Quarterly,* June 1968, pp. 498-507.

21. R. L. Lineberry, "Reforming Metropolitan Governance: Requiem or Reality," *Georgetown Law Journal,* 58 (March-May 1970), pp. 675-717.

22. *Ibid.,* p. 684.

23. The author is indebted to Professor Everett Lee for his assistance in examin-

ing annexation by making available Everett S. Lee and P. Neal Ritchy, "The Prospects for New Cities: The Historical View," paper presented at the annual meeting of the Population Association of America, April 1973.

24. The five COGs are located in the following metropolitan areas: Dayton, Ohio; Washington, D.C.; Denver, Colo.; San Bernadino, Calif.; and Minneapolis–St. Paul, Minn.

25. Grant, *op. cit.*

26. V. L. Marando, "Metropolitan Research and Councils of Government," *Midwest Journal of Public Administration*, 9 (February 1971), pp. 3–15.

27. U.S., Bureau of the Budget Circular A–95, July 24, 1969, attachment C. The A–95 review process applies to the programs of all domestic federal departments. The A–95 review is granted to COGs, allowing them to evaluate builders' requests for federal funds to construct lower-income housing. The A–95 can be utilized by COGs on all lower-income housing projects that have a minimum number of units; single family homes (235) must have 50 or more units, and multifamily projects must have 100 or more dwellings.

28. Scott, *op. cit.*

29. Greer, *loc. cit.*

30. H. Schmandt, P. G. Steinbicher, and G. D. Wendel, *Metropolitan Reform in St. Louis* (New York: Holt, Rinehart and Winston, 1961).

31. Advisory Commission on Intergovernmental Relations, *op. cit.*

32. W. R. McDougall, "Consolidation: How Is It Working?" in National Association of County Officials, *Consolidation Partial or Total* (Washington: National Association of Counties, 1973).

Comment: The Implications of Judicial Decisions for Metropolitan Reorganization

Dennis A. Gilbert

Anyone who feels that the metropolitan status quo is in need of change is bound to be somewhat discouraged by Professor Marando's analysis. His general conclusion is that the citizens affected by metropolitan reorganization are not much inclined to vote in favor of it. Professor Marando cites a number of reasons for this resistance, but says that in most areas the critical catalyst of a pressing public issue simply does not exist. The important factor here is his observation that most citizens are content with the current governmental arrangement of their metropolitan area.

One might well ask, then, if most of the citizens are content with things as they are, why do some people continue to busy themselves agitating for reorganization? The justifications for reorganization normally include mention of particular anomalies and unnecessary inefficiencies, but at the heart of the matter is the continuing existence of many inequities. Reorganization is viewed as an important, if not essential, way to reduce inequities.

The difficulty is that the people benefiting from these inequities are in a majority. And as Professor Marando pointed out, there are very few political incentives for the haves to relinquish any of their advantages to the have-nots.[1] So Professor Marando's summary seems quite correct: if inequities are to be substantially altered by reorganization, approval of the change cannot be left to local voters.

Professor Marando suggests two possible ways around local referenda. One approach would settle for less than complete reorganization. Annexation and/or mechanisms like councils of governments could be used instead. However, as he notes himself, except for a few scattered instances these devices simply lack the political and other resources needed to do something meaningful about the difficult problems of inequity.

The second alternative would create what Professor Marando calls "new arenas" at the state level. Yet if these arenas are political, then a number of troublesome questions arise. For example, are the politics of transferring an activity to the state level so different from local politics that a pressing issue will be less necessary at that level? In light of the mutual back scratching that often makes state legislators reluctant to impose state will on resisting local communities, could state legislators actually be expected to ignore strong local sentiment and order reorganization? And with one-man, one-vote redistricting having increased suburban power in state legislatures, is it not likely that the capacity of the state to mandate reorganization will be reduced still more?

Other questions might be asked, but the point is simply that political mechanisms appear to offer, at best, a rather limited hope for minorities who are now on the short end of the status quo. In other situations, when the institutional safeguards have proven inadequate to protect the rights and interests of our nation's minority segments against the sentiments of the majority, the aggrieved sought relief not at the ballot box with referenda, but in the courts. I suggest that under these circumstances the courts may be a very helpful means for breaking the present political impasse.

A Federal Appeals Court case that is receiving increasing attention in both legal and academic communities is *Hawkins v. Town of Shaw*.[2] The plaintiffs in the case pointed out that in Shaw, Mississippi, 98 percent of the homes facing on unpaved streets were occupied by blacks, and 97 percent of the homes without sanitary sewers were occupied by blacks. When new street lights were installed, they were erected only in the white part of town. In the white neighborhood there were 6-inch water mains; in the black neighborhoods there were only 2-inch water mains. Citing these facts and others, the plaintiffs argued that the situation was discriminatory and a violation of their constitutional right to equal protection of the law. The Appeals Court agreed. And in a much-quoted passage the decision stated:

> In order to prevail in a case of this type it is not necessary to prove intent, motive, or purpose to discriminate on the part of city officials. . . . We now firmly recognize that the arbitrary quality of thoughtlessness can be as disasterous and unfair to private rights and to public interest as the perversity of a willful scheme.

The only argument the court was willing to hear to the contrary was compelling state interest. In other words, if there exists a vastly inequitable status quo that is not required by compelling state interest, it is discriminatory and an unconstitutional violation of rights—regardless of intent. And in *Swann v. Charlotte-Meckenlenburg Board of Education*[3] the U.S. Supreme Court said that

> Once a right and a violation have been shown, the scope of a district's equitable powers to remedy past wrongs is broad, for breadth and flexibility are inherent in equitable remedies.

Who can seek relief? Most of the cases brought and most of the cases won are seeking relief from discrimination based on race. But a Federal Appeals Court decision in Atlanta[4] recognized that race and low income are frequently overlapping categories. And in the *Hawkins* case in a concurring opinion, Judge Wisdom wrote, "By our decision in this case we recognize the right of every citizen regardless of race to equal municipal services." A dissenting judge in the same case was alarmed by this line of reasoning. He said if Judge Wisdom were correct, then "the disparity would be irrelevant to race. . . ." The matter is still far from settled. Both sides in the argument cite cases as precedents in support of their positions. The point is that even though the issue has not been finally resolved, the potential impact is enormous.

In what service areas can remedies be sought? Education and housing have received considerable judicial attention. With the *Hawkins* decision, nearly every municipal service becomes fair game. However, the courts will want to draw some lines. Quoting Judge Wisdom in the *Hawkins* case once more,

> The line will, of course, have to be drawn between those disparities which create a right of action in federal court and those which do not. Case by case development will define the contours of a federal cause of action; this case is not a vehicle for precise definition.

Again, the issues are not fully developed, but the potential impact is great.

Finally, as the subject here is metropolitan reorganization, what does all this mean for jurisdictional lines? The *Hawkins* case required equity within a given jurisdiction. A Federal Appeals Court case in Cleveland[5] compelled a county housing authority that spanned central city lines to reduce inequities in the form of racial discrimination. And, in *Serrano v. Priest*,[6] the California Supreme Court found that vastly unequal tax bases for different school districts were in violation of the California state constitution. In short, equity is being required within a single jurisdiction, within a jurisdiction that spans other jurisdictional lines, and also between coequal and autonomous jurisdictions—the sort of relation that exists between governments of the central cities and the surrounding suburbs. Of course, the *Serrano* precedent received a setback with the failure of the *Rodriques* case[7] in the U.S. Supreme Court. However, there are always state constitutions to which to appeal and other ways to establish the principle using another function or using education in a different way.

This cursory review has provided only the barest outline of a very large number of highly complicated issues. The intention has been to show that the camel's nose is now under the tent. It is not possible to tell from the nose exactly what shape this camel will be, but the indications are that he will be quite large. That is why *Hawkins* has been cited in so many decisions and why *Serrano* caused such a storm. These decisions, and others like them, represent the first parts of a camel that may eventually be able to leap jurisdictional lines with a single bound and carry all sorts of aggrieved citizens on its back, attacking any inequitable municipal function in sight.

If and when we see this beast bounding around the countryside, we will probably find a lot of old political warhorses getting up off their duffs and swinging into action. For example, *Serrano* caused many states to take a hard look at the way they finance their schools. This is not to say that activity is the same as progress, but moving the political process off dead center is no mean feat in itself.

It should also be noted, though, that there are potential pitfalls along the judicial road. In the *Hawkins* case, equity is defined as equality. Yet many proponents of change would want to see equity defined in terms of need, so that those who require more services than the average will receive them. Since equity can be defined in several ways, even if cases brought to reduce inequities are successful, they may not produce the final result intended. Plaintiffs will need to understand thoroughly the legal, political, fiscal, and social ramifications of the changes they seek to cause.

Any progress won in the courts will be deliberate, and decisions will be circumscribed. No decision will be a panacea. There will be setbacks, as there was with *Rodriquez*. However, there are always state as well as federal courts, and in light of the decisions already handed down, there are countless possible approaches.

One or a number of decisions are not apt to be as comprehensive in any given metropolitan area as a massive reorganization. Yet because decisions set a standard for all similar areas, the total impact of a single significant decision may be much greater than that of a single important reorganization. Consequently, given Professor Marando's description of the political problems confronting attempts to improve equity in metropolitan areas through governmental reorganization, given his explanation of the present and possible future alignment of political forces, and given the new ground being broken by recent court decisions, it seems likely that reformers who are concerned about equity in metropolitan areas will turn their efforts to the courts.

NOTES

1. For a discussion of the possibility that a permanent minority is emerging in American society, see Alan K. Campbell, "Breakthrough or Stalemate?" in Campbell, A. K., *The States and the Urban Crisis* (Englewood Cliffs, N.J.: Prentice-Hall, 1970), pp. 146–204.
2. 437 F. 2d 1286 (5th Cir. 1971), affirmed *en banc* 461 F. 2d 1171.
3. 402 U.S. 1, 15, 91 S.Ct. 1267, 28 L.Ed. 2d 554 (1971).
4. *Crow v. Brown*, 332 FS 382 (N.D. Ga. 1971), affirmed 457 F. 2d 788 (5th Cir. 1972).
5. *Mahaley v. Cuyahoga Metropolitan Housing Authority*, 355 FS 1245 (N.D. Ohio 1973).
6. Cal 3d 584, 487 P. 2d 1241, 96 Cal Rptr 601 (1971).
7. *San Antonio Independent School District v. Rodriguez*, 411 U.S. 1, 93 S.Ct. 1278, 36 L.Ed. 2d 16 (1973).

3. Metropolitan Governance: The Intergovernmental Dimension

Joseph F. Zimmerman

While students of local government and citizen reformers advocate and debate the need for and the political feasibility of local government restructuring, the system is constantly undergoing incremental change. It is continuously being changed by the use of intergovernmental service agreements, upward transfer of functional responsibility to the county and state levels, direct provision of services by state-controlled public authorities, and federal preemption.

INTERGOVERNMENTAL AGREEMENTS

Formal and informal service compacts have increasingly been utilized by local governments during the past 25 years and have lessened pressures for a more major change in the local governmental system. The reasons for the popularity of interlocal service agreements are easy to understand—municipalities often are able to obtain a service or a product that they can not provide themselves, costs may be lower and the quality of the service may be higher, the freedom of action of the parties to the agreements is not reduced significantly, and the structure of the local governmental system is not altered in a fundamental way.

In 1972, 1,393 (61 percent) of 2,248 responding municipalities of over 2,500 population reported that they were parties to formal and informal service agreements.[1] Although these agreements can involve any service, formal agreements with another governmental unit usually involve joint facilities, water supply, and sewage treatment. Most informal agreements relate to mutual assistance in emergencies and maintenance of bridges and highways. It must be pointed out, however, that mutual aid agreements do not provide for the rendering of a service on a regular basis.

Larger municipalities and council-manager municipalities have the greatest propensity to enter into agreements for the receipt of services. Central cities and suburban communities enter into agreements with about the same degree of frequency—75 percent and 71 percent, respectively. Service compacts are most common in the West (78 percent) and least common in the East (53 percent) and the South (53 percent). Cities, towns, and villages enter into agreements most frequently with counties (61 percent) and other municipalities (40 percent). State governments and public authorities are also major providers of services—28 percent of the respondents receive services from the state and 16 percent receive services from authorities.

Relatively few intergovernmental service agreements—13 percent—call for the provision of a package of services. Most agreements involve only two governments and one service, and the services provided—fire and police mutual aid, jails, civil defense, and water supply—tend to be relatively noncontroversial. The explanation for the small number of package agreements is that few municipalities have the ability or the desire to provide several services to another local government.

With only a few exceptions, the reason given by respondents for entering into service agreements was to take advantage of economies of scale rather than to improve the quality of the services. Not surprisingly, the survey revealed that there was general satisfaction with service compacts when measured by discontinuance—only 5 percent of the municipalities had terminated agreements.

Joint service provision agreements are relatively common, with 35 percent, or 679 of 1,939 responding municipalities reporting the existence of such agreements. Most common in the West (48 percent) and least common in the South (28 percent), joint agreements most often involve council-manager cities and central cities.

In a number of metropolitan areas, particularly in the South, the central city and the county have consolidated functions on a gradual basis over a period of years. The city of Charlotte and Mecklenburg County in North Carolina, to cite only one example, have consolidated school, public health, and public welfare systems, and jointly finance a single agency responsible for elections.

Provision of services and products by agreements may be viewed as a limited and temporary form of consolidation with policy making decentralized and administration centralized. The major problems with the use of intergovernmental agreements to solve area-wide service problems are the desultory nature of this approach to service provision and the accompanying complication of the local government system, which may make it less responsive to the needs and wishes of the citizenry. One can reasonably argue that it would be preferable to shift the legal responsibility for the provision of a number of services to higher-level units of government.

TRANSFER OF FUNCTIONAL RESPONSIBILITY

The great difficulty experienced in mobilizing public support for a major re-structuring of the local government system in metropolitan areas has promoted interest in the upward shift of responsibility for functions perceived to be performed best on an area-wide basis. An intergovernmental service agreement and the upward transfer of responsibility for the same function differ in that the former is a temporary arrangement, subject to termination either on the expiration of a written contract or at the will of one or both of the parties, whereas the transfer of responsibility is usually permanent and is not subject to revocation.

The major arguments for the shifting of responsibility for a function upward are the achievement of economies of scale, more even service provision throughout the entire metropolitan area, and a more equitable system of financing the service. Economies of scale, however, may not result from the transfer, even though unit costs generally tend to decrease with an increase in output, because diseconomies of scale may be encountered as output continues to increase. A study by the Advisory Commission on Intergovernmental Relations concluded that no significant economies or diseconomies of scale are associated with a city in the population range of 25,000 to 250,000.[2] The law of diminishing returns, the Commission reports, applies as size exceeds 250,000, resulting in major diseconomies of scale. The largest diseconomies in the Commission's study were associated with police protection.

Whether efficiency and equity will be improved by the transfer of functional responsibility depends, of course, on the quality of the service provided by the upper-tier unit and on the method of financing the service, compared to the quality of the service provided by and the method of financing employed by cities, towns, and villages.

Few data exist on transfer of functional responsibility. This situation will be remedied soon as a national survey will be completed which has collected data on the frequency of transfers, the reasons for the transfers, and the impact the transfers have had on the perceived need for subcounty special districts, a modernized county government, a multicounty regional service agency, and a council of governments (COG).[3]

Role of the State

The states have played one of three roles relative to the formation of metropolitan governments—inhibitor, facilitator, or initiator. Most states have abdicated their responsibility to help solve problems transcending local political boundary lines, and this is the major factor accounting for the small degree of progress made in reorganizing the local governmental system compared to the progress made in consolidating local school districts to form regional ones. Furthermore, the formation of a regional governmental entity is impeded by the constitution in many states. To cite only one illustration, the New York State constitution requires the separate approval of voters of cities as a unit, and the voters of towns as a unit within a county, before responsibility for a function can be transferred to the county.[4] And a triple concurrent majority—separate affirmative votes in referenda by city voters, town voters, and village voters— is required for the approval of a proposed transfer of a village function to the county.

The state legislature can facilitate the creation of metropolitan governments by establishing or authorizing the establishment of metropolitan study commissions and enacting the necessary enabling legislation for the creation of such governments. Interest in the study commission approach peaked in the 1950s. Of the 112 surveys initiated between 1923 and 1957, 79 were launched between 1948 and 1957, compared to one or two per year from 1923 to 1948.[5]

A significant change in the number and nature of surveys occurred in the 1960s, primarily as the result of conditions attached to various federal grant-in-aid programs. A sharp rise in transportation and comprehensive land-use surveys occurred. The number of transportation studies rose from 15 to 118 in 1966, to 154 in 1967, and to 198 in 1968. Comprehensive land-use studies increased from 15 in 1960 to 48 in 1966 and 73 in 1967, but decreased to 71 in 1968. Studies concerned with governmental organization declined from 40 in 1960 to 34 in 1966 and 29 in 1967. In 1968, 36 such studies were launched. Although no national survey of study commissions has been conducted since 1968, it is apparent that today the number of active commissions concerned with governmental reorganization is small.[6]

The state government initiated the formation of metropolitan governments in the nineteenth century in Massachusetts and New York. Numerous towns were annexed to the city of Boston by mandate of the General Court, and New York City was formed in 1898 by a legislatively directed amalgamation of all local governments within a five-county area. No other major consolidation was ordered by a state legislature without provision for a popular referendum until 1969, when the Indiana State Legislature enacted a law merging the city of Indianapolis and Marion County.[7] The new governmental system, however, remains a federated one as two small cities, a town, 16 townships, school corporations, Marion County Health and Hospital Corporation, and Indianapolis Airport were all excluded from the consolidation.

There is little evidence suggesting that state legislatures will often order the merger of local governments to form a metropolitan government. On the contrary, there is a movement to break up large Northern cities into federated cities, with a city-wide level and a neighborhood level.[8]

An interesting state-initiated organizational response to growing area-wide problems is the Metropolitan Council, which was established for the 7-county

Twin Cities area in 1967 by the Minnesota State Legislature.[9] The governor appoints the chairman and 14 other members for overlapping six-year terms, with the advice and consent of the Senate. No provisions were made for a public referendum on the question of creating the Council, and no units of local government were amalgamated.

The Twin Cities model of metropolitan governance is basically a federated one with powers divided between the Council and counties, municipalities, and metropolitan special districts. The Council is the comprehensive metropolitan planning agency. It possesses the power to review and indefinitely suspend plans of each metropolitan special district in conflict with the Council's development guide, and appoints the Metropolitan Sewer Board.[10] The 1969 legislature created a Metropolitan Park Reserve Board[11] and provided for its appointment by the Council. The Board's role as an operating service body was terminated in 1970 by a Minnesota Supreme Court ruling invalidating laws passed on the 121st day (one day past the constitutional limit) of the 1969 legislative session.[12] The Board has been retained as an advisory body, but reenactment of the original Park Reserve bill has been blocked by opposition from the Inter-County Council and the Hennepin County Park Reserve District.

The separation of policy execution from policy making is a distinguishing characteristic of the Twin Cities model. It provides for the Council to determine regional policies which are to be carried into execution by service boards appointed by the Council. In theory, it can devote its full attention to broad policy making for the region and leave routine administrative problems to the service boards.

Although glowing accounts have been published,[13] the Twin Cities governmental system remains fragmented. This model suffers from three major weaknesses. First, major problems, as in the past, generally are being attacked on a piecemeal basis, with the Legislature continuing in the role of major referee between competing regional bodies and interests.

Political fragmentation on the regional level is responsible for a second and related operational weakness of the model—deadlocks between various regional entities failing to operate on the basis of comity. The Council has twice exercised its power to indefinitely veto a site for a new jetport proposed by the Metropolitan Airport Commission, yet the Council lacks the power to order the Commission to construct the jetport at a site selected by the Council.

Third, the Twin Cities model may have an inherent defect—the possibility of disputes between the Council and its service boards. A dispute of this nature, involving the Council and the Sewer Board, occurred relative to the Board's 1971 construction program.[14]

Turning to New York State, a decision was made in the 1960s to use the plenary authority of the state to directly solve areawide problems by the establishment of state-controlled public authorities. Both statewide and regional authorities have been created for special purposes: Urban Development Corporation (UDC), Environmental Facilities Corporation, Job Development Authority, Metropolitan Transportation Authority (MTA), Niagara Frontier

Transportation Authority, Capital District Transportation Authority, Central New York Regional Transportation Authority, Rochester-Genesee Regional Transportation Authority, and others. Currently, there are 31 state-controlled public authorities—14 of transportation, 5 for commerce and development, 4 for port development, 4 for finance and housing, 2 for recreation, and 2 for marketing.

One of the major problems associated with the use of state-controlled authorities stems from their creation on an ad hoc basis. Fractionalization of responsibility on the regional level results in nearly total neglect of essential coordination as these authorities are independent of each other and of local governments in terms of planning, financing, and programming. To reduce the fractionalization problem within a given metropolitan area, the device of the interlocking directorate can be utilized, as it has been in the New York City metropolitan area since 1967 to coordinate transportation authorities. The board of directors of the newly created MTA was made the *ex officio* board of directors of the Long Island Rail Road, New York City Transit Authority, Manhattan and Bronx Surface Transit Operating Authority, and Triborough Bridge and Tunnel Authority.[15] Since 1967, the MTA board has been made the *ex officio* board of the Staten Island Rapid Transit Operating Authority, Metropolitan Suburban Bus Authority, and Stewart Airport Land Authority. The use of the interlocking directorate in the New York City area is somewhat similar to the Twin Cities model, but differs in that the Metropolitan Council has no direct operating responsibilities.

In addition to voluntarily initiating action to solve area-wide problems, state governments are being pressured by partial federal preemption to play a more major metropolitan governance role.

THE FEDERAL ROLE

Although the United States Bureau of the Census accorded recognition to metropolitan areas in 1910 by establishing 25 metropolitan districts for data collection purposes, the federal government's concern with area-wide problems was minimal until the 1960s. Beginning with the Federal Aid Highway Act of 1962, the federal government began to place heavy emphasis upon regional planning as a device for promoting interlocal cooperation in solving area-wide problems, and in 1965 it began to partially preempt the authority to abate environmental problems, which tend to be most serious in metropolitan areas.

The Ecumenical Approach

Congress concluded in 1965 that metropolitan planning had been largely ineffective because the planning commissions were not controlled directly by the local elected decision makers. Consequently, a provision was added to the Housing and Urban Development Act of 1965, making organizations of public officials in metropolitan areas eligible to receive federal grants for the preparation of comprehensive area-wide plans.[16] The following year Congress provided another incentive for integrating metropolitan planning with local decision making by enacting a requirement—popularly known as Section 204 review—that all local government applications for grants and loans for 30 specified projects must be submitted for review to the organization responsible for area-wide planning "which is, to the greatest practicable extent, composed of or responsible to the elected officials of a unit of areawide government or of the units of general local governments."[17] Section 204 promoted the formation of numerous COGs and metropolitan planning commissions composed of local elected officials.

The importance of metropolitan planning has been further enhanced by the passage of the Intergovernmental Cooperation Act of 1968[18] and the National Environmental Policy Act of 1969.[19] Parts of these two acts and Section 204 are implemented by United States Office of Management and Budget Circular A-95, which broadens the coverage of the review of grant applications by the planning agency to 106 programs and extends the review to nonmetropolitan areas and the state level.

We conclude our brief discussion of COGs by pointing out that the cooperative or ecumenical approach as epitomized by COGs has been unable to solve a major problem in any area, and that the federal government has increasingly exercised its powers of preemption to help solve metropolitan problems.

Preemption by the Federal Government

The federal government in the 1960s decided that certain metropolitan problems—environmental ones in particular—could not be solved by reliance upon state and local governmental action encouraged by the "carrots" of federal grants-in-aid. Consequently, Congress enacted the Water Quality Act of 1965, which required each state to adopt "water quality standards applicable to interstate waters or portions thereof within such state," as well as an implementation and enforcement plan.[20] The Secretary of the Interior, now the Administrator of the Environmental Protection Agency (EPA), is authorized to promulgate interstate water standards, which become effective at the end of six months should a state fail to establish satisfactory standards. The federal role subsequently has been strengthened, particularly by Federal Water Pollution Control Act Amendments of 1972.[21]

Although Congress has totally or partially preempted several other fields of regulation, we will limit our comments to one additional field. In 1967, Congress completely preempted the right to establish automobile exhaust emission standards for 1968 and subsequent model vehicles by enacting the Air Quality Act.[22] It also partially preempts other air pollution abatement activities of state and local governments by following the general procedure embodied in the Water Quality Act of 1965. Municipal, state, and interstate air pollution abatement programs are encouraged provided that they meet minimum federal standards, but federal enforcement action is authorized in the event of state inaction.

The Clean Air Amendments of 1970 represent a sharp break with the earlier approach to air pollution abatement, relying upon state and local governments to provide the necessary leadership and taking into consideration the economic and technical feasibility of abatement controls.[23] Protection of public health by direct federal action was made national policy, and explicit dates for adoption of standards and abatement plans were specified.

The amendments stipulated that 1975-model automobiles must achieve a 90 percent reduction of the 1970 standards for emissions of carbon monoxide, hydrocarbons, and nitrogen oxides.[24] In contrast to earlier standards, the new ones were mandated without considering the economic and technical feasibility of pollution abatement systems. On April 18, 1973, the EPA Administrator granted the automobile industry's request for a one-year extension to meet the standards established in the amendments for automotive emissions of carbon monoxide and hydrocarbons.

Of particular importance to metropolitan areas is the provision in the amendments directing the EPA Administrator to publish in the *Federal Register* within 90 days a list of categories of stationary sources of air pollution, subject to the performance standards established under the amendments. He was given an additional 120 days following publication of the list to include in the *Federal Register* proposed regulations establishing federal standards for new sources of air pollution. Every state was authorized to submit to the Administrator a procedure for implementing and enforcing standards of performance for new sources located in the state, and the Administrator was empowered to delegate authority to each state to implement and enforce the standards for other than new, United States–owned sources. In February 1974, the Administrator published in the *Federal Register* final regulations for reviewing the air quality impact, prior to construction, of new facilities that may generate significant amounts of automobile traffic.[25]

The 1975 automotive emission standards and the regulation of new major sources of air pollution—electric power generating plants, factories, and shopping centers are examples—have major land-use implications. In any air quality control region where stationary source controls combined with new motor vehicle emission controls cannot ensure the attainment of statutory ambient air quality standards, transportation controls must be adopted. Such controls will necessitate a significant change in life styles for residents of metropolitan areas.

On June 11, 1973, the United States Supreme Court, by a four-to-four vote, let stand a District Court decision that states cannot permit significant deterioration of existing air quality.[26] As the Supreme Court's decision was without opinion and as the District Court[27] did not elaborate upon its ruling, EPA has been forced to execute a nondegradation policy without judicial guidelines.

To implement the courts' decisions, EPA proposed that four steps be taken including the establishment of clean air and polluted air zones. Although pollution levels cannot exceed federal standards in either zone, only minor increases in the degree of pollution would be allowed in the former zones, whereas larger increases would be allowed in the latter zones. If implemented, this proposal will rule out any further spreading of "Spread City," as development would not be allowed in the fringe areas if it would contribute to a degradation of the areas' existing air quality. Allowable growth may have to be accommodated within developed areas.

CONCLUSIONS

Projecting the experience of the last 10 years into the future, one is on safe ground in concluding that proposals revamping the local government system in metropolitan areas seldom will receive voter sanction. City-county consolidation, however, is apt to occur occasionally in less politically complex Southern metropolitan areas. Intergovernmental service agreements and the upward transfer of functional responsibility will become increasingly popular, thereby alleviating pressures for the creation of general-purpose metropolitan governments.

States with a high percentage of their citizens residing in metropolitan areas will play a more important role in the metropolitan governance system during the next decade by directly intervening to solve area-wide problems. Unfortunately, this intervention probably will be taken on an ad hoc basis and involve the creation of single-purpose, state-controlled public authorities.

The federal government, through revenue sharing, will help to perpetuate the existing balkanized local government system, while at the same time preempting additional areas of regulation and tightening standards in areas already partially preempted. Congress, however, is unlikely in the forthcoming decade to adopt the Douglas Commission's recommendation that federal revenue sharing be utilized as a catalyst to encourage small units to consolidate by restricting shared revenue to local governments with a population in excess of 50,000.[28] General revenue sharing, unless modified, will reduce the pressures for the amalgamation of small units of local government but will not reduce the pressures for the upward shift of responsibility for certain governmental functions.

NOTES

1. For further details, see Joseph F. Zimmerman, "Meeting Service Needs through Intergovernmental Service Agreements," *The Municipal Yearbook: 1973* (Washington: International City Management Association, 1973), pp. 79–88; Joseph F. Zimmerman, "Intergovernmental Service Agreements for

Smaller Cities," *Urban Data Service Reports,* January 1973; and Joseph F. Zimmerman, "Intergovernmental Service Agreements," in Advisory Commission on Intergovernmental Relations, *Substate Regionalism and the Federal System,* vol. 3 (Washington: Government Printing Office, 1974).

2. "Size Can Make a Difference: A Closer Look," *ACIR Information Bulletin,* Sept. 16, 1970.

3. The results of the survey by the author will appear in an information bulletin to be published by the Advisory Commission on Intergovernmental Relations in the summer of 1975. A preliminary report by the author appears in "Municipal Transfer of Functional Responsibility," *Urban Data Service Report* Int'l City Management Assoc. Vol. 7, No. 9 Washington Sept. 1975.

4. *Constitution of the State of New York,* art. IX.

5. Daniel R. Grant, "General Metropolitan Surveys: A Summary" in *Metropolitan Surveys: A Digest* (Chicago: Public Administration Service, 1958), p. 3.

6. Joseph F. Zimmerman, ed., *Metropolitan Surveys* (Albany: Graduate School of Public Affairs, State University of New York at Albany, 1966–68.

7. *Indiana Acts of 1969,* chap. 173.

8. For details, see Joseph F. Zimmerman, *The Federated City: Community Control in Large Cities* (New York: St. Martin's, 1972).

9. *Minnesota Statutes,* chap. 473B.

10. *Ibid.,* chap 473C.

11. *Ibid.,* chap. 473E.

12. *Knapp v. O'Brien,* 179 N.W. 2d 88 (1970).

13. Stanley Baldinger, *Planning and Governing the Metropolis: The Twin Cities Experience* (New York: Praeger, 1971); "Twin Cities Metropolitan Council Anticipates and Supplies Orderly Growth," *Urban Action Clearinghouse,* Case Study No. 20 (Washington: Chamber of Commerce of the United States, 1971); and John Fischer, "The Minnesota Experiment: How to Make a Big City Fit to Live In," *Harper's Magazine,* April 1969, pp. 12, 17, 18, 20, 24, 26, 28, 30, and 32.

14. For additional information on the Council, see Joseph F. Zimmerman, "Metropolitan Governance and the Twin Cities Model," a paper presented at the National Conference on Government, Minneapolis, Minn., Nov. 28, 1972.

15. *New York Laws of 1967,* chap. 717 (McKinney).

16. *Housing and Urban Development Act of 1965,* 79 Stat. 502 (1965), 40 U.S.C.A. § 461(g) (1965).

17. *Demonstration Cities and Metropolitan Development Act of 1966,* 80 Stat. 1255, 42 U.S.C.A. §§ 3301–14 (1966).

18. *Intergovernmental Cooperation Act of 1968,* 82 Stat. 1103, 42 U.S.C.A. §§ 4201–43 (1970).

19. *National Environmental Policy Act of 1969,* 83 Stat. 852, 42 U.S.C.A. § 4321 and §§ 4331–32 (1972).

20. *Water Quality Act of 1965,* 79 Stat. 903 33 U.S.C.A. 1151 *et seq.* (1969).

21. *Federal Water Pollution Control Act Amendments of 1972,* 70 Stat. 498, 33 U.S.C.A. § 1151 (1972).

22. *Air Quality Act of 1967,* 81 Stat. 485, 42 U.S.C.A. §§ 1857–18571 (1969).

23. *Clean Air Amendments of 1970,* 84 Stat. 1676, 42 U.S.C.A. §§ 1857 *et seq.,* 49 U.S.A. §§ 1421 and 1430 (1970).

24. *Ibid.,* 49 U.S.A. §§ 1421 and 1430.

25. *Federal Register* 7271 *et seq.*

26. *Fri v. Sierra Club,* 41 U.S.L.W. 4825 (1973).

27. *Sierra Club v. Ruckelshaus,* 344 F. Supp. 253, 4 ERC 1205 (D.D.C. 1972).

28. National Commission on Urban Problems, *Building the American City* (Washington: Government Printing Office, 1968), pp. 378–82.

Comment: Efficiency and Other Economic Aspects of Metropolitan Governance Reform

Jerry Miner

Joseph Zimmerman's review and analysis of the recent history of reform of metropolitan governance lead him to rather pessimistic conclusions. He takes the position that the most widely adopted measures of metropolitan reform—intergovernment service agreements, state public authorities, and federal preemption of certain state and local standards—are largely unresponsive to the major problems of metropolitan areas. At the same time, upward transfer of functional responsibilities through consolidation, the reform which would best meet these problems, has proven virtually impossible to achieve. In fact, the very success of the other reforms, coupled with measures such as general revenue sharing, may be hampering the achievement of more basic changes in the intergovernmental structure by reducing pressures for consolidation. As a result, irresistible pressures for state assumption of functional responsibilities are likely to emerge in the near future.

Zimmerman's thesis poses two obvious questions. One concerns the relative efficacy of the various alternatives with respect to the objectives of governmental reform. The other involves the prospects for implementation of each of these reforms, given the expected political and economic climate. I have only a little to add to Zimmerman's conclusions regarding the latter, but application of some of the principles of public economics, especially those of fiscal federalism, may help in clarifying the potential contribution of alternative reforms.

As a necessary background it is essential to specify the primary objectives behind the reform of metropolitan governance. These are not fully spelled out in the article, but in referring to the arguments in favor of shifting responsibilities, Zimmerman mentions achievement of economies of scale, more even service provision, and a more equitable system of financing services. These would apply as objectives, I should think, not only to the upward transfer of functions but to the other reforms as well. I would add to this list of objectives corrections for spillovers, responsiveness to special local needs and other circumstances, and improvement in decision-making processes while expanding economies of scale to include other sources of cost reduction.

What can we say about the various reforms? The salient advantage of intergovernmental service agreements, despite the responses to Zimmerman's survey, seems to me to be a lower-cost solution to the "peak-load problem" rather than the achievement of economies of scale. Local governments have a regular, normal need for police, fire, water, jail, and similar facilities and services. Under unusual and unpredictable circumstances normal levels of need may be greatly exceeded for short periods of time. Each government that provides such services must decide how much it will be prepared to deliver, in case of emergency, above the normal need. The cost of maintaining a capacity in excess of normal needs is reduced if an agreement for "mutual aid" can be reached with a nearby government. Emergency capacity can thereby be reduced by all parties, and yet the ability to meet a peak-load requirement is still present.

The limits of such agreements now become clear. First, the usefulness of the compact declines with the interdependence of the probabilities of peak-load demand among the parties. Thus, for example, if a decline in water pressure of one party to the agreement generally is caused by the same forces that reduce pressure in another, the agreement is not terribly useful. Second, and perhaps more important, this kind of sharing of facilities or services can occur only for those services where excess capacity can be "stored" and is not regularly in full use. Genuine economies of scale, on the other hand, occur when the normal magnitude of output is large enough to justify using a method of production that employs at least one efficient, but large and indivisible, input. To take advantage of economies of scale in local government service delivery, if indeed there are any such economies, would instead require production over a larger area attained either through consolidation, upward transfer of the function, or, as we shall see, public authorities, if the service is amenable to user charges.

The technical limitations on the accomplishments of service agreements reinforce Zimmerman's conclusions regarding their shortcomings as a basic metropolitan reform. They may reduce certain costs and even promote some more even service provision across neighboring communities; but their impact, even here, is relatively small, and they do not contribute at all to reducing fiscal disparities.

While service agreements have limited impact because the activities to which they are subject have to be transferable among jurisdictions on short notice, state-public authorities have limited effectiveness primarily because they can only provide services where user charges can be applied. Zimmerman, in discussing the characteristics and deficiencies of public authorities, emphasizes their ad hoc nature and the resultant fragmentation of responsibility. Yet a far more significant obstacle to authorities having a major impact on metropolitan problems is that they do not receive appropriations from a legislature, but instead are self-financing through borrowing and repayment out of fees or other user charges. As a consequence, authorities cannot and do not provide services for which it is either not feasible or too costly to charge (*e.g.*, public health, streets and roads) or not desirable (*e.g.*, local schools).

At the same time, there are those who argue that a far larger proportion of goods and services which are now publicly supplied without direct charge could be provided more effectively by fee-charging authorities. Were this policy under serious consideration as a fiscal reform, which it does not seem to be, Zimmerman's objection on the grounds of fragmentation would be more relevant than it is under the present situation where public authorities are so restricted in their areas of activity. Still, the financial status of the authority raises further questions about its effectiveness in solving even the restricted range of problems with which it is capable of dealing. The issue here is that as a fiscally autonomous and self-financing entity (although subsidized by low interest rates), it lacks incentives to take proper account of spillovers and other externalities that result from its actions, and it may not follow optimal (marginal-cost) pricing in an effort to increase revenues so as to amortize its debt. Here again, normative economic considerations support Zimmerman's more political analysis.

Federal government policies of preemption and persuasion are further remedies discussed by Zimmerman. The scope of these policies is limited to efforts to secure regional planning and to regulate certain external effects of private activities. Potentialities for the direct provision of services by the federal government presumably are considered as an aspect of the upward transfer of functions, and thus are implicitly considered under that policy. Efforts to persuade various local governments to coordinate policies through the establishment of planning requirements as a condition of the receipt of higher-level grants has not proven an effective means of promoting regional planning and policy. Zimmerman simply asserts that no major problem has been solved by this method without suggesting any reasons for its failure. The essentials of an explanation follow from closer examination of two aspects of this approach.

First, with regard to the preparation of area-wide plans, the availability of funds for planning does not contribute to the reduction of fiscal disparities or to the resolution of conflicts over the distribution of any of the costs of compliance among jurisdictions. Thus, while federal funding for planning is likely to be taken up by intergovernmental bodies, the actual implementation of plans by the local governments in the absence of grants for capital and operating expenses is highly unlikely.

Second, with respect to granting review and veto power over federal grants to a regional planning body, the technical capacity of such bodies and their will to face the political consequences of rejecting a grant proposal are extremely limited. These bodies usually have barely sufficient funds to operate and are dependent upon local as well as federal funds. They cannot afford to reject projects in which their local sponsors have an interest, nor can they hire adequate staffs to do professional reviews. Furthermore, their powers extend only to rejecting unsatisfactory projects; they cannot initiate projects.

Zimmerman sees federal preemption as an alternative to persuasion. The problems with which preemption deals are, like those encompassed by regional planning, issues of coordination and control of private resource use rather than public service delivery. Thus preemption is applied to achieve uniform environmental standards, but not to the provision of equal public education or health services across communities or states. Zimmerman does not elaborate on the prospects for the extension of preemption, but clearly an extension of this approach will not achieve the objections of metropolitan reform even for those areas where preemption is feasible. For example, where environmental standards are applied to local public sector activities and require significant expenditures for compliance, how are localities with inadequate revenue sources to meet their legal obligations? Also, uniform standards do not take local conditions into account. Furthermore, there is considerable controversy over whether environmental controls should be centered around the establishment of standard codes or should be based on the application of a schedule of pollution charges. Here too, on the basis of economic considerations, preemption offers the prospect of only modest gains.

Now, finally, we come to the favored policy—upward transfer of functions. Zimmerman sharply contrasts the negative prospects of achieving this reform through consolidation with the positive chance for the state, and perhaps the federal, government to take over functional responsibilities where coordination and disparities are serious problems. The issues here go to the heart of the theory and practice of federalism. This, however, is not the place to enter into a discussion of these issues. Instead, I wish to raise only two points. First, I think Zimmerman is too sanguine about the chances for the upward shifting of responsibilities. The resistance to such a shift by those local governments that are in an advantageous position with regard to the existing system is a very considerable impediment to change. These governments tend to be those with considerable influence in state legislatures. Perhaps future research can provide a classification of functions (e.g., service delivery, transfer payments, environmental control, regional planning) such that constituencies in favor of and opposed to transfer to higher levels may be distinguished. Then we may have a better idea of the future of this reform.

Second, it seems essential in evaluating the prospects and consequences of functional transfer to distinguish aspects of functional control. That is, all aspects of governance of a function need not be transferred to remedy one particular defect. For example, if primary concern lies in the unequal fiscal capacities of local governments, transfer of finance to a higher level, while leaving control over service characteristics to local governments, may be both more efficient and more politically feasible. If inequity, impropriety, or discrimination is practiced in the provision of services, either grants-in-aid with conditions attached or administrative regulation and supervision by the state rather than full transfer may, again, be a superior and a politically more acceptable solution.

In appraising Zimmerman's expectations regarding state assumption of full responsibility for particular functions, it should be noted that this reform would require an extensive state-directed system of local field administration foreign to our mode of federalism. Also, while state assumption is likely to attain certain objectives of reform (equity, cost reduction, and reduction of spillovers), it probably violates others (conformance to individual preferences, avoidance of excessive bureaucracy). Thus, while this type of restructuring of metropolitan governance may have its attractions, its variance with present traditions and interests hardly makes it the most likely wave of the future.

4. Multipurpose Districts, Modernized Local Governments, and a More Systematic Approach to Servicing Assignments: A Tripartite Strategy for Urban and Rural America

Robert E. Merriam

A prime intergovernmental challenge of the seventies is how we will respond to the functional, fiscal, and institutional pressures that have combined to establish a new but very real level of governmental activity at the substate regional level. For over two years the Advisory Commission on Intergovernmental Relations probed the multiple districting developments, the local governmental reorganization efforts, and the shifting servicing assignment patterns that provide the raw materials out of which this substate regional level is being fashioned. In February 1974, the Commission took final action on a series of recommendations which—when linked with the districting decisions made in June 1973—constitute a new and bold strategy for coping with the structural, servicing, and regional systems quandary now confronting most of urban and rural America.

THE SUBSTATE REGIONAL SETTING

This tripartite package of reform proposals grew out of the research findings set forth in the six volumes constituting this study. Unlike the situation 10 years ago, we identified more institutions, more programs, more coordinating efforts, more comprehensive and functional planning, and even more servicing and governmental reorganization efforts at this ill-defined sector—below the states but larger than the cities and frequently larger than the counties. In all this, we discovered clear evidence of major federal involvement, of lesser state concern, and of basic local governmental anxiety. Above all, we found more confusion and more conflict at this level than ever existed before. And no wonder!

Districting Developments

The rapid growth of recent regional council and districting developments has transformed the jurisdictional terrain of nearly all the nation's metropolitan areas and most of its nonmetropolitan regions. Over 600 regional councils of governments, largely controlled by city and county representatives, have come into being in approximately 350 metropolitan and nonmetropolitan areas. This is due largely to federal 701 funds, the Section 204 requirement of the Metropolitan Development Act of 1966, and the Intergovernmental Cooperation Act of 1968. In all, 450 A-95 clearinghouses (212 metropolitan and 238 nonmetropolitan) have been designated pursuant to these acts, most of them having a council-of-governments format. About 1,800 federally encouraged districts have been established at the substate regional level under 19 separate categorical and block grant programs (e.g., comprehensive health planning, law enforcement, transportation, air pollution). Independent special districts and authorities nearly surpassed the 25,000 mark in 1972, making them the fastest-growing unit of local government; but only about one-quarter of these had boundaries that matched those of county or city governments. Finally, and partially in response to some of the federally encouraged districting efforts, 44 states now have at least designated substate districting systems, and one more state is ready to move on this front. By way of contrast, a decade ago there were only about 25 councils of governments, a handful of area-wide transportation units, three or four states with substate districting systems, and 5,564 fewer special districts and authorities.

The Reorganization Record

Such were some of the basic dimensions of the rash of regional council and districting developments as of 1973. But what of the local and area-wide reorganization and servicing issue? This rapid growth of regional councils, area-wide coordinating procedures, state-established substate districts, federally supported unifunctional districts, and traditional special-purpose operating districts is, after all, only one huge intergovernmental footnote to the fact that the present jurisdictional and functional assignment pattern at the multicounty, county, and municipal levels, in all but a handful of instances, is ineffective, inadequate, and frequently insensitive to popular control. At the same time, the pace of change on the reorganization front has been more rapid than many would believe. For example:

- More city-county consolidations (11) took place between 1962 and 1972 than during the previous century and a half, though out of every four attempts, only one, on the average, succeeded, and the bulk of these were in the Southeast.
- The two- and three-tier approaches to local and area-wide governmental reorganization now are being tried in the United States. Miami-Dade represents an example of a deliberate chartering of a federated urban county. A few states now permit the incorporation of metropolitan multipurpose servicing districts, and a handful are functioning at present. State-supported regional councils, best represented by the Twin Cities Metropolitan Regional Council, are the decade's major innovation in the three-tier approach; this general-purpose policy-making unit has responsibility for developing area-wide plans, coordinating the major functional agencies operating in the region, and guiding the area's development.
- At the county level, one-fifth of these area-wide or subareal governments now have some form of separate executive leadership, and about one-fifth of the expenditures of metropolitan counties now go for other than state-mandated and traditional services.
- Nearly two-thirds of all urban municipalities annexed territory during the sixties, and more than 6 million people were affected by such actions; most of these annexations were small, however, and in only a few instances provided a means of achieving a *de facto* metropolitan government.
- In terms of positive state involvement, six (Iowa will soon make it seven) have established broad-gauged boundary control boards or commissions on a statewide or single-county basis, and a number of these are contributing to orderly expansion of municipal boundaries and a slower growth rate for new special districts and municipal incorporations.

Efforts to strengthen and modernize area-wide, county, and municipal units obviously are part of recent substate regional and subregional developments. Moreover, they are stronger today than they were a decade ago. At the same time, the success record in every instance included only a minority of the jurisdictions involved. Institutional change clearly comes slowly in America. Shifts in functional assignments, on the other hand, are occurring much more rapidly, but with confusing, not clarifying, results.

Functional Assignments in Flux

The Commission found that the present servicing patterns within states are largely and haphazardly a product of diverse fiscal pressures on local and state governments; the varying historical and legal status of different local units; the numerous but largely unrelated federal and state program initiatives, especially at the substate regional level; and a general reluctance to face the challenge implicit in the "form follows function" formula. With "ad-hocracy" in the ascendancy, inappropriate and conflicting servicing assignments have resulted among state, regional, and local governments and units. Conflicting centralization and decentralization trends are rampant, and any systematic sorting out of the economic efficiency, fiscal equity, managerial effectiveness, and popular accountability dimensions of the overall state-local servicing system is generally lacking.

SOME QUESTIONS NEEDING ANSWERS

This cluster of findings raises basic questions regarding the future of substate regional development—indeed, regarding the very functioning of the federal system itself. Turning first to the regional council-districting dilemma, what are the broader ramifications of the multiplication of these mechanisms at the substate level?

- Organizationally, the various governmental policies and actions at this level have been characterized by ambivalence in terms of the territory, functional scope, and decision-making processes of these districts. This has resulted in overlapping boundaries, duplicating functions, and confusing responsibilities, and has contributed to further jurisdictional fragmentation in both urban and rural America.
- Functionally, substate districts reflect the growing impatience of policy makers at both the federal and state levels with the areal—hence the functional—inadequacies inherent in the local governmental jigsaw puzzle.
- Bureaucratically, districting can be viewed as an effort on the part of middle-management program specialists to establish functional planning, coordinating, and fund-disbursing counterparts at the substate level. Although the jury is still out, there is considerable evidence that the functionalists are winning out against politically accountable elected officials and their generalist allies, given the general absence of genuine regional governments, the nonauthoritative nature of most regional councils, the continuing attractiveness of special districts, the separate status of a majority of federally supported substate districts, and the completely embryonic character of most districting systems established by the States.
- Politically, in some localities, substate districts alone are an innovative, long-term goal; in others, they are a short-range response to a cluster of immediate problems; to still others, they are a vital transitional mechanism out of which might emerge more fundamental institutional changes at a

later date; and finally, in some, they are merely a way of dealing with relatively minor and noncontroversial multicounty issues, but not with the critical structural and functional difficulties facing city and county governments.

As the foregoing suggests, the debate over districts ultimately becomes a debate over the prospects and possible programs for local and especially area-wide governmental reform. And here three basic questions are raised by the record to date:

- Will the accelerating acitvity at the substate level strengthen efforts to achieve local governmental modernization and regional reorganization?
- Can a districting strategy be developed that does not ignore the governmental reorganization issue, both at the regional and subregional levels?
- Can a complementary and commonsense reorganization program be devised that recognizes the wide political and jurisdictional variations of regions across the country, as well as the uneven pace of and the uncertain sentiment for reform efforts?

Our response to each of these is "yes," but more on that in a moment.

When the functional assignment angle is added to the districting and governmental reorganization angles of this substate regional triangle, the interdependence of the three issues becomes even more apparent. After all, the chief institutional and procedural obstacles to achieving more effective functional assignments include:

- The voluntary but selective character of most intergovernmental service agreements and functional transfers and consolidations
- The unwillingness to use federal grant-in-aid management procedures, such as the A-95 project notification and review system, to sort out eligible area-wide and local service providers
- The lack of authoritative and generalist substate districts and regional councils generally that can provide various area-wide services
- The continued proliferation of independent, unifunctional, area-wide, and local special districts that do not coordinate their services with established local governments
- The slow pace of county modernization and the resultant inability or unwillingness of most counties to assume various local and regional service responsibilities
- The continued defeat of most local and regional governmental reorganization proposals that would involve a clearer sorting out of local and area-wide service responsibilities
- The lack of decentralization of state-administered services and the inability of most state-local governmental systems to devolve service responsibilities from county or regional to municipal and neighborhood subunits of government

Clearly, institutional forms cannot be analyzed apart from their functions, and public functions cannot be treated systematically—apart from a range of state, area-wide, and local formal institutions. This, in the final analysis, is the basic pair of issues raised by the servicing dimension of the substate regional challenge.

A TRIPARTITE REFORM STRATEGY

With these issues and background findings in mind, the Advisory Commission on Intergovernmental Relations has developed a strategy designed to eliminate much of the present confusion in area-wide affairs, to link planning with implementation, to produce more authoritative regional decision making, to mesh districting with local governmental modernization efforts, and to link servicing assignment efforts to both. This strategy is rooted in recommendations adopted by the Commission at its June 1973 and February 1974 meetings. In the ACIR's judgment, districting should be viewed as an integral part of an overall effort to bring greater effectiveness, efficiency, and accountability to governmental operations at the area-wide and the local levels. This means that substate districting should be viewed as one basic component of a three-pronged approach to regional reform, which includes local governmental reorganization and the systematic reassignment of responsibility for performing various substate functions between and among cities, counties, and regional bodies.

The UMJO Component

When the Commission tackled the thorny substate districting issue in June 1973, it concluded that what is missing in the vast majority of metropolitan and nonmetropolitan areas is a multipurpose regional unit capable of linking area-wide planning with program implementation and of coordinating the diverse activities of separate unifunctional substate districts—in short, a unit that could serve as an effective and responsible regional decision maker.

Hence our adoption of the umbrella multijurisdictional organization (UMJO) as the spearhead of our regional districting reform effort. This approach now is embodied largely in an ACIR model "Statewide Substate Districting Act" and in proposed amendments to Title IV of the Intergovernmental Cooperation Act of 1968.

What is the essential nature of this new breed of regional entity? Once established, the umbrella multijurisdictional organization would occupy a pivotal position at the substate regional level. Although its operations would be heavily intergovernmental, the UMJO would be basically an agency of local government. All general-purpose local units would be required to be members of and make financial contributions to the umbrella body in their district, and at least 60 percent of the governing board would consist of local elected officials appointed by their respective governments. Any state agency dividing the state for planning, administration, or service delivery would be required to conform its boundaries to those of the officially designated substate districts and to "piggyback" the UMJO unless it could demonstrate that compliance would be detrimental to the accomplishment of its purposes. As this umbrella organization would be responsible for certain decentralized state programs and activities and would receive substantial state financial assistance, the governor would select officials to represent the state on its governing board.

The UMJO would use a dual voting system. Although the one-government, one-vote principle would probably apply to most issues, the bylaws would specify the circumstances under which any local member could call a population-weighted voting procedure into effect and the formula to be used in determining the number of votes to be cast by counties and cities.

The UMJO would be responsible for many of the functions now being performed by regional councils, such as area-wide planning, communications, research, and technical assistance. In contrast to the present situation in most areas, the umbrella organization would not have to compete with other regional bodies for federal funds, program assignments, local official participation, and public visibility. As a consequence of a series of federal, local, and especially state actions, the UMJO would be empowered to:

- Promote mutual problem solving among counties and cities, and provide such technical assistance and services as these units may singly or jointly request.
- Adopt and publicize regional policies and plans along with a program for their implementation.
- Provide planning and programming inputs into the state's planning and budgeting process.
- Serve as its region's A-95 clearinghouse, with authority to resolve conflicts as well as to review projects.
- Assume responsibility for implementing all federally supported area-wide planning, programming, coordinating, or districting programs, as well as for similar state undertakings.
- Resolve differences between certain state agency and local government programs and projects that have spillover effects on adopted regional policies and plans.
- Act as the policy board for multijurisdictional special districts. *And*
- Assume direct operating responsibilities for regional functions upon the affirmative vote of a majority of local members representing at least 60 percent of the district population.

The Commission's UMJO strategy clearly relies on the building blocks already in place at the substate level. But this strategy goes well beyond the status quo in a systematic effort to provide an effective overarching unit that can cope with the growing demand for better management, coordination, and implementation —in short, decision making—in those programs and policies that are area-wide in nature.

A Local and Area-wide Reorganization Agenda

The umbrella multijurisdictional organization proposals are but one element in the Commission's overall substate regional strategy. No analysis of the complexities and challenges of recent substate regional developments would be complete, after all, without full consideration of the local and area-wide governmental reorganization and functional assignment issues.

The Commission has done this. At our February, 1974, meeting we studied the relationship between our substate districting strategy and our concern with local governmental modernization and the performance of functions; we pondered the record to date on the reorganization and service assignment fronts; we deliberated and acted on proposals relating to local and area-wide governmental reform and to systematic functional assignment policies.

As we view them, there is full compatibility between our UMJO recommendations and our new proposals for general local governmental reform. An overall effort in both areas must be mounted to bring the structure and functions of units below the state level to a point where they can cope with the electorate's current and future servicing needs and in a more efficient, effective, and accountable fashion than now prevails generally.

In some large substate regions, the UMJO would be the only politically feasible regional reform proposal—either now or in the future—yet local government modernization would still be possible and needed to facilitate many of the UMJO's difficult assignments. In other smaller, less complicated areas, the UMJO might be only a short-range response to the immediate problems of mushrooming districts, and here area-wide governmental reorganization efforts might be strengthened by the umbrella organization—to the point that some form of regional government eventually would supersede it. In a few substate regions, a regional government already is in place and no UMJO would be necessary. Quite clearly, the differences among all these regions as to size, jurisdictional complexity, political attitudes, and servicing problems preclude any across-the-board generalizations as to the specific relationship between our UMJO and general local governmental modernization proposals.

But despite this diversity, four facts stand out:

- All substate areas require an authoritative regional decision maker, whether an UMJO or a government.
- All but a handful of these areas require a strengthening of their subregional local units.

- Certainly a majority of them face major hurdles in achieving area-wide governmental reform in the near future.
- All of the interstate metropolitan areas confront insurmountable regional reorganization hurdles, save perhaps for the UMJO option.

These are the factors that explain the linkages and form the line between the UMJO and local governmental modernization parts of our triangular substate regional strategy. What, then, is the ACIR's new program for local and area-wide governmental reform? In February 1974 the Commission adopted an action agenda in this field that encompasses a half-dozen broad but interrelated goals:

First, this agenda seeks to place the clear sanction of state statutory authority behind a set of enforceable standards relating to municipal incorporation, local governmental viability, and annexation.

Second, it recommends that states establish local government boundary commissions to apply these standards in specific instances and to assume a continuing responsibility in such matters as the modification of substate district and county boundaries and the dissolution or merger of special districts and of nonviable general local governmental units.

Third, it contains a packet of nine reform proposals that are geared to revitalizing the structure of county governments, to sorting out and reconciling county and municipal servicing responsibilities, and to carving out a new state role that is supportive of these efforts.

Fourth, it calls for state enactment of permissive legislation authorizing five different regional home rule options—multicounty consolidation, city-county merger, the modernized county, the multipurpose regional service corporation, and conversion of an UMJO into a general-purpose government. The distinctive features of each of these governmental options are designed to meet the special problems of different types of substate regions.

Fifth, it provides for the formation of broadly representative, permanent state advisory commissions on intergovernmental relations to probe on a continuing basis the structure, functions, finances, and relationships of lower-tier, middle-tier, and state governments.

Finally, it urges the Executive Branch of the federal government and the Congress to adopt policies that accommodate state and local efforts to reorganize governments at the substate regional and local levels.

A Servicing Assignment Component

Turning to the third component of this substate regional strategy, the Commission found that the present pattern of functional assignments at the state, area-wide, and local levels is a patchwork product of largely uncoordinated, separate actions taken by all levels, including the federal government. To achieve a more consistent and logical determination of responsibilities and to round out its UMJO and reorganization proposals, the ACIR called upon the states to enact legislation creating an ongoing assignment of functions policy and process, including the formulation of general criteria to help provide more balanced and systematic answers to basic assignment questions and of classification standards to be developed on a function-by-function basis that would sort out what level is responsible for what. The Commission urged that a state-local unit, preferably a state ACIR, be assigned the tough task of developing the criteria and classification standards. In addition, this broadly representative unit would be empowered to issue "intergovernmental impact statements" on federal, state, or local proposals involving significant changes in service assignment responsibilities and to recommend specific functional reassignment policies to appropriate decision-making bodies.

CONCLUSION

State-designated but locally controlled districts, local governmental modernization, and more systematic assignment of functions processes—these are the three top items on the ACIR's current implementation program in the nonfiscal area. None will be easy, because none has a strong, "built-into-the-system" constituency.

One hundred and forty years ago, De Tocqueville wrote in his *Democracy in America,* "A nation may establish a free government, but without municipal institutions it can not have the spirit of liberty." Today, the very vitality of our local governmental institutions is at stake. And the manner in which we solve the substate regional dilemma, in no small measure, will determine whether or not they will continue to be strong, resourceful, and responsive foundations of our libertarian tradition.

5. State Assumption of Urban Responsibilities: Exception to the Rule or Wave of the Future?

John J. Callahan and
Ruth M. Bosek

The states are the pivotal level of government in a federal system. They are constitutionally coequal with national government and are the legal stewards of local government.[1] Consequently, they face few legal bounds as to the functions that they might assume in a federal system.

The theory of federalism, however, provides no quick and sure guide to the functions that state government might be responsible for. In the words of one observer,

> . . . the federal principle does not prescribe any physical, moral, or qualitative conditions for the distribution of functions. It is indifferent to the precise content of the division [of functions], and it argues that there is no *a priori* principle by which a distribution of functions could be effected. The definitive element of the federal state is simply in the form of the division, not its substance; in the creation of a specific kind of jural relationship between law-making authorities, not in the material quality of functions vested in the general and regional governments.[2]

Legal bases for a systematic division of functions among a state and its constituent localities are equally hard to fathom.[3] States, therefore, have little *a priori* guidance as to the functions that they might assume in a modern federal system, though certain legal mandates do require states to provide, directly or through delegation, adequate levels of some services, most notably education.[4]

While states have little analytic guidance as to the functional assignment policies that they might pursue,[5] some observers have noted their unwillingness to take the political leadership in this area, particularly in assuming more urban functional responsibilities.[6] Some attribute this to the fact that states, as a middle tier of government, are relatively invisible to most people.[7] Others note the glaring disorganization of many state executives and legislatures and contend that states are ill-equipped to assume more functional responsibilities than they now have. Still other recent evidence, however, suggests that states perform functions that the public expects them to perform;[8] therefore, they wisely have refrained from assuming additional functions. The low repute of state government, the need for structural modernization,[9] and state reluctance to deal with pressing urban policy problems,[10] in the opinions of many, continue to keep state governments a distinctly secondary force on the functional assignment front.

On the other hand, states still are regarded as the public policy laboratories of federalism. In a variety of areas—air pollution, land-use control, workmen's compensation—states are or have been in the forefront of the federal scene. Recent state advances in educational finance, property tax assessment reform, and even local government reorganization cannot be discounted. States sometimes, if not inevitably, stand ready to alter the functional assignment pattern of American federalism. Indeed, if one views some of the currents of new federalism—block grants, revenue sharing that has bolstered state government budgets, national unwillingness to pursue uniform solutions of pressing policy problems,[11] even adverse federal court rulings such as *Rodriguez,*[12] which contend that the solution to many policy problems must be found at the state level—it is readily apparent that state governments will have to play a significant role, for ill or good, in functional assignment policies in years to come.

The issue, then, is how states will meet their problems of service allocation. Will they assume more responsibility for directly providing services? Will they reorganize and restructure local and regional governments to better meet urban service demands? Will they bolster the fiscal, structural, and personnel capabilities of existing units of local government to meet various service allocation problems, or will they do nothing? The task of this paper, therefore, is to set out the record of state assumption of service responsibilities, to assess in preliminary terms how well state assumption has worked, to suggest some of the political, economic, and administrative issues of state assumption, and to offer proposals that set forth assignment policies that states might wish to pursue in the latter part of this decade.

STATE ASSUMPTION: THE RECORD

How states actively pursued the assumption of more functional responsibilities within their state-local systems of government? Fiscal data for 1958 and

1972 indicate that states generally have expanded their revenue-raising capabilities more rapidly than their direct expenditure responsibilities. During these 14 years, the state proportion of state-local expenditure responsibility increased from 35 to 37 percent, while the state share of state-local revenue-raising responsibilities increased from 49 to 55 percent. States considerably expanding their revenue-raising capacity include Illinois, Kansas, Minnesota, New York, and Rhode Island. States that have raised markedly their expenditure responsibilities include Idaho, Nebraska, Pennsylvania, West Virginia, and Wisconsin. States that both have raised their shares of expenditure and revenue-raising responsibilities include Kentucky, Massachusetts, New Jersey, Utah, and Vermont.

Is there any pattern within these general data that suggests how different states have approached the service assumption problem? Data from the 1957 and 1967 Census of Governments presented in Table 5-1 indicate that there has been relatively little movement in states' assuming additional expenditure responsibilities during this period. Rather, what has occurred is that most states with major expenditure responsibilities in 1957 continued to maintain them as of 1967 (*e.g.,* Vermont and Utah). In contrast, states that exhibited relatively few assumed responsibilities in 1957 also showed few assumptions of responsibility by 1967 (*e.g.,* Colorado, Kansas, Nebraska, New York, Ohio, South Dakota, Texas, and Wyoming). (See Table 5-1.)

What are the prospects for urban expenditure assumption from this record? Looking at the functions assumed by state governments in both 1957 and 1967, it appears that states frequently take over two types of expenditures: (1) those that have substantial impact on urban *populations* (welfare, unemployment compensation, and other education) and (2) those that generally benefit rural *areas* (highways and natural resources). Only a few states have moved into those areas of expenditure responsibility that primarily benefit urban *areas* (health, hospitals, and corrections, for example).[13] At the same time, other analysis shows that innovative states' governments—those altering local structures and reassigning local functions—are often those that do not assume direct expenditure responsibilities in their state-local system.[14]

There are a few states that have both passed innovative legislation affecting urban problems and assumed significant expenditure responsibilities within their state-local system (Connecticut, Hawaii, Alaska, Rhode Island, and Vermont, for example). These latter jurisdictions are assuming more functional and structural responsibility for dealing with the urban problem. Other larger urban states (New York, California, Wisconsin, New Jersey) seem to be dealing with structural rather than expenditure facets of urban problems. Finally, there are a few states that seem to be dealing with neither the expenditure nor the structural dimensions of urban problems (Ohio and Texas).

The fiscal and legislative outputs of different state political systems indicate that they may view significant tradeoffs in dealing with urban problems on a structural or fiscal basis. Larger urban states may shy away from assuming more expenditure responsibilities because of the enormous fiscal burdens involved

TABLE 5-1. *State Assumption of Functional Expenditure Responsibilities, 1957–67*

State	Number of Functions Wholly or Predominantly Financed at State Level		State Percent of General Expenditure		Functions Assumed or (Devolved) between 1957 and 1967
	1957	1967	1958	1972	
Alabama	10	11	42.5	50.0	Natural resources[1]
Alaska	n.a.	16	n.a.	67.8	n.a.[2]
Arizona	7	6	38.3	38.6	(Higher education)[2]
Arkansas	5	8	51.3	52.0	Public welfare, insurance trust
California	8	6	27.1	28.6	(Higher education)
Colorado	6	5	32.5	39.4	(Higher education), natural resources[3]
Connecticut	9	12	53.7	43.8	(Highways),[3] other education, other hospitals, water transport, corrections
Delaware	16	16	64.6	51.5	(Highways),[2] insurance trust
Florida	6	5	36.0	35.6	(Higher education),[2] other education
Georgia	8	8	39.2	42.2	—
Hawaii	n.a.	15	n.a.	79.3	n.a.
Idaho	7	7	44.2	51.3	(Higher education),[2] other education, corrections
Illinois	6	8	33.6	38.8	(Higher education),[3] other education, natural resources[2]
Indiana	5	7	30.4	35.8	Other education, water transport
Iowa	6	7	38.6	38.5	Other education
Kansas	5	4	33.6	34.7	(Higher education),[2] other education
Kentucky	10	10	47.9	59.4	(Higher education),[1] other public assistance

State					
Louisiana	6	52.1	8	48.2	Other education, other public assistance
Maine	12	51.6	10	54.8	(Natural resources[1] highways)[3]
Maryland	9	35.2	4	36.0	(Higher education),[2] other education, natural resources,[2] corrections
Massachusetts	8	31.6	10	45.3	Other education, airports
Michigan	5	34.2	7	37.3	(Higher education),[3] other education, water transport, unemployment compensation
Minnesota	5	29.7	6	29.8	Other education
Mississippi	8	45.5	6	48.2	(Higher education)[2]
Missouri	6	42.3	7	38.2	(Higher education),[2] other public assistance, natural resources[2]
Montana	6	46.4	8	51.4	Other education, highways[3]
Nebraska	5	33.8	4	40.3	Higher education[1]
Nevada	8	44.4	9	35.2	Natural resources[3]
New Hampshire	10	51.0	10	48.1	(Corrections), highways[3]
New Jersey	6	22.2	6	31.0	(Higher education)[3] natural resources[3]
New Mexico	10	52.8	9	49.8	(Corrections)
New York	5	22.7	5	23.1	(Natural resources),[1] other education
North Carolina	10	57.0	9	42.1	(Higher education),[1] natural resources,[3] corrections
North Dakota	10	54.2	9	51.1	(Corrections)
Ohio	5	32.0	4	35.2	(Higher education),[2] other education
Oklahoma	10	52.5	7	52.7	(Natural resources,[2] corrections)
Oregon	6	41.5	6	44.9	(Higher education),[3] other education
Pennsylvania	9	36.8	10	44.5	(Higher education),[3] other education hospitals[3]

(continued)

TABLE 5-1 *continued*

State	Number of Functions Wholly or Predominantly Financed at State Level		State Percent of General Expenditure		Functions Assumed or (Devolved) between 1957 and 1967
	1957	1967	1958	1972	
Rhode Island	15	16	50.6	54.2	Hospitals[1]
South Carolina	9	12	47.7	48.4	Natural resources,[3] highways[2] water transport
South Dakota	8	6	47.2	48.8	(Corrections, natural resources)[3]
Tennessee	9	8	37.9	41.7	(Natural resources)[3]
Texas	6	5	35.8	40.1	(Higher education),[2] other education
Utah	9	11	41.3	55.0	(Corrections), other education Highways,[3] other public welfare
Vermont	9	14	49.0	65.6	Natural resources,[3] hospitals[1] highways,[3] health, employee retirement
Virginia	7	9	43.5	40.7	(Natural resources),[3] highways,[3] categorical public assistance, hospitals[1]
Washington	6	9	44.2	43.3	Other education, other public assistance, other public welfare
West Virginia	11	11	54.3	61.5	(Natural resources),[3] employee retirement
Wisconsin	6	6	22.8	33.5	(Natural resources),[3] other education
Wyoming	7	5	47.9	47.9	(Higher education)[2]

[1] Current expenditure.
[2] Capital and current expenditure.
[3] Capital expenditure.
Source: ACIR tabulation from 1957, 1967, and 1972 Census of Government materials.

while at the same time moving to modernize local governmental structure or pass new, urban-directed, state-aided programs. Smaller urban states—Rhode Island, Delaware, Hawaii—may be able to move simultaneously on both fronts, state expenditure takeover and development of new urban, locally controlled programs. In these latter states, action to resolve urban problems may succeed due to the manageable character of the urban crisis in these states and the lack of local fears of strong state government. In other larger urban states, however, the opposite may be true. In these latter jurisdictions urban crises and state and local governmental structures both may be unmanageable. This size characteristic combined with growing political struggles and shifting coalitions between urban, suburban, and rural interests in these states may mean that state-directed solutions to urban problems in large, metropolitan states will be complex and even counterproductive to urban interests on occasion.[15]

STATE ASSUMPTION: AN EVALUATION IN THREE FUNCTIONAL AREAS

State functional assumption and its resulting impact on both state and local governments cannot be evaluated easily. Rarely does a state completely preempt a function, leaving no local role. Nor do states take over identical components of a function or perform them on easily comparable terms. Therefore analysis of state takeover or devolutions of functions must be tempered by an understanding of unique conditions in each state.

Education

Currently only one state, Hawaii, fully finances its elementary and secondary school systems. In other states localities support their schools through the local property tax with varying degrees of state assistance. Full state financing of schools has been urged for a variety of fiscal and educational reasons.

The main argument for full state funding of education concerns the inadequacies of local finance. The property tax is a regressive tax and is the major source of revenue for local governments. It produces considerable inequalities in the level of education throughout a state because of the maldistribution of wealth among local governments. Most states, in an effort to minimize these disparities, have instituted programs of state educational assistance. However, most of these assistance plans fall short of their fiscal equalization goals.[16]

In New York, for example, state assistance is largely a function of property values per pupil. Consequently, central cities, with traditionally higher property values, receive less state aid than their suburban neighbors. Simultaneously, central cities generally spend a smaller percentage of their own tax revenues on education because of the cost of funding other service requirements not found in suburban areas.[17] Moreover, state educational aid to the central cities sometimes does not increase educational spending; rather, it frees up more local money for other badly needed services, while in the suburbs it usually is a stimulus to more educational spending.[18] However, central cities contain the majority of students with the greatest educational needs, and they should be spending at least as much per pupil as the suburbs, if not more.

Full state financing could eliminate the resource disparities among school systems and relieve the burden on local revenues. As state government has a more varied tax capacity than local governments, it can spread this fiscal burden across a broader tax base. Local communities would also benefit by having the education dollars directly targeted to their individual needs, and the equalizing of education spending through full state funding might encourage decentralization by providing the necessary funds to make community control meaningful.[19]

Land-Use Management

Until recently, land-use controls were primarily a local function. However, increasing numbers of states have begun to institute land-use controls ranging from nearly complete state control of certain types of development or natural areas to greater supervision of local land-use controls.

Hawaii's land-use program provides the strongest state role, with only those land areas classified as "urban" by the state coming under any control by local governments. Vermont's law allows the state to regulate any industrial or commercial development over 10 acres even if there are local plans in effect—the state can regulate development over 1 acre if there are no local plans. Maine's Site Location Law authorizes the state to control the location of certain types of development which might be damaging to the environment. At least 12 states have laws protecting coastal zones or wetlands. Some state land-use laws hinge on local inaction—in Oregon the governor can develop a comprehensive land-use plan and zoning controls for any unregulated land, while in Wisconsin and Minnesota the lack of satisfactory local controls places shorelands under state regulation.[20]

The assumption by the states of significant land-use controls may be partly a product of the environmental movement and partly the result of traditionally strong state involvement in the natural resource area. Visible and forceful application of significant state land-use controls can have the salutary effect of making the average citizen more aware of potential development hazards and the means for controlling development. However, while many state laws are aimed at encouraging local governments to adopt their own land-use controls, this does not always happen. Some geographic areas, such as coastal zones and wetlands, are beyond the jurisdiction of any single locality and require consistent state policy. Moreover, in those states that act only when the local governments do not, some local governments may opt out of this difficult functional responsibility. They may choose not to go through the time-consuming, costly process of developing land-use controls or through the politically hazardous process of enforcing them. There are indications that some local governments in Vermont, for example, are not developing local plans, as the state is expected to control land use even if they do not.[21]

Mental Health Care: Back to the Locals

In 1963 Congress passed a law creating community mental health centers on the premise that many hospitalized mental health patients could function better if they were given proper local supervision and outpatient treatment. This encouragement, combined with the budget crunches of the early 1970s, prompted many states to begin closing down their mental institutions and returning patients to home communities. However, federal funds have not been sufficient to provide proper housing and treatment for the released patients, and the states have not taken up the fiscal slack. The result has been the development of "psychiatric ghettoes" in many local areas. Former patients, many old and unable to care for themselves, live in rundown boarding houses or hotels. No one level of government—federal, state, or local—is willing to accept program responsibility for these former inmates.[22]

What has happened in the field of mental health is an example of the possible consequences of an unclear and unsupervised assignment of functional responsibility. If the program is expensive and not "glamorous," if its constituency is not articulate and powerful, then the responsibility for the function is likely to be sloughed from one governmental level to another, to the detriment of both the program and the people it serves.

Summary

The main advantages of state assumption of a function are fiscal ones: resources can be equalized, money can be concentrated where it is most needed, and tax burdens can be better distributed among various types of taxes. The state also is better situated to handle problems with a geographic scope exceeding that of local governments. Some disadvantages are that state assumption can lead to overcentralization of decision-making power, and may encourage local governments not to take action on difficult problems.

The key questions in considering state assumption of functions, then, concern the components of functions the state should assume and the form that state assumption should take. Depending on the function and the mode of assumption, state takeover could either increase or decrease political accountability, fiscal equity, economic efficiency, and administrative effectiveness of a state-local service system.

STATE ASSUMPTION: SOME GENERAL POLICY PROBLEMS

How should public policy makers evaluate the desirability of state assumption of urban functions? A brief review of some pertinent economic, political, and administrative issues suggests the strengths and weaknesses of any service assignment strategy.

Economically, state assumption of functional responsibilities has been held to be a key to resolution of metropolitan fiscal disparity problems. Certainly it appears that the provision of fiscal equity in state and local government is a state responsibility. However, some economists have contended that state centralization of expenditure responsibilities may lead to a leveling effect on public expenditures[23] or to protracted political struggles, as different geographic areas try to have their diverse expenditure preferences met at a single, heterogeneous level of government.[24] Other expenditure benefits, such as those resulting from economies of scale, seem more likely to be realized on a regional rather than a statewide basis.

Administratively, many doubt that large-scale state-local bureaucracies will be more innovative in public policy development. Indeed, experience with some state environmental reorganizations indicates that resultant state superdepartments have had difficulty in meeting relatively straight-forward public policy goals. Moreover, state agencies have yet to effectively deal with substate districting problems that will inevitably be part of state takeover of a functional responsibility.[25] On the other hand, large-scale, professional state bureaucracies might be a force for more planned experimentation in public policy than now exists.

Politically, state assumption will not be an easy task. State legislators often show a marked disinclination to deal with complex urban problems. Indeed, rural and suburban political coalitions, both national and state phenomena, may be very unwilling to redistribute fiscal resources of programmatic power to large urban areas. Nor is it likely that such legislators will look with favor on radical local governmental reorganization policies. Finally, many state legislators and governors probably feel that they should not bear all the political risks in dealing with urban problems. Rather, they believe that local officials, often in new regional organizations, should still bear the main responsibility for finding solutions to these pressing urban concerns.[26] This, of course, can change if local officials are unwilling or incapable of finding cooperative solutions to urban issues.

What this seems to add up to is that states—as Ohio, Florida, and New Jersey are now doing—may investigate whether they can better affect the service allocation problem by sharing powers over functions rather than by fully assuming local expenditure responsibilities. Our recently concluded two-year ACIR study on substate regionalism suggests, for example, that a three-part strategy of regional districting, local governmental reorganization, and more sophisticated functional assignment policies may be the key to new approaches to dealing with the urban problem.[27]

States may analyze those functions and components that they can best directly provide while delegating other functions and services to regional and local governmental instrumentalities. In this manner, a state will be able to conserve its fiscal, political, and administrative resources and target its efforts on service allocation problems that are most amenable to state administration. Without such a policy, states and local governments will precipitously shift services up and down the functional assignment system with consequent political, economic, and social disruption. A state can join with its constituent local governments in designing a functional assignment scheme that is more equitable, efficient, accountable, and effective than the present one.

CONCLUSIONS

State assumption of functional responsibilities may be a counterproductive means of solving the functional assignment problems of urban federalism. Rather, what may be needed is a jointly (state-local) developed assignment policy that will systematically allocate powers over functions and their components among state, regional, and local governments.

State assumption has tremendous political, economic, and administrative risks. While it is advocated by many on equity grounds, many believe other consequences outweigh the good that could come from state assumption of various functional responsibilities. Economically, state assumption may lead to leveling effects on public expenditures, heightened political conflict about expenditure policy, and further unwillingness to exercise state expenditure control. City exploitation at the hands of rural and suburban legislatures cannot be discounted. State legislatures still do not have adequate staff to evaluate the consequences of their actions. State executives are still fragmented and limited by archaic constitutional and legislative restrictions on their powers, and the general public often has little attachment to or interest in the state political process. State bureaucracies, like all large organizations, still have to overcome severe administrative limitations on their ability to find new and innovative solutions to pressing public service problems.

Greater state involvement in functional assignment problems, however, is a must. The development of new governmental forms and decision-making processes at the substate regional level stands out as a prime hope for effective state action in the functional assignment area. A few states—New Jersey, Florida, Ohio—are now studying new functional assignment possibilities, and their experience may uncover new, effective state approaches to the service allocation problem.

One exception to the preceding paragraph concerns greater state responsibility for the development of a fairer system of intergovernmental fiscal relations. Fiscal equity in the financing of almost any function can probably be best pursued through such policies as unconditional state revenue sharing, development of progressive state revenue structures, expanded local nonproperty taxation, and interlocal fiscal transfer systems—all designed to reduce the interjurisdictional and interpersonal fiscal inequities that characterize most state-local fiscal systems. An exception to this general route to fiscal equity may be required if local or area-wide governments are unwilling or unable to provide adequate local or metropolitan services after a specified period of time. In that case, full state assumption will be necessary. Fiscal equity and service adequacy stand out as two primary goals for state functional allocation policy during the late 1970s.

States also have a prime responsibility for letting area-wide and local governments experiment more with their governmental structures and service delivery programs, which would enhance what is now known about metropolitan service delivery systems. We still do not know much about the equity, efficiency, and accountability tradeoffs in different types of functional assignment systems. A state must encourage debate about its service allocation and encourage public choice among different assignment systems. This is not easy territory to venture into, but it is in keeping with the state's overriding legal responsibility as the steward of its local governmental system and purveyor of many constitutionally required services.

NOTES

1. Anwar Syed, *The Political Theory of Local Government* (New York: Random House, 1966).

2. Rufus Davis, "The Federal Principle Reconsidered" in Aaron Wildavsky, ed., *American Federalism in Perspective* (Boston: Little, Brown, 1967), p. 7.

3. See Frank I. Michelman and Terrance Sandalow, *Materials on Governments in Urban Areas* (St. Paul: West Publishing Co., 1970), p. 299 ff.

4. Recent state court cases on equalizing educational opportunity are brought on the basis that state constitutions frequently require provision of "thorough and efficient" educational services.

5. For an exception see California Council on Intergovernmental Relations, *Allocation of Public Service Responsibilities in California* (Sacramento: Council on Intergovernmental Relations, 1970).

6. Alan K. Campbell, ed., *The States and the Urban Crisis* (Englewood Cliffs, N.J.: Prentice-Hall, 1970).

7. York Willbern, "The States as Components in an Areal Division of Powers" in Arthur Maass, ed., *Area and Power* (New York: Free Press, 1959), pp. 70–89.

8. U.S. Senate Committee on Government Operations, *Confidence and Concern: Citizens View American Government* (Washington: Government Printing Office, 1973).

9. Committee for Economic Development, *Modernizing State Government* (Washington: Committee for Economic Development, 1967).

10. Campbell, *op. cit.*

11. James Sundquist, *Making Federalism Work* (Washington: Brookings, 1969).

12. *San Antonio Independent School District v. Rodriguez*, 411 U.S. 1, 93 S.Ct. 1278, 36 L.Ed. 2d 16 (1973).

13. Michael C. LeMay, "The States and Urban Areas: A Comparative Assessment," *National Civic Review,* December 1972, pp. 542-8.

14. Similar policy tradeoffs between fiscal and program policies work at the national level. See Richard Lehne, "Benefits in Federal-State Relations," *Publius,* II, 2 (Fall 1972), pp. 75-94.

15. John J. Callahan, William H. Wilken, and M. Tracy Sillerman, *Urban Schools and School Finance Reform: Promise and Reality* (Washington: National Urban Coalition, 1974).

16. See Joel Berke, Alan Campbell, and Robert Goettel, *Financing Equal Educational Opportunity: Alternatives for State Finances* (Berkeley, Calif.: McCutchan Publishing Corp., 1972), p. 130.

17. U.S. Advisory Commission on Intergovernmental Relations, *City Financial Emergencies: The Intergovernmental Dimension* (Washington: Government Printing Office, 1973), app. B.

18. Berke, Campbell, and Goettel, *op. cit.,* p. 130.

19. *Ibid.,* p. 136.

20. William S. James, "Why a Role for State Land-Use?" *State Government,* Summer 1973, p. 169.

21. Elizabeth H. Haskell and Victoria S. Price, *State Environmental Management: Nine Case Studies* (New York: Praeger, 1973), p. 191.

22. Sharland Trotter and Bob Kuttner, "The Mentally Ill: From Back Wards to Back Alleys," *Washington Post,* Mar. 3, 1974, pp. C-1 and C-4.

23. Seymour Sacks *et al., City Schools—Suburban Schools? A History of Fiscal Conflict* (Syracuse, N.Y.: Syracuse University Press, 1972).

24. Robert Bish, *The Public Economy of Metropolitan Areas* Chicago: Markham Publishing Company, 1971).

25. Melvin B. Mogulof, "Federally Encouraged Multijurisdictional Agencies in Three Metropolitan Areas" in U.S. Advisory Commission on Intergovernmental Relations, *Regional Governance: Promise and Performance* (Washington: Government Printing Office, 1973).

26. U.S. Advisory Commission on Intergovernmental Relations, *Substate Regionalism and the Federal System* (Washington: Government Printing Office, 1973-74), a report in six vols.

27. *Ibid.*

Comment: The Need for Measuring the Effects of Reorganization

Yong Hyo Cho

Public policies have traditionally been adopted and changed without systematic analysis of their implications. This still happens today, in most cases. Municipal reforms, for example, have long thrived on justifications based on *a priori* logic, moralistic assertions, and political instinct, rather than on objective evaluation. Only recently has systematic, empirical analysis become an important element of the study of public policy outcomes.

The idea of state assumption of urban responsibilities, to which the Callahan-Bosek paper is addressed, has not yet gained the intellectual currency it deserves. However, there is evidence of a growing awareness among social scientists that state governments will play a pivotal role in the resolution of subnational fiscal problems.

The emergence of the idea of state assumption of urban responsibilities symbolizes the "rediscovery" of the states in the 1970s as more promising partners in the American federal system. As Callahan and Bosek point out, while the states are constitutionally empowered to be the cornerstone of the federal system, they nevertheless have been a target of relentless criticism for many decades. The critics argue that the states are the weakest link in the federal system, for they are incapable of, inactive in, and unresponsive to facing the challenge of urban, industrial America. This criticism is based on past performance—state governments have made little contribution to the more progressive, urban-oriented, contemporary social policies, *e.g.,* antipoverty programs, manpower training programs, or model cities programs. But it is also a fact that the states have greatly expanded their role in financing or administering some of the more important domestic service functions, including public assistance programs, higher education, local school financing, highways, and natural resources.

State assumption of urban responsibilities, one of several reform ideas intended to enhance metropolitan governance, is a centralization measure, while an alternative reform concept, neighborhood government, is a decentralization measure. The middle-of-the-road approach is metropolitan or substate regionalism, which provides a way of creating an integrative metropolitan mechanism for public service delivery. Each of these reform approaches has distinct advantages and disadvantages. Thus no one of these reform measures should be expected to be fully effective in dealing with the multidimensional urban governance problems.

The remainder of this comment is addressed to the following two points: (1) the policy implications of state assumption, and (2) the political feasibility of state assumption.

POLICY IMPLICATIONS

A number of issues are crucial in the assessment of the policy implications of state assumption: (1) equity, (2) leveling up of public services, (3) enhancing governmental capacity to deal with urban problems, (4) economies of scale, and (5) bureaucratic innovativeness.

It is widely believed that fiscal inequities among local governments will be resolved by state assumption of urban responsibilities. However, it is possible that state assumption of urban responsibilities may obliterate, rather than eradicate, the inequities. This is because the problem of inequities is as much an intrajurisdictional problem as it is an interjurisdictional one, as exemplified in the *Hawkins v. Shaw*[1] case. In fact, while inequities within local jurisdictions will likely remain in the event of state assumption of urban responsibilities per se, previous interlocal inequities may not disappear, but rather may add to these existing intrajurisdictional inequities.

For a number of reasons, state governments are believed to be better equipped to raise taxes than are local governments, and therefore, that state assumption will result in an overall leveling up of public expenditures. The state assumption of financing responsibilities will enable states to tap resources throughout each state, presumably because state governments are less vulnerable to the pressure for competitive undertaxation than are local taxing jurisdictions. Cross-section evidence, however, does not support this expectation. For example, a comparison of the 50 states shows that when state-local tax responsibilities are more state-centralized, the per capita level of state and local taxes tends to be lower.[2]

State assumption of urban responsibilities is expected to strengthen the ability to effectively govern the urban areas by weakening the structural impediment of jurisdictional fragmentation of local governments. Many problems requiring concerted area-wide effort, such as public education, environmental pollution, and housing, suffer from jurisdictional fragmentation of local governments. State assumption of urban responsibilities will provide an institutional framework capable of allowing area-wide approaches to urban problems. Again, however, there is no assurance that such structural reassignment is going to deal with the forces underlying intrametropolitan political conflict.

Another frequent criticism of the existing state of urban governance is that fragmented local governments in metropolitan areas lead to diseconomies of scale. Callahan and Bosek seem to believe that state assumption of urban responsibilities may achieve the desired economies of scale. However, it should be noted that there is little, if any, empirical evidence to support the economy-of-scale contention.

Finally, Callahan and Bosek indicate the possibility that the large state bureaucracy that would result from state assumption of urban responsibilities would not become an innovative force in policy development. The evidence on this contention is scarce and mixed. With respect to the latter characteristic, some studies, such as the public housing policy analysis by Michael Aiken and Robert R. Alford[3] have demonstrated that a larger bureaucracy can be more innovative than a smaller one in terms of its propensity to adopt policy changes.

POLITICAL FEASIBILITY

State assumption seems to be easier to achieve politically than are other reform alternatives. Both substate regionalism and neighborhood government approaches, for example, suffer from the fact that a region or a neighborhood is an abstract concept rather than a concerte political jurisdiction and, therefore, neither has any identifiable political constituency.

To mobilize political support for a regional government mechanism and to sustain its viability, it is necessary to have a regional constituency, namely, "regional citizenship", as it is labeled by the Metropolitan Fund, Inc., of the Detroit area.[4] The sense of "regional citizenship" does not yet exist in metropolitan areas because the concept of "regionality" has never been cultivated into a fact of political life.

"Neighborhood" is a concept almost as ambiguous as "region," and almost as difficult to define. To decentralize urban service delivery mechanisms through neighborhood government seems to be more reactive than creative in dealing with the governance problems of metropolitan mass society. The reform concept of neighborhood government grows out of a strong preference for local autonomy, i.e., citizen participation in and citizen control of public policy decision making. That reform benefit of decentralization must be weighed against the possible losses in equity, in scale economies, in the lower level of resources which may result, and in the potential for the return to the corruption of the political ward system.

Compared to the regionalism and neighborhood government approaches to reform, state assumption enjoys some important political advantages. First, as Callahan and Bosek note, the states have constitutional powers. Second, the states have the historical, political, and emotional identity as a key institution in the American system of government. Third, the states have been highly consistent in expanding their responsibilities for domestic services throughout the twentieth century. In fact, the states have been "the most dynamic sector" among both the public and private sectors of the economy. All considered, state assumption seems to be much less difficult to achieve than other reform alternatives.

CONCLUSION

Undoubtedly, state assumption is not a panacea for urban ills. Nevertheless, this idea has important merits, including a partial liquidation of some of the problems that result from existing antiquated systems of local government. In spite of the fundamental changes that the society has undergone, the United States has too long remained "a nation of political villages." State assumption seems to be a natural vehicle to create "a nation of states," where the union can become more perfect rather than where the fragmentation can become more complete.

The Callahan-Bosek paper is valuable and timely, for it raises questions and offers insights concerning a central issue, the role of the states, in rearranging the intergovernmental relations for the last quarter of this century. The paper lays an excellent agenda for future research on this subject.

NOTES

1. 437 F. 2d 1286 (5th Cir. 1971) affirmed *en banc* 461 F. 2d 1171.
2. Alan K. Campbell and Seymour Sacks, *Metropolitan America: Fiscal Patterns and Governmental Systems* (New York: Free Press, 1967.)
3. Michael Aiken and Robert R. Alford, "Community Structure and Innovation: The Case of Public Housing," *American Political Science Review,* 64, 3 (September 1970), pp. 843–64.
4. Kent Mathewson, "A Regional Ethic," in Kent Mathewson, ed., *The Regionalist Papers,* (Detroit: Metropolitan Fund, 1974), pp. 41–55.

6. State and Regional Government Financing of Urban Public Services

Roy W. Bahl and
Walter Vogt

The fiscal problems of American cities have been attributed to a multiplicity of factors, including the revenue implications of a declining economic base, the expenditure implications of a heavy concentration of "high cost" citizens, the high cost of replacing an antiquated public infrastructure, and suburban exploitation.[1] Whatever the underlying factors, the rate of increase in core city expenditure requirements has continued to strain local tax bases and has forced an increasing reliance on external financing of urban public services.

The trend towards financial centralization has at once stimulated the use of several different mechanisms for state and federal assistance to local governments: categorical federal aids, general revenue sharing, increased and reformed state aid programs, and direct state government assumption of financial responsibility for local government functions. The choice of a proper mix of these alternative methods for relieving the urban fiscal crisis requires careful study of the impact of each program on the local government budget, on the distribution of expenditures among the various functions, and on the distribution of resident tax burdens.

This study focuses on the analysis of programs that would shift financial responsibility from central city governments to either state or regional governments. Specifically, this study attempts to deal with the following question: if a state or regional government were to assume full financial responsibility for a heretofore locally financed service (*e.g.,* education or welfare), what would be the effects on the local government budget and on the overall tax burdens of local area residents? The answer to these questions is derived here from a comparison of the results of a set of case studies carried out in nine Urban Observatory (UO) cities. The policy usefulness of these results is enhanced because these studies are based on the study of city government functions that are "feasible" candidates for state or regional government financial assumption, and on consideration of "realistic" tax structure changes.

Immediately below is a brief summary of the arguments usually put forward as support for state or regional government financial assumption as a remedy for urban fiscal ills. Attention is then turned to a general socioeconomic and fiscal profile of the UO cities studied, to a description of the case study methodology, and to the results of the analysis. Finally, the policy implications of these results are briefly explored.

THE FINANCIAL ASSUMPTION ALTERNATIVE

The direct assumption of financial responsibility by a higher level of government is widely supported as an effective means of easing the fiscal plight of central city governments. It would seem useful here to briefly trace the information that advocates of this alternative have drawn on in citing its benefits.

There appear to be three central arguments. First, the area-wide financing implied by state or regional assumption would result in *eliminating the interjurisdictional fiscal disparities,* which are due to differences in taxable capacity. Second, it is argued that financial assumption, particularly by the state government, would result in a *more elastic state-local government tax system*[3] and hence a revenue growth that is more likely to be adequate in meeting expenditure needs. This conclusion is justified because the major state taxes, *i.e.,* sales and income, are more elastic than the major local tax, the property tax. Though there is considerable disagreement about the relative size of the income elasticity of these taxes, ACIR estimates show the elasticity of the income tax to be between 1.3 and 1.9 and that for the property tax to be between 0.8 and 1.[4] Third, proponents argue that state financial assumption would *produce a less regressive*[5] *overall state-local tax burden,* and therefore would shift some of the costs of government services from lower- to higher-income residents. This conclusion is based on the thesis that state government taxes are characterized by a less regressive tax burden pattern than is the local property tax.[6]

THE OBSERVATORY CITIES

The case study approach is particularly appropriate for studying the impact of transferring the financial responsibility for certain local government functions to a higher level of government. First, actual case studies carried out jointly by city government officials and local researchers assure that only realistic policy alternatives will be studied, and that the peculiar features of individual cities will be given adequate consideration. Second the diversity of the cities studied allows for a statement about the effects of financial centralization in a wide variety of socioeconomic and fiscal settings. More generally, the results of such analysis allow a realistic estimate of what the overall effects of state or regional government financial assumption could mean.

Socioeconomic Structure

The nine Urban Observatory cities studied here—all metropolitan central cities—display a wide variation in socioeconomic and demographic characteristics. For example, per capita income is one-third lower in Baltimore than in Denver; population density in the most crowded city is nine times that of the least crowded, and the proportion of the central city population that is nonwhite ranges from 7 to 51 percent. In spite of this wide variation, there are "trends" which most of the nine cities share. Three such trends that appear common are the following: (1) each city is becoming a less dominant force in its Standard Metropolitan Statistical Area (SMSA), despite annexation; (2) city residents are becoming increasingly poorer than their suburban counterparts; and (3) central cities are gaining increasing concentrations of the very low-income population group—the group which places relatively high expenditure demands on local governments and generates relatively few resources.

The data in Table 6-1 indicate that central city (CC) populations grew at a much lower rate than suburban (OCC, or outside central city) populations, with extreme examples being Atlanta, Baltimore, and Denver.[7] Of the nine cities studied, only Kansas City, Kansas, shows an increasing population share for the metropolitan area, and this is largely due to annexations. There are two important implications of this declining population dominance of observatory cities. First, the pattern is similar for all large cities in the nation, suggesting that the observatory cities are representative. Second, the declining population dominance of these metropolitan cities is generally reflective of the total relationship between the city and the SMSA; *i.e.*, city-suburb disparities in income and education have grown.

Two structural changes in central city population appear common to the UO cities as well as to major U.S. cities in general: an increase in the percentage of the nonwhite population and in the percentage of the population over 65 years of age. The nonwhite concentration increased in all the UO cities—except Kansas City, Kansas—with particularly large increases in Atlanta and Baltimore. In general, these central cities have received almost all of the growth of the SMSA's nonwhite population. For example, the CC portion of the Milwaukee SMSA accounted for about 98 percent of the total SMSA growth in nonwhite population over the past decade. A similar pattern is observed with respect to the growth in the percentage of population over 65—all cities except Kansas City, Kansas, experienced increases, and the largest increases are observed for Atlanta,

TABLE 6-1. *Selected Socioeconomic Characteristics of Urban Observatory Cities, 1960 and 1970*

City[1]	Annual Rate of Change of Population, 1960 to 1970		Central City Population as a Percent of SMSA Population		Population per Square Mile (1970)	Percent of Nonwhite Population	
	CC	OCC	1960	1970		1960	1970
Atlanta	0.2	6.8	47.9	35.8	3,779	38.3	51.3
Baltimore	-0.3	3.4	52.1	43.7	11,568	34.7	46.4
Boston	-0.8	1.4	26.9	23.3	13,936	9.1	16.3
Denver	0.4	6.4	53.1	41.9	5,406	6.1	9.1
Kansas City, Kans.[2]	3.3	2.4	11.2	13.4	2,961	23.1	20.4
Kansas City, Mo.	0.6	2.1	43.5	40.4	1,603	17.5	22.1
Milwaukee	-0.3	2.8	58.0	51.1	7,548	8.4	14.7
San Diego	2.0	4.4	57.8	51.3	2,199	6.0	7.6
Average[3]	0.2	2.7	48.7	41.0	6,125	17.9	23.4

City	Percent of Population over 65		Central City Median Family Income as a Percent of SMSA Median Family Income		Median Family Income (1970)	Percent of Families with Incomes under $3,000 (1970)	
	1960	1970	1960	1970		CC	OCC
Atlanta	7.9	9.2	80.3	71.4	$6,275	18.0	10.0
Baltimore	9.0	10.5	87.7	78.3	6,796	20.0	7.0
Boston	12.3	12.8	77.0	67.7	5,921	19.0	5.0
Denver	10.8	11.4	105.7	82.4	6,920	18.0	10.0
Kansas City, Kans.	10.9	10.3	88.5	87.4	7,667	n.a.	n.a.
Kansas City, Mo.	10.8	11.8	87.5	85.2	7,474	20.0	10.0
Milwaukee	9.6	11.0	92.3	85.1	8,138	13.0	7.0
San Diego	7.6	8.8	94.6	94.4	6,223	17.0	14.0
Average	9.8	10.7	89.2	81.4	6,923	18.0	9.0

[1] Metropolitan Nashville–Davidson excluded because of the incomparability of the 1960 and 1970 data.
[2] The relatively large population growth rates are largely a reflection of annexation.
[3] Unweighted.
Source: Advisory Commission on Intergovernmental Relations, *City Government Financial Emergencies* (Washington: July 1973), A–42, app. B.

Baltimore, and San Diego. These trends have particularly important implications for this study, as increasing concentrations of the poor do suggest a growing revenue-expenditure mismatch and heighten the concern about regressive local tax structures. Indeed, if the 1970s hold an extension of these trends, financial centralization would seem to be an almost essential intergovernmental reform.

The same picture of relative decline for central cities may be observed when the level and distribution of income is examined (see Table 6-1). These data show that the central city median income as a percent of SMSA median income declined over this 10-year period in all cities; *i.e.*, the CCs became relatively poorer. Here Denver is the extreme case, with Atlanta, Baltimore, Boston, and Milwaukee also showing large relative declines. This disparity in the relative levels of CC and OCC resident incomes may be underlined by comparison of the percentage of families with incomes below $3,000. In every city the CC percentage is greater, and only in San Diego is the disparity not substantial.

In sum, the UO central cities are growing slowly, and their residents are becoming poorer in relation to their OCC counterparts. Furthermore, the composition of the CC population is changing dramatically—with growing concentrations of nonwhites, the aged, and the poor in general.

Fiscal Structure

It would be difficult, if at all possible, to develop a set of measures that would enable strict comparison of the magnitude of the fiscal problem among the UO cities. However, a comparison of fiscal structures and trends, and of fiscal disparities, may give some indication of the nature of fiscal problems facing these cities, and specific characteristics of individual cities may give some indication of the sources of such fiscal problems.

The wide variation in functional responsibility among the UO cities is the key to understanding the relative severity of their fiscal crisis. All have responsibility for the education function, while only Baltimore and Denver are responsible for welfare (see Table 6-2). All cities have a set of functions in common —police, fire, sanitation, street maintenance, parks and recreation, financial administration, and general control—referred to here as the "common functions." The remainder of noneducation expenditures, excluding welfare, may be noted as "optional" functions. In general, the more functional responsibility a city has, the greater its potential fiscal problems, and the more likely it is to benefit from financial centralization.

Three cities in particular—Baltimore, Boston, and San Diego—stand out as interesting in terms of fiscal structure and trends. Some mention of these special circumstances may shed light on the nature of the urban fiscal crisis in general and on its relationship to population characteristics and functional responsibility in particular. First, Baltimore stands out as having the highest level of per capita expenditures, primarily because it has the financial responsibility for the welfare

TABLE 6-2. *Expenditure Structures and Trends, 1962–70*

Expenditures from City Budgets	Baltimore	Boston	Atlanta	Denver	Milwaukee	Kansas City, Mo.	Kansas City, Kans.	San Diego
Per Capita Expenditure 1970								
Education	$222	$139	$218	$170	$183	$169	$127	$186
Noneducation	417[1]	414	204	306[1]	218	245	117	137
Total	$639	$553	$442	$476	$401	$414	$244	$323
Common Functions[2] as a Percent of Noneducation Expenditure	42.4[1]	39.2	43.2	35.5[1]	58.2	37.9	61.0	67.6
Welfare Expenditures as a Percent of Noneducation Expenditures	22.9	2.4	—	18.9	—	—	—	—
Education Expenditures as a Percent of Total Expenditures	34.7	25.1	49.3	35.7	45.6	40.8	52.0	57.5
Average Annual Percent Change in Education Expenditure per Capita								
1962–67	10.5	10.8	19.0	8.0	10.7	4.4	9.7	2.3
1967–70	25.8	15.9	26.4	11.4	22.6	26.5	8.5	12.6
1962–70	15.1	12.3	21.2	9.0	14.2	11.0	7.9	5.4
Average Annual Percent Change in Noneducation Expenditure per Capita								
1962–67	4.4	12.3	13.3	17.2	10.8	13.7	7.9	4.6
1967–70	22.2	0.1	18.8	12.8	6.0	21.4	4.9	4.6
1962–70	9.7	8.6	14.9	15.8	9.3	16.0	7.0	4.6

[1] Includes welfare.

[2] Common functions are those which all cities tend to finance from their general budgets. These include streets, police, fire, sanitation, parks and recreation, financial administration, general control, and general public buildings.

101

TABLE 6-3. *Per Capita Expenditures and Locally Raised Taxes for the Central*

	Expenditures[2]					
	Noneducation			Educational		
City[1]	CC	OCC	$\frac{CC}{OCC}$	CC	OCC	$\frac{CC}{OCC}$
Baltimore	$417	$134	3.10	$222	$215	1.03
Boston	392	188	2.08	139	177	0.78
Atlanta	336	124	2.70	218	191	1.14
Kansas City, Mo.	316	153	2.06	169	194	0.87
Nashville-Davidson	210	57	3.68	168	115	1.46
Milwaukee	379	263	1.60	183	250	0.73
Denver	332	111	2.99	170	195	0.87
San Diego	298	245	1.21	186	227	0.81
Eight UO SMSAs[3]	335	159	2.10	182	196	0.93
37 Largest SMSAs[3]	341	174	1.96	183	211	0.87

[1] Kansas City, Kans., is omitted because it was not possible to present data by overlapping governments.
[2] These data include expenditures from all overlapping governments in the SMSA.
[3] Unweighted.
Source: Computed from Advisory Commission on Intergovernmental Relations, *City Financial Emergencies: The Intergovernmental Dimension* (Washington, July 1973), app. B.

function. Nearly 23 percent of noneducation expenditures are for the welfare function, and, furthermore, the changing composition of Baltimore's population (see Table 6-1) indicates that continued responsibility for this function will induce an even more severe drain on the city budget. By comparison, while most other cities' expenditures on noneducational services slowed down, particularly during the 1967-70 period, Baltimore's skyrocketed. It is interesting to compare Baltimore's experience with that of Boston. In 1960 both cities were responsible for the welfare function. However, in 1969 Boston's welfare function was shifted to the state. As a result, Boston's growth in noneducation expenditures was almost zero over the 1967-70 period, even though the change in the composition of Boston's population during this period was similar to that experienced by Baltimore. Thus it appears that removal of the responsibility for welfare finance from the city of Boston permitted a much less drastic increment in expenditures than would have resulted otherwise.

San Diego's fiscal structure and experience is also instructive. Of all the cities studied, San Diego showed the smallest CC-OCC disparities in socioeconomic characteristics. In fact San Diego, in terms of income, population composition, population density, etc., appears more suburban than urban compared with the other cities (see Table 6-1). The absence of a heavy concentration of the

City and Outside Central City Portion of the SMSA, 1970

			Locally Raised Taxes					
Total			*Per Capita*			*As Percent of Income*		
CC	*OCC*	$\dfrac{CC}{OCC}$	*CC*	*OCC*	$\dfrac{CC}{OCC}$	*CC*	*OCC*	$\dfrac{CC}{OCC}$
$639	$349	1.82	$221	$195	1.13	8.0	5.1	1.57
531	365	1.45	369	263	1.40	11.6	6.4	1.81
554	315	1.75	252	122	2.06	7.1	3.4	2.08
485	347	1.40	253	157	1.61	7.5	3.9	1.92
378	172	2.19	163	62	2.62	5.5	2.7	2.03
562	513	1.10	306	179	1.70	8.9	4.4	2.02
502	306	1.64	272	180	1.51	7.4	5.4	1.37
484	472	1.02	206	198	1.04	5.7	5.9	0.97
517	355	1.46	255	170	1.51	7.7	4.7	1.66
524	385	1.36	258	190	1.36	7.4	5.1	1.45

poor and the presence of a relatively strong resource base, together with financial responsibility for relatively few of the "optional" functions, lead to San Diego's relatively strong fiscal position. The city of San Diego is able to devote nearly 68 percent of its noneducational expenditures to the common city functions—police, fire, sanitation, streets, parks and recreation, financial administration, and general control—and still spend over 57 percent of its total resources on education. In total, it has the second lowest per capita total expenditures ($323) of the UO cities.

While the structure and trend of city fiscal activities give some notion of the underlying sources of the urban fiscal problem, another dimension is the fiscal disparities issue—the disparities in expenditure levels and tax burdens that exist between city and suburban governments. To gain an overall picture of fiscal disparities in the UO SMSAs, expenditures by all CC and OCC overlapping jurisdictions are compared (see Table 6-3).[8] The results are quite similar to those obtained by Sacks in his comparisons of the 37 largest SMSAs.[9] In the UO SMSAs, noneducational expenditures are up to three times as great in the CC as in OCC portions of the SMSA. Again, Baltimore and San Diego are the two extremes. The disparities in education expenditures are mixed: three central cities show higher per capita expenditures than do the OCC portions of the SMSAs.

On the other hand, the cities of Boston, Kansas City, Milwaukee, and San Diego have relatively low per capita expenditures compared to their suburban counterparts. It would appear that one trend of the national disparities—higher noneducational and lower educational expenditures in central cities than their suburbs—is present in at least four of the Urban Observatory cities.

Some characteristics are common. In all of the cities studied, per capita locally raised taxes are much higher in CCs than OCCs; the ratio of per capita locally raised taxes in the CC to those in the OCC ranged between 2.06 in Atlanta and 1.04 in San Diego, with a mean ratio of 1.67. The ratio of locally raised taxes to income, which gives a crude measure of tax effort, shows a uniformly higher effort by CC than OCC jurisdictions. In at least three SMSAs, the core city tax burden is over twice as high.

STUDY APPROACH AND ASSUMPTIONS

This study evaluates the impact on city government budgets and on the distribution of tax burdens of central city residents which results from fiscal centralization. The term "fiscal centralization," as used in this study, means the shifting of financial responsibility for a function or group of functions to a higher level of government, e.g., to a regional authority or to the state government.

Two sets of assumptions are critical to this analysis. One is the functions to be considered for shifting, and the other is the choice of taxes to be reduced by the city government shifting the function and to be increased by the government receiving the function. With respect to the choice of functions, the decision was made by the local observatories following only the criteria of political feasibility and the general guidelines offered by the ACIR (see Table 6–4).[10] The choice of taxes to be considered was also left to the local observatory, and the choice was generally based on the nature of the existing tax structure and on political feasibility.

In fact, the observatory cities considered numerous functions as candidates for financial assumption by state or regional government (see Table 6–5 for a listing of the specific functions shifted). Generally, these may be grouped into three categories: education, welfare, and a group of functions which, for convenience, we refer to as the "service package." The latter include public transit, airports, cultural institutions, hospitals, health care and recreation, libraries, etc. The "service package functions," if considered individually, often represent less than 1 percent of a city's budget. As a package, however, they can represent a considerable percentage (e.g., up to 28 percent of a city's locally raised revenues).

In most case studies, it was proposed that the financing of the service package

TABLE 6-4. *Criteria Suggested by the Advisory Commission on Intergovernmental Relations for Proper Assignment of Functions to Governments*

1. The governmental jurisdiction responsible for providing any service should be large enough to enable the benefits from that service to be consumed primarily within the jurisdiction. Neither the benefits from the service nor the social costs of failing to provide it should "spill over" into other jurisdictions.

2. The unit of government should be large enough to permit realization of economics of scale.

3. The unit of government administrating a function should have a geographic area of jurisdiction adequate for effective performance.

4. The unit of government should have the legal and administrative ability to perform services assigned to it.

5. Every unit of government should be responsible for a sufficient number of functions so that its governing processes involve a resolution of conflicting interests, with significant responsibility for balancing governmental needs and resources.

6. Performance of functions by the unit of government should remain controllable by and accessible to its residents.

7. Functions should be assigned to that level of government which maximizes the conditions and opportunities for active citizen participation and still permits adequate performance.

Source: Advisory Commission on Intergovernmental Relations, *Performance of Urban Functions: Local and Areawide* (Washington: ACIR, September 1963).

be moved to a regional government, with the objective that such a move would force all beneficiaries to pay for service benefits. Where welfare and education were considered as candidates for functional shifting, direct state government financial assumption was proposed. As may be seen from Table 6-5, the most commonly suggested candidates for transfer to state or regional levels of government are education and mass transit.

The set of taxes considered by the nine UO cities were generally similar. In all cases, it was assumed that the transfer of a function away from the local government would be accompanied by a reduction in the local property tax. The increased expenditures of the receiving government were generally assumed to be financed by additional state or regional government income taxes and general sales taxes.

The analysis itself involves three distinct steps. First, an appropriate income concept was developed. This income concept is referred to here as "economic" income. It is more inclusive than the normal census definitions of income in that it includes money incomes not counted by the census, such as realized capital gains and nonmoney incomes, and the imputed rental value of owner-occupied housing. It was necessary to develop this more inclusive measure of income so

TABLE 6-5. *Functions Proposed for Financial Assumption by State or Regional Governments*

Function	Boston	Denver	Baltimore	Atlanta	Kansas City, Kans. and Mo.	Mil-waukee	San Diego	Nashville-Davidson
Education			S¹		S	S	S	S
Welfare	S	S	S		S	S²		
Mass Transit		R¹					R	
Crime Labs							R	
Airports							R	
Cultural Institutions		R					R	
Sanitary Fills							R	
Flood Control							R	
Hospitals	S			R				
Health Care	S			R				
Recreation	S	R		R				
Libraries	S			R				
Public Safety	S							
Waste Disposal	S							
Courts and Correction	S	R						
Veterans Assistance	S							
Vocational Education	S							
Air Pollution Control	S							
Regional Ammendments	S							
Roads		R						

[1] S denotes a proposed shift to state government financing, R to regional government financing.

[2] In Wisconsin, welfare is a county function. The shift in welfare financing shown for Milwaukee from the city to the state does not indicate that Milwaukee city government is responsible for welfare. In the Milwaukee study, the portion of the county welfare budget that is paid by Milwaukee residents was estimated and hypothetically shifted to the state.

that the changes in taxes implied by financial centralization could be related to a more realistic measure of a family's ability to pay taxes. The distribution of income based on this broader concept was computed for each of the UO cities.

Second, a set of assumptions concerning the incidence of taxes and the expenditure effects of shifting the financing of certain functions to higher levels of government were standardized. The tax incidence assumptions used here are the standard assumptions employed in most empirical tax burden studies: property taxes on residential property are borne by owner-occupiers or renters in line with housing consumption, nonresidential property taxes and sales taxes are passed on to consumers in the form of higher prices, and income taxes are borne by the income recipient. One city, Milwaukee, did not employ the standard property tax incidence assumption and, instead, allocated residential property taxes to owners of capital. Therefore, the Milwaukee results are not strictly comparable, but they do serve to illustrate the drastic difference in policy implications that emerges if the property tax is, in fact, shifted backward.[11]

Third, a simulation model of fiscal centralization was developed and implemented on the data provided by each city. The simulation model for fiscal centralization is standardized in several respects. The city tax that is assumed to be reduced is always the property tax. Only the Kansas City case study deviates in any way from this assumption. In that case study, only residential property taxes are assumed to be reduced by the city. This does not render the Kansas City study incomparable; rather, it adds another dimension to the possibilities for reassigning the financing of urban public services.

The model is also standardized in that it is assumed that the state or regional government always uses some combination of the following taxes to finance its new expenditure responsibility:

1. An income tax
2. A sales tax
3. A combination of income and sales taxes
4. A property tax
5. A motor fuels tax

It is also assumed (1) that the city government reduces its property tax collections by the amount of budget relief[12] it experiences from fiscal centralization, and (2) that the state or regional government has no surplus revenues and must increase tax rates to raise new revenues equal to its new expenditure responsibility. The new financial responsibility for the state or region is equal to the sum of locally raised revenues by *all* local government units within the state or region, and it is assumed that total expenditures in the state on the shifted functions do not increase after fiscal centralization.[13] The results presented here, then, are roughly comparable between cities, and permit an evaluation of the effects of state or regional government financial assumption on central city government budgets and on central city government taxpayers. Moreover, they permit such comparative evaluation under a wide range of central city fiscal and economic circumstances. The range of implications for central city taxpayers, of this overall increase in financial responsibility to the receiving government, should be emphasized. For example, if education financing is shifted from local property taxation to state income taxation, the city under study could be subject to these effects:

1. Overall city government budget relief
2. A less regressive tax burden
3. An overall increase in average resident tax liability

RESULTS

As noted above, the central city functions that are considered candidates for financial reassignment to the state or regional government may be divided into three groups: education, welfare, and the service package. Six cities evaluated the effects of shifting education financing and the effects of shifting welfare financing to the state government, while four cities considered the shifting of service package financing to either state or regional government. Below we examine the impact of each of these shifts on central city budgets and on the tax burdens of central city residents. The analysis is carried out as though the fiscal centralization programs studied had been implemented in fiscal 1969-70. The impacts are compared below according to the function shifted to the state or regional government.

The Education Function

Six of the nine cities under study proposed that education financing be shifted to the state government:

- *Baltimore* proposed two alternatives for state financing: shifting financing to a state income tax, which would require an income tax surcharge of 80 percent; and shifting financing to a state sales tax, which would require that the sales tax rate be increased from 4 to 7.5 percent.
- *Nashville-Davidson* proposed a shift in financing to the state sales tax, which would require that the sales tax rate be increased from 3 to 5.6 percent.
- *Milwaukee* proposed a shift in financing to the state income tax, which would require a state income tax surcharge of 156 percent.
- *San Diego* proposed shifting financing to a combination of the state income and sales taxes, which would require an increase in sales tax rate from 4 to 5.3 percent and a 153 percent income tax surcharge.

• *Kansas City, Missouri,* and *Kansas City, Kansas,* proposed a shift in financing to a combination of state sales and income taxes. In Missouri, the state sales tax would rise from 3 to 3.75 percent, while the income tax rate would rise by 1 percent of income per income class. In Kansas, the respective figures are from 3 to 4.25 percent and 1.5 percent.

The effects of state government assumption of education finance on the central city fisc, summarized in Table 6-6, vary widely among the UO cities studied —largely depending on the breadth of the city government's functional responsibilities. The greatest relief to a city budget is experienced in Milwaukee, where education expenditures use up 47.5 percent of all locally raised revenues, and the least, 15.2 percent, is in Kansas City, Kansas. Still, in the absolute, the amount of property tax liability relief to the city government is substantial for all cities studied; *i.e.,* the range is from approximately $106 per capita in Baltimore to about $18 per capita in Kansas City, Kansas.

Whether or not the city government is able to tap these "freed-up" resources will depend in large part on what happens to the overall tax bill facing city residents. It is clear that residents' tax bills will not fall by the full amount of education financial responsibility assumed by the state government, because city residents will be subjected to new state taxation to meet the increased state government education expenses. In fact, the results here show *increases* in overall resident tax liability in Baltimore, Milwaukee, San Diego, and Kansas City, Kansas. In these cities, residents apparently would finance a portion of education expenditures now made by local governments in the rest of the state. The size of this increased tax liability is striking. Per capita tax liabilities rise by as much as 51 percent in Baltimore if the state sales tax is the means of finance, 46.4 percent in Milwaukee if financed by the state income tax, and 46.5 percent in San Diego if financed by a combination of the state sales and income taxes. Thus there is evidence that centralization of education would act to increase the aggregate tax liabilities of central city residents.

There are two effects operating that cause the aggregate tax liabilities of city residents to increase as a result of state government financial assumption of the education function. One is the shifting of taxes away from a combination of business and individual taxes (*e.g.,* local property tax) and toward taxes strictly on individuals (*e.g.,* individual income and retail sales taxes). Whereas under the local property tax residents in the city really pay only a fraction of their education bill, under the state government taxes the possibilities for exporting are eliminated. The other effect has to do with intrastate disparities in the level of education expenditures. If education expenditures in the city are relatively lower than those in the rest of the state (a common pattern for central cities), then it is likely that the city's share of state taxes to finance total education expenditures will, in amount, exceed its previous level of locally raised education expenditures. In this respect, note in Table 6-6, that Nashville-Davidson and Kansas City are the only cities that have higher per capita expenditures from

TABLE 6-6. *Change in Tax Liabilities due to State Assumption of Education Financing*

| | Type of State Financing | | | | | | |
| | State Sales Tax | | State Income Tax | | State Sales and Income Tax | | |
	Baltimore	Nashville-Davidson	Baltimore	Milwaukee	San Diego	Kansas City, Mo.	Kansas City, Kans.
Aggregate Tax Liability of City Residents[1]							
Before State Assumption	36.4	26.0	36.4	76.6	49.7	15.9	3.0
After State Assumption	55.0	20.9	47.0	112.2	65.5	12.8	3.9
Change	18.6	-5.1	10.6	35.6	20.8	-3.1	0.9
Per Capita Tax Liability							
Before State Assumption	$40.19	$61.02	$40.18	$106.83	$64.15	$31.35	$17.83
After State Assumption	60.72	49.05	51.89	156.48	94.00	25.24	23.18
Change per Capita	20.53	-11.97	11.71	49.65	29.85	-6.11	5.35
Percent Change	51.0	-19.6	29.1	46.4	46.5	-19.4	30.0
Effect on Locally Raised Revenues for City Government Budget	-$75.8	-$33.0	-$75.8	-$83.0	-$52.7	-$15.9	-$3.0
Locally Financed Education Expenditures as a Percent of Total Revenues from Local Sources[2]	29.0	26.0	29.0	47.5	42.1	15.4	15.2

[1] In millions of dollars. The tax liability of city residents differs from the amount of taxes raised for education by the amount of tax exported to nonresidents. For example, locally raised taxes for education are shown as $75.8 million, while $36.4 million of this was paid by Baltimore residents. This means that $39.4 million of locally raised revenues for education were exported to nonresidents. The same type of effect is shown in Tables 6–9 and 6–11 below.

[2] "Total Revenues from Local Sources" in this case denotes revenues raised locally for all city government functions including education.

local sources than other local governments in the state, and that they also show a decline in the aggregate tax liabilities as a result of state government financial assumption.

Though aggregate tax liabilities in some cities rise as a result of centralization, it does not necessarily follow that families in all income brackets experience tax burden increases. The data in Table 6-7 show the change in tax payments per dollar of income that result from state government assumption of education finance. For example, if the state of Maryland assumed total financial responsibility for the education function and financed its increased expenditures with an income tax, a Baltimore family with an income between $3,000 and $3,999 would experience a tax reduction of 1.15 cents per dollar of income. If this family's income were $3,500, its total annual tax reduction would be $40.25.

In general, these results show that state assumption tends to result in tax increases only for family units in the higher income classes. However, this generalization requires qualifications, for the results vary considerably among cities. Most of the variation appears to be due to the choice of the state tax to be used, and to the structure of the state tax. In this respect, three of the six cities proposed a mix of state income and sales taxes. The general consensus was that sole use of the sales or income tax would require rate increases that would be difficult to obtain. The mixing of two state taxes avoids the high rates necessary if only one tax is used.

There is a dramatic difference in results between Baltimore and Nashville-Davidson, even in the case where both would finance education expenditures with the state sales tax. In Baltimore, those below the $5,000 income level experience tax decreases, while residents of Nashville-Davidson with incomes below $3,000 experience tax increases. This effect is a reflection of the differences in the sales tax base used in Maryland and Tennessee. In Tennessee, food purchases are not exempt as they are in Maryland. Because food expenditures account for approximately 25 percent of total expenditures made by low-income families, the results simply reflect the greater regressivity of the sales tax in Tennessee than in Maryland. Although this comparison of the interpersonal equity effects is for only two cities, it does serve to illustrate that state financial assumption via state sales taxation can produce very different effects on interpersonal equity.

In general, however, there is a consistency in the conclusions reached. The results presented in Table 6-7 indicate that the state assumption of education financing generally results in tax decreases for families with lower income and tax increases for families with higher income. Moreover, the tax decreases are inversely related to income, while the tax increases rise as income rises; *i.e.,* the poorer a family, the greater the tax relief, and the richer a family, the greater the tax increment. San Diego stands out among this group in that its proposed financial centralization program would afford the greatest tax relief to families with low incomes, *i.e.,* below $7,000, and impose the largest tax increases per income class of any city to families with incomes above $12,000. Thus in San

TABLE 6-7. *Change in Tax Payments Per Dollar of Economic Income Resulting from State Government Assumption of Education Finance, by Income Class (in cents)*

Income Class ($)	State Sales Tax		State Personal Income Tax			Combination of State Personal Income and Sales Tax	
	Baltimore	Nashville-Davidson	Baltimore	Milwaukee	San Diego	Kansas City, Mo.	Kansas City, Kans.
0– 999	-0.66	+2.35	-3.29	-0.50	-5.9	-1.92	-1.09
1,000– 1,999	-0.66	+0.06	-3.29	-2.64	-3.4	-0.29	-0.09
2,000– 2,999	-0.66	+0.05	-3.29	-1.38	-2.6	-0.54	-0.05
3,000– 3,999	-0.58	-1.15	-1.15	-0.99	-2.1	-0.14	-0.03
4,000– 4,999	-0.58	-0.78	-1.15	-0.83	-1.6	-0.08	-0.01
5,000– 5,999	+0.60	-0.63	-0.77	+2.06	-1.1	-0.06	-0.01
6,000– 6,999	+0.60	-0.58	-0.77	+1.98	-0.8	-0.05	0.00
7,000– 7,999	+0.57	-0.39	-0.05	+1.73	-0.5	-0.05	+0.01
8,000– 8,999	+0.57	-0.37	-0.05	+3.41	-0.3	-0.04	+0.02
9,000– 9,999	+0.57	-0.31	-0.05	+2.87	-0.2	-0.04	+0.02
10,000–11,999	+0.56	-0.30	+0.47	+2.16	+0.1	-0.02	+0.03
12,000–14,999	+0.56	-0.23	+0.99	+2.71	+0.6	-0.03	+0.03
15,000–24,999	+0.65	-0.18	+0.99	+1.38	+1.5	-0.01	+0.03
25,000 and over	+1.03	-0.16	+1.19	-1.03	-2.1	+0.01	+0.01
Average	+0.55	-0.27	+0.31	+1.17	+0.10	-0.14	+0.15

Diego this type of centralization would do more to redistribute income through the tax structure than in any other city considering this shift.

The conclusions to be drawn from these case studies of state assumption of education finance are:

1. Central city budgets receive large amounts of expenditure relief, but it is not likely that the city may view these as freed-up resources for other use.
2. The aggregate tax increases experienced by central city residents depends on the state tax used and the CC-OCC disparity in locally raised revenues for education. In the cases where locally raised revenues for education are higher outside than inside the central city, aggregate tax payments made by city residents increase from 30 to 50 percent.
3. The tax burden of lower-income city families declines, and that of higher-income city families rises. The degree of this heightened progressivity of tax burdens depends on the state government tax which is used.

The Welfare Function

Two cities, Milwaukee[14] and Denver, considered the impact of centralization of welfare financing. In both cases a complete transfer to state government financing was proposed. Milwaukee proposed shifting of local welfare financing from the county property tax to the state income tax. This shift would require that state income tax rates be increased by 7 percent. Denver proposed shifting from a city property tax to a state income tax. This would require that a state income tax surcharge of 25 percent be levied. The data in Table 6-8 show that in terms of welfare expenditures as a percent of locally raised revenues, there is a considerable difference in the potential budget relief to the two cities. In Denver locally raised welfare funds represent only 6.8 percent of the total locally raised revenues, while in Milwaukee the comparable figure is 12.6 percent. If the shift is to a state personal income tax, as proposed here, Milwaukee residents would *decrease* their average per capita tax liabilities for welfare by 53.9 percent (over $8 per capita), while the decrease for Denver is 11.4 percent (over $1 per capita). Setting aside for the moment the size of these changes in per capita taxes, one conclusion is clear: the aggregate tax liability of central city residents is lower after centralization than before. This results for exactly the opposite reason that city resident tax liabilities for education are higher after centralization: Central city expenditures on welfare *from local sources* are higher than expenditures in the rest of the state, whereas for education they are lower. Because of this, after centralization, residents in the balance of the state pay some portion of the central city's welfare cost.

The interpersonal equity effects of centralization of welfare financing are shown in Table 6-9. The interpersonal equity effects on Milwaukee and Denver residents are similar in that most residents experience tax decreases. However,

TABLE 6-8. *Change in Personal Income Tax Liabilities Due to State Assumption of Welfare Financing*

	Milwaukee	Denver
Aggregate Tax Liability of City Residents[1]		
Before State Assumption	11.5	6.1
After State Assumption	5.3	5.4
Change	−6.2	−0.7
Per Capita Tax Liability		
Before State Assumption	$16.03	$11.85
After State Assumption	7.39	10.49
Change Per Capita	−8.64	−1.36
Percent Change	−53.9	−11.4
Effect on Locally Raised Revenues for City Government Budget[1]	13.2	7.5
Locally Raised Welfare Expenditure as a Percent of Total Revenues Raised from Local Sources	12.6	6.8

[1] In millions of dollars.

the patterns vary. In Milwaukee, the tax burdens in all income classes are reduced; *i.e.,* the shift to a more progressive state tax is more than offset by the net shift of total statewide welfare costs from Milwaukee to other local governments in the state. It may also be noted here that there is no monotonic relationship between tax burden changes and family income level. This is because of the assumption, in the Milwaukee study, that property taxes are borne by property owners rather than by occupiers in terms of housing consumption.

The results for Denver show that tax burdens decline below an income level of $15,000 but rise thereafter, due to the traditional property tax incidence assumption used in the Denver study and to the progressive structure of the Colorado income tax. These results for Denver show that even in the face of a reduction in aggregate tax liability for welfare, central city families in the higher-income classes could realize tax increases.

The conclusions to be drawn from these two case studies of the impact of state assumption of welfare financing are:

1. Central city residents, in aggregate, will experience large amounts of tax relief.
2. Most central city residents will experience tax decreases per dollar of income; however, there is the possibility that certain high-income groups would face tax burden increases.

TABLE 6-9. *Changes in Income Taxes per Dollar of Economic Income Due to State Assumption of Welfare Financing (in cents)*

Income Class ($)	Milwaukee	Denver
0- 999	-0.44	-14.02
1,000- 1,999	-0.22	-0.51
2,000- 2,999	-0.43	-0.40
3,000- 3,999	-0.44	-0.31
4,000- 4,999	-0.34	-0.31
5,000- 5,999	-0.22	-0.23
6,000- 6,999	-0.20	-0.18
7,000- 7,999	-0.18	-0.17
8,000- 8,999	-0.10	-0.15
9,000- 9,999	-0.10	-0.11
10,000-11,999	-0.10	-0.12
12,000-14,999	-0.10	-0.12
15,000-24,999	-0.16	+0.22
25,000 and over	-0.42	+0.08
Average	-0.20	-0.03

The Service Package

Lumped together as the "service package" are a variety of public functions. Their inclusion here as a group enables us to estimate the impact of financial centralization of a smaller group of subfunctions which are thought to be feasible candidates for financial centralization. While the larger and seemingly more troublesome functions—education and welfare—receive the bulk of reform attention, there is a wide range of local government activities the removal of which from city government budgets could bring marked fiscal relief.

The shifting of the service package to a higher government level is complicated by the fact that two different "higher" levels of government are considered as the receiving government. In San Diego, Atlanta, and Denver, a metropolitan government is proposed as the receiving government. On the other hand, Boston considered shifting the service package to the state govenment. The proposed taxes to be used by the receiving government are:

- San Diego: A shift to a regional property tax would require an increase in regional property tax rates of 6 percent. A shift to a regional sales tax would require a new regional tax with a yield of $3.6 million to be instituted.
- Denver: A shift to a regional sales tax was proposed.
- Atlanta: A shift to a regional sales tax was proposed.
- Boston: Two types of shifts in service package financing to the state gov-

ernment were proposed. The first would require a state income tax surcharge of 65 percent and an increase in the state motor fuel tax from 6.5
to 7.4 percent. The second alternative would require a state sales tax increase from 3 to 5 percent, a state income tax surcharge of 32 percent, and
an increase in the state motor fuel tax from 6.5 to 7.4 percent.

The effects of these programs on the central city tax liabilities are shown in
Table 6-10.

Expenditure for the service package represented approximately 28 percent
of locally raised revenues in Boston and Atlanta, but only between 7 and 8 percent for San Diego and Denver. In any of the cities studied, shifting of the service package would theoretically free up a sizable portion of locally raised
revenues. Assuming that the freed-up revenues are used to grant tax relief, the
effect on the aggregate tax liabilities of city residents is sizable. In per capita
terms, the tax *relief* experienced by central city residents in San Diego, Atlanta,
and Denver from a shift to a regional property tax ranges between 32.8 and 61.5
percent of the original expenditure. A shift to a regional sales tax (the option
considered in Denver and Atlanta) results in per capita tax decreases of 28.5 and
47.1 percent respectively. The shift to a package of income, sales, and motor
fuel taxes in Boston would lower per capita tax liabilities to half their previous
levels.

The implications here are clear. The shifting of the service package to either
regional or state government allows central city residents to shift a portion of
the cost of providing urban public services to people residing outside of the city.

The interpersonal equity effects of centralization are shown in Table 6-11. In
general, the results are consistent in implying tax decreases for most or all families.

Denver and Atlanta evaluated the interpersonal equity effects due to a shift
from the city property tax to a regional sales tax. The results of this type of centralization are similar, in that lower-income family units experience tax increases. However, these tax increases turn to decreases at a low level of family
income—with the distributional effects "better" in Atlanta.

The Boston study considers a shift to a combination of state taxes. Two alternatives considered were shifting the service package either to a combination of
the state income and motor fuel tax or to a combination of state income, motor
fuel, and sales taxes. The interpersonal equity effects are similar for the two alternatives in that both result in tax decreases throughout most of the income
distribution; however, the second alternative results in smaller tax decreases up
to the $7,000 income level and in general would appear to heighten the pro-
gressivity of the system by a lesser degree.

Of the four alternatives shown in Table 6-11, three have similar effects. Shifting to a regional property tax (the alternative used in San Diego, Denver, and
Atlanta) produces results similar to those of a shift to state income and motor
fuel tax or to an income, sales, and motor fuel tax (the alternative used in Boston). All three alternatives result in tax decreases that are inversely related to
income. The alternative of shifting financing of the service package to a regional

TABLE 6-10. *Change in Tax Liabilities due to Fiscal Centralization of the Service Package*

	Type of Tax after Centralization						
	Regional Property Tax			Regional Sales Tax		State Income and Motor Fuel Tax	State Sales, Motor Fuel, and Income Tax
	San Diego	*Atlanta*	*Denver*	*Denver*	*Atlanta*	*Boston*	*Boston*
Aggregate Tax Liability of City Residents[1]							
Before Centralization	3.9	24.2	7.0	7.0	24.2	47.0	47.0
After Centralization	1.5	15.4	4.7	5.0	12.8	27.6	23.1
Change	-2.4	-8.8	-2.3	-2.0	-11.4	-19.4	-23.9
Per Capita Tax Liability							
Before Centralization	$5.60	$48.70	$13.60	$13.60	$48.70	$94.57	$94.57
After Centralization	2.15	30.98	9.13	9.74	25.75	55.53	46.48
Change per Capita	-3.45	-17.72	-4.47	-3.86	-22.95	-39.04	-48.09
Percent Change	-61.5	-36.3	-32.8	-28.5	-47.1	-42.1	-50.8
Effect on Locally Raised Revenues for City Government Budget[1]	4.7	23.7	8.7	8.7	23.7	73.8	73.8
Locally Raised Financing of the Service Package as a Percent of Total Revenues from Local Sources[2]	7.0	28.3	7.9	7.9	28.3	27.00	27.00

[1] In millions of dollars.
[2] "Total Revenues from Local Sources" in this case denotes only revenues raised for local noneducational expenditures. However, cities with dependent school districts include education revenues raised locally.

TABLE 6-11. *Changes in Taxes per Dollar of Economic Income due to Fiscal Centralization of the Service Package (in cents)*

| | Type of State or Regional Financing | | | | | | |
| | Regional Property Tax | | | Regional Sales Tax | | Personal Income and Motor Fuel Tax | Personal Income, Sales, and Motor Fuel Tax |
Income Class ($)	San Diego	Atlanta	Denver	Denver	Atlanta	Boston	Boston
0– 999	-0.20	-1.08	-5.2	+1.3	+5.38	n.a.	n.a.
1,000– 1,999	-0.12	-0.39	-0.19	+0.08	+0.22	-5.42	-5.36
2,000– 2,999	-0.09	-0.31	-0.15	+0.09	+0.02	-3.98	-3.76
3,000– 3,999	-0.07	-0.45	-0.12	+0.01	-0.56	-2.92	-2.66
4,000– 4,999	-0.07	-0.54	-0.13	+0.01	-0.93	-2.34	-2.07
5,000– 5,999	-0.07	-0.58	-0.11	0.00	-1.07	-1.94	-1.80
6,000– 6,999	-0.06	-0.58	-0.10	-0.01	-1.05	-1.57	-1.52
7,000– 7,999	-0.06	-0.54	-0.10	-0.01	-0.96	-1.00	-1.16
8,000– 8,999	-0.06	-0.58	-0.10	-0.06	-0.93	-0.89	-1.03
9,000– 9,999	-0.06	-0.57	-0.10	-0.05	-1.03	-0.77	-0.92
10,000–11,999	-0.05	-0.51	-0.12	-0.13	-0.83	-0.64	-0.76
12,000–14,999	-0.05	-0.38	-0.12	-0.16	-0.49	-0.48	-0.65
15,000–24,999	-0.04	-0.34	-0.11	-0.17	-0.44	-0.17	-0.43
25,000 and over	-0.03	-0.34	-0.04	-0.05	-0.57	+0.11	-0.29
Average	-0.08	-0.43	-0.10	-0.08	-0.56	-0.75	-0.93

sales tax has distributional effects (the alternative evaluated by Atlanta and Denver) that are quite different from the other three alternatives, *i.e.,* tax *increases* in the lower income classes.

The general conclusions to be drawn from these three case studies are:

1. A sizable amount of budget relief is gained by central city budgets when the service package is shifted, *e.g.,* from 7 to 28 percent.
2. In aggregate, the tax liabilities of central city residents decrease significantly.
3. Lower-income central city residents may or may not experience tax decreases depending on the type of state or regional tax used.

POLICY IMPLICATIONS

If the reforms proposed here were undertaken in all nine cities, there would indeed be a sweeping change in intergovernmental relations in these nine states. Assuming for the moment that such a change were politically feasible, the pattern of tax burden distribution both among jurisdictions within the state and among families in different income classes would be markedly altered. There would, as well, be a substantial relief of pressures on the core city budget.

To quantitatively demonstrate these effects, assume that *all* functional reassignments proposed above are carried out. In such a case, the effects in question are (1) changes in the short- and long-term budgetary position of the city government; (2) changes in the overall tax liabilities of central city residents; and (3) changes in the distribution of tax burdens across income classes within the city.

These effects are clear, and are summarized by the data in Tables 6-12 and 6-13. With respect to city budget relief, the amount of resources "freed up" by fiscal centralization are substantial. They range from a high of over half of all locally raised revenues in Milwaukee to a low of about 14 percent in Denver. Whether or not these resources may be captured by the city government is a question not answered here. But even if city governments do not augment tax resources because of functional reassignment, there clearly will be long-term budget relief. The shifting of "high growth" functions (education, welfare) to a higher level of government brings about a better balance between the growth in expenditure requirements and the growth in the property tax base.

While the city budget is relieved by financial centralization, the aggregate tax liability of central city residents may actually rise. Primarily because of the typically lower level of education spending in large central cities than in the rest of the state, one result of financial centralization is to increase the average tax liability of central city residents in San Diego, Milwaukee, and Baltimore. Only for the cities of Boston and Atlanta, which propose shifts in the service package, are there major declines in average resident tax liability as a result of

TABLE 6-12. *Change in Tax Liabilities due to Fiscal Centralization of City Government Functions*

	Atlanta	Baltimore	Boston	Denver	Milwaukee
Aggregate Tax Liability of City Residents[1]					
Before Centralization	24.2	36.4	47.0	10.0	88.1
After Centralization	15.4	47.0	27.6	6.9	117.5
Change	-8.8	+10.6	-19.4	-3.1	+31.4
Per Capita Tax Liability					
Before Centralization	$48.70	$40.18	$94.57	$25.45	$122.83
After Centralization	30.98	51.89	46.48	19.62	163.87
Change	-11.72	+11.71	-48.09	-5.83	+41.04
Percent Change	36.3	29.1	-50.8		
Effect on Locally Raised Revenues for City Government Budget[1]	23.7	75.8	73.8	16.2	96.2
Locally Raised Revenues for the Functions Centralized as a Percent of Total Locally Raised Revenues	28.3	29.0	27.0	13.8	51.4[3]

	Kansas City, Kans.	Kansas City, Mo.	Nashville-Davidson	San Diego
Aggregate Tax Liability of City Residents[1]				
Before Centralization	3.0	15.9	26.0	53.6
After Centralization	3.9	12.8	20.9	67.0

Change	0.9	-3.1	-5.1	+13.4
Per Capita Tax Liability				
Before Centralization	$17.83	$31.35	$61.02	$69.75
After Centralization	23.18	25.24	49.05	96.15
Change	+5.35	-6.11	-11.97	+26.40
Percent Change	30.0	19.4	-19.6	
Effect on Locally Raised Revenues for City Government Budget[1]	3.0	15.9	33.0	57.4
Locally Raised Revenues for the Functions Centralized as a Percent of Total Locally Raised Revenues[2]	15.2[2]	15.4[2]	26.0[2]	45.9[2]

[1] In millions of dollars.
[2] Revenues raised locally for all functions including education.
[3] Including revenues raised by county from Milwaukee residents for education.

TABLE 6–13. *Changes in Taxes per Dollar of Economic Income due to Fiscal Centralization of City Government Functions (in cents)* [1]

Income Class ($)	Milwaukee	Denver	San Diego	Boston	Kansas City, Kans.	Kansas City, Mo.	Nashville-Davidson	Baltimore	Atlanta
0– 999	-0.94	-19.22	-6.10	n.a.	-1.09	-1.92	+2.35	-3.29	-1.08
1,000– 1,999	-2.86	-0.70	-3.52	-5.36	-0.09	-0.29	+0.06	-3.29	-0.39
2,000– 2,999	-1.81	-0.55	-2.69	-3.76	-0.05	-0.54	+0.05	-3.29	-0.31
3,000– 3,999	-1.43	-0.33	-2.17	-2.66	-0.03	-0.14	-1.15	-1.15	-0.45
4,000– 4,999	-1.17	-0.44	-1.67	-2.07	-0.01	-0.08	-0.78	-1.15	-0.54
5,000– 5,999	+1.84	-0.34	-1.17	-1.80	-0.01	-0.06	-0.63	-0.77	-0.58
6,000– 6,999	+1.78	-0.28	-0.86	-1.57	0.00	-0.05	-0.58	-0.77	-0.58
7,000– 7,999	-1.55	-0.27	-0.56	-1.16	+0.01	-0.05	-0.39	-0.05	-0.54
8,000– 8,999	+3.31	-0.25	-0.36	-1.03	+0.02	-0.04	-0.37	-0.05	-0.58
9,000– 9,999	+2.77	-0.21	-0.26	-0.92	+0.02	-0.04	-0.31	-0.05	-0.57
10,000–11,999	+2.06	-0.24	+0.95	-0.76	+0.03	-0.02	-0.30	+0.47	-0.51
12,000–14,999	+2.61	-0.24	+0.55	-0.65	+0.03	-0.03	-0.23	+0.99	-0.38
15,000–24,999	+1.22	+0.11	+1.46	-0.47	+0.03	-0.01	-0.18	+0.99	-0.34
25,000 and over	-1.45	+0.04	-2.13	-0.29	+0.01	+0.01	-0.16	+1.19	-0.34

[1] Functions centralized in Table 6–13:
Denver: welfare to state income tax; service package to regional property tax.
San Diego: education to a combination of state sales and income taxes; service package to a regional property tax.
Milwaukee: welfare and education to state income tax.
Baltimore: education to state income tax.
Boston: service package to a combination of state sales, income, and motor fuel taxes.
Nashville-Davidson: education to state sales tax.
Kansas City, Mo. and Kans.: education to a combination of the state income and sales taxes.

122

financial centralization. Finally, in all cities it would appear that financial centralization results in a marked improvement in the distribution of tax burdens (see Table 6-13). In some cases, *e.g.,* San Diego and Boston, the size of the tax burden reduction in the lowest income classes is substantial. In sum, the major effects of such a program are clearly an improvement in the equity of the state-local tax system, and probably a statewide or region-wide equalization of public service levels.

Quite apart from the question of the budgetary and tax burden effects of state and regional government financial assumption, there are implications of this reform which may have more far-reaching effects on the system of state-local finances. At least in the short run, there are reasons to expect that the net effect of centralization will be an increase in the level of state and local government expenditures. There are a number of reasons for this. For one, by shifting financing from less elastic (property) to more elastic (income, sales) tax bases, it will probably increase the overall growth in state and local government revenues. For another, the centralization of financial responsibility, particularly to the state government, implies some "leveling up"; *i.e.,* state government financing implies that disparities among local units in the level of expenditures would be eliminated. In such a case, a reasonable expectation is that expenditures of all local governments would tend to rise toward the higher levels. For example, it would be expected that wage rates, pension benefits, etc., for the shifted functions would tend to be standardized at the higher levels currently existing within the state, and this would, of course, induce an overall cost increase. On the other hand, there are factors that would suggest that in the long run fiscal centralization will have a dampening effect on the level of state and local government expenditures. For one, any trend toward an increased size of the state-local sector would tend to be offset somewhat by the replacement of state grants-in-aid with direct state expenditures, as grants-in-aid are thought to be "high-powered" funds which generate local matching efforts. For another, state financial control would likely reduce innovative and/or experimental programs at the local level. Though such programs may ultimately result in increased government sector productivity, their elimination would lower overall local government costs.

Questions about expenditure levels aside, this program of financial centralization would imply a centralization of the management of local government costs at the state or regional government level.

For example, it would be expected that full state government financial assumption would result in the state government's standardization of wage rates, pensions and fringe benefits, work rules, etc., on a statewide basis, and therefore the collective-bargaining process for these functions would be carried out at the state level. What this amounts to is the suggestion that financial centralization would markedly reduce the fiscal and administrative importance of city governments in the delivery of public services. The "costs" of such loss in local autonomy will have to be properly detailed and weighed carefully against the equity gains that are shown here to result from financial centralization.

NOTES

1. For different approaches to studying the urban fiscal problem, see William B. Neenan, *Political Economy of Urban Areas* (Chicago: Markham Publishing Company, 1972); Dick Netzer, *Economics and Urban Problems* (New York: Basic Books, 1970); Roy W. Bahl, *Metropolitan City Expenditures: A Comparative Analysis* (Lexington: University of Kentucky Press, 1969); and Alan Campbell and Seymour Sacks, *Metropolitan America: Fiscal Patterns and Governmental Systems* (New York: Free Press, 1967).

2. These case study results are reported fully in James Kitchen, W. Richard Bigger, and George Babilot, *A Study of Local Government Finance in the San Diego SMSA*, Urban Observatories Municipal Finance Study Project (San Diego: Urban Observatory of San Diego, June 1972); K. Hubbell, J. Olson, J. Ward, and S. Ramenossky, *Alternative Methods for Financing Public Services: The Cases of Education and Welfare, Kansas City, Missouri*, Urban Observatories Municipal Finance Study Project (Kansas City: Urban Observatory of Kansas City, August 1973); William A. Perry, Robert A. Horton, and J. Edmund Newman, *The Impact of State Assumption of Selected Metropolitan Nashville Expenditure Programs*, Urban Observatories Municipal Finance Study Project (Nashville: Urban Observatory of Metropolitan Nashville-University Centers, February 1974); Arthur P. Becker, *Local Government Finance in the Milwaukee SMSA*, vol. 2, Urban Observatories Municipal Finance Study Project (Milwaukee: Urban Observatory of Milwaukee, forthcoming); James D. Evans, *Expenditure and Revenue Analysis 1956-1971* (Metropolitan Nashville–Davidson County: Office of the Mayor, January, 1974); Larry D. Schroeder and David L. Sjoquist, *The Burden of Atlanta's Property Tax Relative to Alternative Tax Sources*, Working Paper 7374-06 (Atlanta: Georgia State University, October 1973); David L. Sjoquist and Larry D. Schroeder, *A Method for Constructing Distributions of Broad-based Income for Metropolitan Areas and Central Cities*, Working Paper 7374-04 (Atlanta: Georgia State University, October 1973); William Winter, Cris Tomasides, James Adams, and John Richeson, *Local Government Finance in the Denver Metropolitan Area*, First-Year Report, Urban Observatories Municipal Finance Study Project (Denver: Denver Urban Observatory, April 1972); William Winter, Cris Tomasides, James Adams, and John Richeson, *Local Government Finance in the Denver Metropolitan Region*, Second-Year Report, Urban Observatories Municipal Finance Study Project (Denver: Denver Urban Observatory, November 1973); Joseph S. Slavet, Katherine Bradbury, and Philip Moss, *Reallocation of Selected Municipal Services to the State: A Municipal Finance Alternative*, Urban Observatories Municipal Finance Study Project (Boston: Boston Urban Observatory, October 1973); William H. Oakland and Eliyaher Borukhov, *Incidence and Other Fiscal Impacts of the Reform*

of Educational Finance: A Case Study of Baltimore, Urban Observatories Municipal Finance Study Project (Baltimore: Baltimore Urban Observatory, 1974). A more detailed analysis is in Roy Bahl and Walter Vogt, *Fiscal Centralization and Tax Burdens: State and Regional Financing of City Services* (New York: Ballinger, 1976).

3. An income-elastic tax is one whose revenues increase more than in proportion to increases in personal income. Conversely, the revenues from an inelastic tax increase less than in proportion to increases in personal income.

4. Advisory Commission on Intergovernmental Relations *Federal-State-Local Finances: Significant Features of Fiscal Federalism* (Washington, February 1974), M–70, p. 53. It is important to note that these estimates are statewide and that more variation has been shown to exist for the taxes on a local level; *e.g.,* the elasticity of the property tax is estimated at only 0.34 for Albany, N.Y.

5. The term "regressive" means that taxes paid per dollar of income are lower for higher-income individuals or families.

6. Some empirical evidence supporting this thesis may be found in Donald Phares, *State-Local Tax Equity* (Lexington, Mass.: Lexington Books, Heath, 1973), p. 53; and Advisory Commission on Intergovernmental Relations, *loc. cit.*

7. The small growth observed for the city of Atlanta occurred only because of annexations during this period. Without the annexations, Atlanta's central city population would have declined.

8. Comparison in terms of overlapping jurisdictions removes any distortions caused by intercity differences in functional responsibility.

9. As reported in the appendix to Advisory Commission on Intergovernmental Relations, *City Financial Emergencies* (Washington: ACIR, September 1973).

10. Advisory Commission on Intergovernmental Relations, *Performance of Urban Functions: Local and Areawide* (Washington: ACIR, September 1973).

11. There is a debate over the incidence of the property tax, which in no way is resolved here. We have simply made the traditional assumption, which implies a regressive property tax. To the extent this assumption is not valid and the property tax is actually progressive, the policy implications of this research are considerably different. In this respect, a comparison of the Milwaukee results with those obtained in the other cities is particularly instructive. For a survey of the current status of this debate, see Henry Aaron, Harvey Brazer, Richard Musgrave, Dick Netzer, Earl Rolph, Ann Friedlander, and George Peterson, "The Property Tax: Progressive or Regressive," *Papers and Proceedings of the American Economic Association,* May 1974, pp. 212-34.

12. The budget relief to a city is defined as the amount of locally raised revenues for the function shifted.

13. Clearly, this is a simplifying assumption, since in all probability expenditures will increase after fiscal centralization. This assumption merely allows us to hold the distributional effects of increased expenditures constant

while we examine only the tax distribution effects, *i.e.,* the effects of financing the *same* level of per capita expenditure under a state tax, as opposed to a local property tax.

14. In Wisconsin, welfare is a county responsibility. The amounts referred to as Milwaukee welfare expenditures are estimates of their share of the county welfare expenditures.

Comment: The Spatial Incidence of the Property Tax with Special Reference to the Tax on Housing

Seymour Sacks

The paper by Roy Bahl and Walter Vogt is significant because it raises to an operational level the much-mooted question of the burden of local taxes. The main problem considered centers around the transfer of financing of a function from a local property tax to "additional state or regional government income and general sales taxes." A common methodology is applied to nine large cities. A spatially oriented approach to the incidence of taxation differs very considerably from the recent set of national studies of Pechman and Okner;[1] Musgrave, Case, and Leonard;[2] and Reynolds and Smolensky,[3] as well as the earlier but very influential study by Musgrave, Carroll, Cook, and Frane.[4] The Bahl and Vogt study also differs from the studies of housing and local property taxation by Peterson;[5] Aaron;[6] and Grubb and Hoachlander,[7] to cite some important current examples, in that the former use a comparative framework in their analysis of local property tax incidence.

The Urban Observatory sample, reported by Bahl and Vogt, provides a unique opportunity not only of following through the implications of a given set of assumptions, but of testing, or at least evaluating, the adequacy of the traditional set of assumptions on a jurisdictional level. Unfortunately, in order to preserve comparability throughout their entire analysis, Bahl and Vogt developed a very structured and inflexible framework. Each step of their three-step analysis has implications on the relationship between the level of taxation and the level of income. The first step is to develop "an appropriate income concept"; the second step is to create a standardized "set of assumptions concerning the incidence of taxes and the expenditure effects of shifting the financing of certain functions to higher levels of government;" and finally they develop a "simulation model of fiscal centralization."

THE PROPERTY TAX: DEFINITION

Bahl and Vogt recognize that "there is a debate over the incidence of the property tax, which in no way is resolved. . . ." They make the "traditional assumption—which implies a regressive tax." The very generalized debate, which is currently being carried on by those who side with Harberger, Miezkowski, and McClure[8] and those who find their analysis deficient, does not appear to be appropriate to large city areas where the dominant issues are raised by differ-

127

ences in rates, composition of the tax rolls, housing-income ratios, and tax "exporting."[9] However, some of the difficulties can be seen even on the national level, where Musgrave, Case, and Leonard provide five sets of allocational alternatives in the case of state and local property taxes which, in turn, can be modified by alternative definitions of income.[10]

The property tax is most meaningfully considered as a complex set of taxes on capital values with little or no national meaning. It is the spatial tax par excellence. The tax differs considerably from most other taxes in that there are enormous differences in the structure of the tax when it is considered on a jurisdictional basis. Prior to all other considerations, it should be noted that the fundamental nature of the tax is established on a state basis.[11] Jurisdictions differ in what they may include on their tax rolls depending on state constitutional, legislative, and regulatory provisions; *e.g.*, while all states have a local real property component, the extent to which local personal property, railroads, and public utilities are included is a function of state policy.[12] Similarly, the extent to which the tax is assessed and collected on a state basis is also a function of state policy. And a careful reading will also indicate that one state's personal property may be another state's real property. There are also local differences in assessment practices, rates of taxation, and composition of the tax rolls.

Differences in exemption practices, especially homestead exemptions, and in the amount of other *residential* property, which is exempt from the property tax, are of major importance in evaluating the tax burden by income class. The more localized the area, the more important are differences in the availability of exemptions and in the existence of residential property, primarily low-income public housing, which is exempt from local property taxation.

THE REGRESSIVITY ISSUE

For large cities, and indeed for any local area, a number of special problems centering around the presumed "regressivity" of the local property tax emerge. The extent to which the tax is "exported" or converted into higher prices, or lower returns to the owners of capital, depends on the location of (1) the "consumers" of the specific products and services and/or (2) the owners of capital. Even in the absence of detailed data, a number of aspects of the tax roll seem to be crucially important. The distinction of residential property as owner-occupied or rental is conventional, but what is not integrated into the analysis is the extent to which rental housing may be concentrated in low-income public housing and thus be simultaneously tax-exempt and concentrated in the lower income brackets. Similarly, the extent to which taxes are exported should be recognized as far more extensive than is indicated by the work by McLure[13] and Phares,[14] which is appropriate only to statewide taxes. If nonresidential property taxes are assumed to be passed on, even in part, to local residents as a consumer excise, then a whole set of logical difficulties emerge about firms that do not produce final products. This is independent of whether they fall on the owners of capital who may or may not reside in the taxing jurisdiction.

The Bahl and Vogt analysis, like the recent work of Musgrave, Case, and Leonard[15] questions and then expands the census money income concept ordinarily used in the analysis of the income elasticity of the property tax, *i.e.*, the extent to which it is regressive, proportional, or progressive. "Economic income," as used by Bahl and Vogt, "includes money incomes not counted by the census, such as realized capital gains and nonmoney incomes and the imputed value of owner-occupied housing." The inclusion of the inputed value of owner-occupied housing is of great importance in interpreting the income elasticity of owner-occupied housing.

The issues involved in the determination of the relationship between property taxes and income can be seen by looking at the principal separate elements: owner-occupied residential housing, taxable rental housing, and nonresidential commercial and industrial properties. There are separate issues involved in each case, and for the purpose of illustration only the tax on residential properties will be considered. This type of analysis can be done only by looking at individual jurisdictions, as was done in the case studies, and even then problems emerge where there are other non-coterminous local governments. In contrast to the case of owner-occupied housing, it is not possible to determine the tax incidence directly by looking at the renter or the consumer in the case of nonresidential properties. Instead it is necessary to trace the process through by looking at the initial impact of the tax on the owners of the property and then tracing the extent to which it is shifted. The assumptional method simply does not apply to a local tax on capital values.

BALTIMORE: A CASE FOR PROGRESSIVITY

Using Baltimore as an example, because it is one of the Urban Observatory cities and does not have any overlying local governments, the major components of the local property tax can be shown. According to the Census of Governments,[16] residential property made up 62.5 percent of the gross assessed value of *locally* assessed taxable real property in 1971. However, real property made up only 68.3 percent of all assessed values subject to tax after partial exemptions. State-assessed public utility and railroad property and a small amount of personal property made up the remaining 31.7 percent. Taking these additions into account, residential properties made up 42.7 percent of the base and commercial and industrial properties 24.9 percent of the base, of which a negligible portion was acreage and vacant lots. The residential portion of the tax base in Baltimore is dominated by single-family housing, of which slightly more than one-third is rental and two-thirds is owner-occupied.

The differential between a tax on owner-occupied housing and rental housing, even in the case of single-family dwellings, indicates that for analytic purposes the two should be considered separately. But there are more pervasive reasons drawn from the differing socioeconomic characteristics of owners and renters of single-family dwellings which also press for their separate presentation.[17] Another critical but often neglected aspect involves the extent to which the property is mortgaged. Nonmortgaged property is owned at every level of housing value by households with lower incomes than those with mortgages. An essential difference between the two involves the level of regular payments of interest and/or principal paid on mortgaged property. Furthermore, as shown in Table II, nonmortgaged property dominates the lower value property ownership because of the combined effects of the age of the owner and the value of the property.

For owner-occupiers, as is shown in Table I drawn from Baltimore data in the 1970 Census of Housing,[18] there are two ways of indicating the housing/income patterns. The underlying relationship generates the observed income elasticity of the owner-occupied portion of the property tax. It appears that in order to generate a regressive tax on owner-occupied housing, one has to assume that the income elasticity of housing is very low, or that those households with low incomes have a much greater proportion of housing (capital) relative to their income than those with higher incomes. The observed pattern is a function of the preponderance of low-income, single-person households, generally elderly. Even the inclusion of the imputed value of owner-occupied housing, which has spectacular results in the case of low-income households, does not alter the relationship. It has the curious consequence of adding relatively more to low-income households than to high-income households.

Based on national surveys (Table II) and on an analysis of the Baltimore housing/income ratio, it can be seen that as housing values increase, incomes increase. As shown in the bottom portion of Table I, the two patterns are of the same order of magnitude. Low-value housing is clearly related to, and probably a function of, low income, and high-value housing a function of high income. The higher the value of the house, the higher the ratio between housing values and income. The housing/income ratio increases with the value of housing, *i.e.*, owner-occupied housing is income-elastic.

Assuming the same assessment ratio at all values—an assumption that is roughly consistent with the information in the 1970 residential finance volume of the Census of Housing as shown in Table II—the tax would be regressive if the housing/income ratio were inverse with respect to income. This appears to be the relationship in the upper part of Table I, although it is reduced substantially by the inclusion of the imputed value of owner-occupied housing. On the other hand, if one assumes that the value is positively related to income, as shown in the lower part of Table I, then the major portion of the imputation is on the higher-valued property owned, on the average, by higher-income two-or-more-person households. The pattern is roughly consistent with the assumption that

TABLE I. *Owner-occupied Housing, Baltimore, 1970: Value, Income, and Property Taxes*

Household Income	Median Value Housing	Housing/ Income Ratio	Imputed Value of Housing	Adjusted Housing/ Income Ratio	Tax as Percent Income Rate = 0.033		Percent One-Person Households
					Money	Economic[1]	
Less than $2,000[2]	$ 7,300	7.3:1	642	4.4:1	24.1	14.7	59.9
$ 2,000–$ 2,999	7,800	3.1:1	686	2.4:1	10.3	8.1	41.0
3,000– 3,999	7,900	2.3:1	695	1.9:1	7.5	6.3	32.4
4,000– 4,999	8,400	1.9:1	739	1.6:1	6.2	5.3	24.7
5,000– 5,999	8,800	1.6:1	774	1.4:1	5.3	4.6	19.9
6,000– 6,999	8,900	1.4:1	783	1.2:1	4.5	4.1	14.4
7,000– 9,999	9,500	1.1:1	836	1.1:1	3.7	3.4	7.6
10,000– 14,999	10,600	0.9:1	933	0.8:1	2.8	2.6	3.2
15,000– 24,999	11,900	0.6:1	1,047	0.6:1	2.0	1.9	1.8
More than $25,000[3]	22,900	0.7:1	2,015	0.6:1	2.5	2.4	1.6

(continued)

131

TABLE I *continued*

Value of Housing	Median Income	Housing/ Income Ratio	Imputed Value of Housing	Adjusted Housing/ Income Ratio	Tax as Percent Income Rate = 0.033		Percent One-Person Households
					Money	Economic[1]	
Less than $5,000[4]	$ 5,900	0.7:1	352	0.6:1	2.0	2.0	23.7
$ 5,000–$ 7,499	7,900	0.8:1	550	0.7:1	2.5	2.3	16.6
7,500– 9,999	9,200	1.0:1	770	0.9:1	2.9	2.7	12.2
10,000– 12,499	10,500	1.1:1	990	1.0:1	3.3	3.0	9.5
12,500– 14,999	11,600	1.2:1	1,210	1.1:1	3.7	3.3	7.9
15,000– 19,999	12,300	1.4:1	1,540	1.3:1	4.7	4.2	7.6
20,000– 24,999	14,800	1.4:1	1,980	1.3:1	4.7	4.2	8.1
25,000– 34,999	19,700	1.5:1	2,640	1.3:1	4.7	4.2	11.1
35,000– 49,999	24,900	1.7:1	3,740	1.5:1	5.3	4.6	6.6
More than $50,000[5]	36,600	1.8:1	5,720	1.5:1	5.5	4.8	7.3

[1] Includes imputed value of housing.
[2] Assumed to be $1,000.
[3] Assumed to be $35,000.
[4] Assumed to be $4,000.
[5] Assumed to be $65,000.

Source: U.S. Bureau of the Census, *Census of Housing, 1970 Metropolitan Housing Characteristics, 1970*, and *Taxable Property Values, 1972.*

TABLE II. *Taxes as Percent of Income: United States Mortgaged and Nonmortgaged Single-family Housing*

Value	Mortgaged			Nonmortgaged			
	Income	Tax per $1,000 Value	Computed Tax as Percent Income	Income	Tax per $1,000 Value	Computed Tax as Percent Income	Percent of Mortgaged Properties
Less than $5,000[1]	$ 5,600	$23	1.5	$ 2,800	$20	2.9	464.1
$ 5,000–$ 7,499	6,700	16	1.5	4,100	18	2.7	234.9
7,500– 9,999	8,100	18	1.9	5,400	17	2.8	119.2
10,000– 12,499	9,100	18	2.2	6,000	17	3.2	106.5
12,500– 14,999	10,000	18	2.5	7,100	19	3.0	57.0
15,000– 17,499	10,700	18	2.8	7,300	17	3.9	61.5
17,500– 19,999	11,400	20	3.3	7,800	19	4.6	43.1
20,000– 24,999	12,600	20	3.6	9,600	20	4.7	41.0
25,000– 34,999	14,300	21	4.4	11,100	19	5.1	33.5
34,999– 49,999	18,300	20	4.6	14,900	18	5.1	34.2
More than $50,000[2]	27,400	20	5.4	24,800	18	5.4	43.7

[1] Assumed to be $4,000.
[2] Assumed to be $74,000.
Source: U.S. Bureau of the Census, *Census of Housing, 1970, vol V, Residential Finance.*

higher-income households are able to deduct a portion of the higher property taxes in their federal and state income taxes.

For purposes of comparison only, and recognizing the limitations of national data, a direct measurement of property taxes of the owner-occupiers is shown in Table II. It has the additional attribute of showing the income characteristics of the owners of mortgaged and nonmortgaged properties and the actual tax rates by value of property. This table shows progressivity in both cases.

Similar findings appear to exist in the case of rental housing and are intensified if low-income public housing and its tenants are taken into account. A further ambiguity about the rent-related transfer payments of those recipients of public assistance not residing in low-income public housing must also be resolved if one is to determine the taxes as a proportion of income.

The question of the presumed "regressivity" of the property tax probably should not be reevaluated on the basis of the very general Harberger-Miezkowski-McClure model, but through use of the local housing/income and tax relationships. That some of the results in the case of housing are consistent with the underlying assumptions of that model is a function of the fact that capital values associated with housing do increase more rapidly than income. The underlying issues have to be resolved not by assumption, but by a more careful analysis of the impact, shifting, incidence, capitalization, and exportation of the *local* property tax.

NOTES

1. Joseph A. Pechman and Bernard Okner, *Who Bears the Tax Burden?* Brookings, Washington, 1974.

2. Richard A. Musgrave, K. E. Case, and H. Leonard, "The Distribution of Fiscal Burdens and Benefits," *Public Finance Quarterly,* July 1974, pp. 259–311.

3. Morgan Reynolds and E. Smolensky, "The Post Fisc Distribution: 1961 and 1970 Compared," *National Tax Journal,* December 1974, pp. 515–30.

4. Richard A. Musgrave, J. J. Carroll, L. D. Cook, and L. Frane, "Distribution of Tax Payments by Income Groups: A Case Study for 1948," *National Tax Journal,* March 1951.

5. George Peterson, "The Regressivity of the Residential Property Tax" Working Paper 1207–10, (Washington, D.C.: The Urban Institute, November, 1972).

6. Henry Aaron, "A New View of Property Tax Incidence," *Papers and Proceedings of the American Economic Association,* May 1974.

7. Norton Grubb and E. G. Hoachlander, "Optimal Circuit Breaker Schedules and Their Application in California," Childhood and Government Project. (Berkeley: University of California, 1974).

8. George F. Break, "The Incidence and Economic Effects of Taxation," in

The Economics of Public Finance (Washington: Brookings, 1974), pp. 154–68.

9. Charles McClure, "Tax Exporting in the United States: Estimates for 1962," *National Tax Journal* March 1967, pp. 49–77; and Donald Phares, *State-Local Tax Equity* (Lexington, Mass.: Lexington Books, 1973).

10. Musgrave, Case, and Leonard, *op. cit.,* pp. 264 and 272.

11. Advisory Commission on Intergovernmental Relations, *The Role of the States in Strengthening the Property Tax* (Washington: Government Printing Office, 1963), and Advisory Commission on Intergovernmental Relations, *The Property Tax in a Changing Environment: Selected State Studies* (Washington: Government Printing Office, 1974), provide a discussion of the role of states.

12. U.S. Bureau of Census, *Census of Governments, 1972,* vol. 2, *Taxable Property Values and Assessment: Sales Price Ratio,* part 2, *Assessment: Sales Price Ratio and Tax Rates* (Washington: Government Printing Office, 1973), provides information on the quantitative importance of the various components of the property tax.

13. McLure, *op. cit.,* pp. 49–77.

14. Phares, *op. cit.*

15. Musgrave, Case, and Leonard, *op. cit.*

16. *Ibid.,* footnote 12.

17. U.S. Bureau of the Census, *Census of Housing, 1970,* vol. V, *Residential Finance* (Washington: Government Printing Office, 1973).

18. *Ibid.*

7. Reforming Financing of Education: An Issue of Quality of Services or Fiscal Equity*

Michael W. Kirst

School finance reform is an issue in almost every state. At least 10 states enacted major new legislation in 1973, and others are waiting for pending suits in state courts. The turndown of the Texas-based *Rodriquez* case by the U.S. Supreme Court has merely transferred the legal and political pressure to the state level. A national interlocking directorate has emerged pushing for increased state aid to low-wealth, high-tax school districts and urban-rural districts with special needs. State commissions and study groups abound, supported by national finance experts and legal activists.

On the last day of the 1972 legislative session, the California Legislature passed a property tax relief—school finance bill (Senate Bill 90). Because of the conflict-ridden California political landscape, SB 90 was only a first step in school finance reform. Indeed, in April 1974, a California lower court ruled SB 90 did not meet the *Serrano* criteria and required extensive changes.

Nevertheless, this bill represents a significant improvement with respect to the lowest-wealth and lowest-spending school districts. It provides a maximum aid increase of 15 percent a year for three years in the foundation level plus an additional 7 percent for inflation (federal aid is not included in the base). It also provides for an increase in the property tax exemption for individual homeowners from $750 to $1,750. Moreover, there is direct property tax relief to each renter and additional tax relief for school districts that are taxing themselves at a level substantially above state average. The additional school support provided goes differentially to the lowest-wealth and lowest-spending school

*The author would like to acknowledge the support of the Ford Foundation for the research reported in this paper. Theodore Lobman's help in the quantitative analysis was an important contribution to this effort.

districts. However, school districts with low wealth, high tax rates, and *high expenditures* will only receive tax relief. As we shall see, these direct tax relief provisions dissipated the local pressure for tax relief from money flowing to the school districts.

This paper focuses on the expenditure choices of local districts after they receive unrestricted state aid *i.e.,* on the purposes for which these incremental funds are spent. Local California budget officers agree that a 5 to 7 percent annual aid increment would be absorbed through standard build-in cost increases. Hence an additional 15 percent increase, as provided in SB 90, presents an incremental resource allocation choice—and the underlying reason for this study.

THE POLICY ISSUES

At first glance one would assume that California's reform could have few opponents except entrenched wealthy people who live in low-tax and high-spending school districts. The popular imagery is the stark contrast between palatial Beverly Hills (spending $1,621 per pupil) and the rundown areas of nearby Baldwin Park (spending $821 per pupil) or Newark, New Jersey. What "just" person could oppose changing such situations? The *Rodriquez* decision gives several rationales for judicial restraint, but there is no reason these judicial issues should apply to state legislatures.[1] There has been a strong undercurrent, however, challenging the entire idea of equalizing educational finance. Daniel Moynihan's article in *Public Interest* brings together most of these arguments. First, he addresses the issue of "does money make a difference."

> . . . after a point, school expenditure does not seem to have any notable influence on school achievement. To repeat, after a point, a school without a roof, or without books, or without teachers would probably not be a school in which a great deal of learning went on. But once expenditure rises above a certain zone, money doesn't seem to matter that much in terms of what happens to students.[2]

Moynihan then goes on to cite a Rand study indicating that no "variant of the existing system . . . is consistently related to educational outcomes." The Rand report declares:

> Increasing expenditures on traditional educational practices is not likely to improve educational outcomes substantially.[3]

Given this general view, Moynihan then drops his key thesis as to who will benefit from state school finance reform.

> Teachers will benefit. Any increase in school expenditure will in the first instance accrue to teachers, who receive about 68 percent of the operating expenditures of elementary and secondary schools. That these are estimable

and deserving persons none should doubt, but neither should there be any illusion that they are deprived. . . . In general, they are deservedly well-paid professionals. . . .[4]

Moynihan goes on to speculate that the end result may be to redistribute income from low-income groups to middle-income teachers.

. . . it is also a way of asserting the value, and increasing the value of those services that the middle class dispenses. There is a class economic interest at stake, and that class is pursuing its interest.[5]

This writer is not qualified to analyze the complex technical issues of "do dollars make a difference."[6] In my own view the issue is still an open one and beyond the state of the art to settle conclusively one way or the other. Each side will marshal the data depending on its values and self-interest.[7]

But the California law will enable us to explore several of the crucial issues that Moynihan raises:

- Does new state money flow overwhelmingly to increased teacher salaries— in effect, price increases rather than more school services?
- Will school finance reform intensify existing instructional approaches re- sulting in more of the same?
- How does the process by which low-wealth school districts allocate budgets affect outcomes? For example, do they engage in a rational search for inno- vative alternatives?
- How might federal and state policy improve local budget allocations and discourage use of increased school aid for price increases, *i.e.*, to buy more of the same?
- To what extent will unrestricted state aid merely supplant local expendi- tures financed by the property tax? How can public policy be designed to prevent this?

RESEARCH PLAN

In the next section of this paper, we consider the use of *various* social science models for predictive and explanatory purposes. Then empirical expenditure data and five case studies of budget process will be used to test the several social science models. Finally, these two data sources will be related to the above policy issues.

The case studies are in five suburban districts in Southeast Los Angeles, all with low assessed property value and high tax rates that received the maximum 15 percent increase. Four of the districts have substantial Mexican-American minorities, and one has a large black minority. The districts range in size from 7,220 to 28,020, students in average daily attendance. (ADA)

The quantitative analysis here explores the pattern of school district expenditures (teacher salaries, maintenance, etc.) in Los Angeles County (42 unified school districts). We compare the objects of expenditure before the finance reform was implemented in 1973-74. The results of the quantitative analysis are compared with the findings from five case studies of SB 90's implementation by low-wealth, high-effort, low-spending school districts. It is important to emphasize that the case studies examine behavior both before SB 90 and in the first year that SB 90 was budgeted and spent.† Expenditures on a program basis have been collected from these five cases. The outcomes from the above efforts will then be compared to the predictive and explanatory power of the theoretical models.

Los Angeles County was chosen for this analysis because the 33 elementary school districts, 7 high school districts, and 42 unified districts are a microcosm of the state as a whole. Los Angeles County includes rich districts, poor districts, large districts, urban districts, and even rural districts in the eastern mountains. Moreover, Los Angeles County provides a geographically compact and interrelated market for labor and other input costs. Finally, since we wanted to hold as many factors as constant as possible, this sample would seem superior to one which would require comparison of rural districts near the Oregon border with bigger urban districts in Southern California. This study should be regarded as an exploratory analysis of the behavior of thousands of poor school districts across the United States.

SOCIAL SCIENCE MODELS AND THE ESTIMATION OF LOCAL SCHOOL DISTRICT RESPONSE

The first step in our research is the elaboration of certain predictive models from a variety of social science disciplines. Generally, these theories compromise three major groups: economic, political, and organizational models.

Glenn argues the utility of considering a variety of alternative models to better understand the decision-making process.[8] The model one uses in an analysis has an important impact on what information the observer considers relevant, how the decision process is viewed, and the interpretation of the outcomes of the event under observation. Alternative models used in concert increase the likelihood of a clearer grasp of the whole.

It is important to highlight that the subsequent models have both normative and descriptive uses. The economic model is viewed by many public policy analysts as the "ought" in terms of cost effectiveness and Program Planning Budget Systems (PPBS) budgets. The organizational models do not appeal to many people in a normative sense.

---

†Verified expenditure data for 1973-74 are not available until late in 1974.

Rational Economic Models

The first general class of models is drawn from the theoretical propositions of micro- and macroeconomic theory, particularly the former. Budget action is portrayed as a rational economic choice. The components include a careful elucidation of specific goals and objectives, a series of options or alternatives that will meet the goals and objectives, the evaluation of the various alternatives on the basis of cost and effects, and, finally, a value-maximizing choice. The school district selects the alternative with consequences that rank highest in terms of its goals and its objectives. Both short-term and long-term costs are taken into account, and the maximization at the margin is the presumed decision style. In its purest form perfect information is assumed for the first three components.[9]

If California school districts used this process for making SB 90 allocations, they would set up a hierarchy of goals and objectives. They would then formulate alternatives based primarily on educational research and other types of validated information that would be simulated and tested, costed out and projected for future consequences. Finally, a value-maximizing choice would be made. For example, research has shown that a low-cost effective technique (in terms of achievement) is for older students to tutor younger students who are disadvantaged. The substantial body of research on this issue would have been carefully considered and costed before this position was made. Moreover, since California schools have experimented with PPBS since 1965, it is not unreasonable to expect some Local Education Authorities (LEAs) to employ this model for SB 90 allocations.

All the case studies demonstrated that rational microeconomic concepts are not used by school district budget officials. Cost-effective analysis, PPBS, marginal optimization, and input-output thinking were simply nonexistant. Jesse Burkhead, in his recent article "Economics against Education," helps account for this.

> Apart from the data problems, which will continue to be serious, there are also some conceptual difficulties in the microeconomic analysis of education. In the estimation of production functions in the private sector, it is assumed that a factory manager, for example, has reasonably good knowledge of the marginal productivity of the factors that he utilizes, and thus he is able to optimize factor combinations to maximize profit. But in elementary and secondary education there is no reason to assume that a school principal, or district superintendent, or board of education has knowledge of or interest in the marginal productivity of resource inputs. Even if these were known, it could not be assumed that it would be possible to secure least-cost combinations, given the institutional rigidities of mandates and conventional practice. Neither is there a reasonable substitute for the objective function of profit maximization. Thus the optimization rationale that underlies produc-

tion functions in the private sector is inapplicable for elementary and secondary education.[10]

In sum, rational microeconomic models provide little insight or predictive power for local school budget processes and outcomes. Our cases suggest that new and innovative programs or learning approaches will rarely result from unrestricted state aid.

At least two other economic concepts are particularly relevant to researching LEA response and provide us with another variation of the economic model. The notion of "pent-up demands" is used by business cycle theorists.[11] After World Wars I and II economic booms ensued because productive facilities had been diverted to war needs and businesses were unable to renew capital goods. Moreover, consumers had been restricted to rationing for some goods and other consumer items were simply unavailable. After the war years, such pent-up demands resulted in a large expansion of capital goods and consumer purchases of housing, autos, clothes, and so on. In essence, consumer wants and needs had been present for years. Now that goods were available, consumers did not need to rethink their choices of utility functions.

In a similar fashion, poor school districts have pent-up demands for lower class size, higher salaries, and specialists. Specific proposals may have been made for several years only to be cut out in the budget process. But there is a widespread understanding of what has first priority if and when money comes. There might even be a public commitment by the school board to raise salaries to the county average as first priority if and when money comes. Our cases confirmed this pent-up demand idea. We could trace several of the major new expenditures to programs that had been considered but not funded in the past.

Similar economic concepts with important implications are "the Duesenberry effect", and Friedman's permanent income hypotheses.[12] Duesenberry's relative income hypothesis represents a reformulation of the Keynesian proposition that aggregate consumption in a function of aggregate disposable income. Duesenberry stressed that the difference in consumption behavior during periods of fluctuating income could be explained by differences in the level of relative income, *i.e., income in relation to what one is accustomed to.*

Friedman's "permanent income hypothesis" is an elaboration of Duesenberry's ideas. His notion of distributed lag models would require a longitudinal study of SB 90, and would include whether the initial allocation priorities changed little or much over a period of time.

Almost all low-wealth, low-expenditure LEAs in Los Angeles County experienced a budget deficit in 1970-71. In part, they compensated by depleting reserves, *e.g.,* cutting their "savings" and contingency funds. Duesenberry's and Friedman's theories would predict a replenishing of fiscal reserves and contingency funds in the initial year of SB 90. After these reserves and such things as essential building maintenance projects are restored to prior levels, SB 90 increases in subsequent years will be devoted to other expenditure items like salaries and added educational programs.

Political Models

The first type of political model is based on democratic theory.[13] It starts with an electorate delimited to some criteria of formal position within the system; *e.g.,* there are citizens in a school attendance area or within a school district who have the right to elect board members and approve taxes *and* perhaps budgets.

Decisions are made according to certain procedures:

1. Whenever policy choices are made or representatives elected, the alternative selected and enforced is the alternative most preferred by the electorate.
2. In this choice process, each member of the electorate is assigned an equal value. It is assumed each voter has perfect information.
3. The rule: in choosing among alternatives, the alternative preferred by the greater number of voters is selected.

In some situations and for some purposes voting by ballot or town meeting of the electorate is a natural candidate for meeting this model. Presumably most people vote in their self-interest. The democratic theories allow for coalitions among voters. In many situations, new alternatives have to be created in order to form majority coalitions, and if alternatives are fixed, preference aggregation may be hampered. This theory posits that all members of the electorate should have equal information. The democratic ethic is violated when people with more information persuade people with less information that their preferred alternative does not exist or is not relevant. In voting situations three conditions should be fulfilled:

1. Every member of the electorate performs the acts that we assume constitute expressions of preference among the selected alternative voting.
2. In the tabulation of these expressions (vote), the weight assigned to the preference of *each* voter is identical.
3. The alternative with the greatest number of votes is declared the winning choice.

The properties of the model are normative and most appropriate in referendum or town meeting situations. In other situations, however, decisions are deemed to be democratic if either or both of the following conditions are met:

1. All interelection decisions are subordinated or executory to those arrived at during the election stage; *i.e.,* elections are in a sense controlling on budget policy.

2. New decisions during the interelection period are governed by the preceding conditions operating—however, under rather different institutional circumstances.

If SB 90 expenditure decisions were made according to such a model, voters would be presented with a series of alternative budgets (perfect information assumed). Such models predict that the alternative chosen best reflects the preference of the majority of the citizens. The voters would choose the alternative that maximized their values.

Indeed, some states have a process that approximates this model. New York and Oregon, for example, must get voter approval for school district budgets which exceed a certain percentages increase. Clearly, the 15 percent increase in SB 90 would force a budget election in all Oregon school districts. The pattern in Oregon has been for boards to offer a series of sequential alternatives each with an incremental cut. The Oregon electorate usually turns down at least the first budget proposal. Budget elections in New York and Oregon sometimes go through four cycles before the electorate agrees to a specific budget! There is no automatic provision in California for such budget elections unless a per pupil expenditure limit is exceeded or there is an initiative petition. Neither of these occurred in low-wealth districts in 1973 because of the 15 percent state increase. Consequently, our case studies could not probe the usefulness of this model.

Political Interest Group Theories

Interest group theories stressing external pressures are drawn from considerable research in political science. David B. Truman, one of the major theorists in this tradition, emphasized that society is composed of groups, and that it is impossible to explain or predict policies without taking these constituents into account.[14] These groups make claims concerning the actual policy. This configuration is accounted for by three main clusters of variables:

1. Internal characteristics of the groups
2. Each group's differential strategic position in society
3. Characteristics of the governments or, in this case, school district organization and governance procedures.

With knowledge of these main factors and their dynamic interaction, it is possible to predict policy outcomes. An unpublished paper by Henry Levin, "Serrano-Type Expenditure Increases and Their Effects on Educational Resource Allocation," is a good case of this type of analytic model for education. Levin's paper posits an interest group configuration as portrayed by Table 7-1. The six major groups are local taxpayers, parents of some disadvantaged students, the disadvantaged students themselves, school board, teachers, and the administration.[15] Theoretically, each of these groups would make claims for the SB 90 money, and Levin posits who would win and who would lose. He puts

TABLE 7-1. *Interest Groups and Policy Outcomes*

Constituency	Goal	Power	Coalition	Outcome
1—Local Taxpayer	Minimize local burden	Moderate	With 4	Substitution of outside money for local
2—Disadvantaged Parent	Improve educational outcomes for disadvantaged children	Low	No	No change
3—Disadvantaged Student	Improve educational environment	Low	No	No change
4—School Board	Minimize conflict	High	With 1 and 6	Low conflict
5—Teachers	Increase employment and job benefits	High	With 6	More employment
6—Administrators	Increase employment and minimize conflict	High	With 4 and 5	More employment low conflict

power values on each group and suggests a strong influence factor or ability for the teachers and the administrators. Comparatively weak power is assigned to local taxpayers, parents, and students.

Levin's prediction is that there will be a tacit administrator-teacher coalition and revenues would be devoted to increased employment and job benefits for educational professionals as Moynihan contended. That is, there would be little evidence of this decision derived from a thoughtful and extensive plan to improve the education of disadvantaged youngsters, even though these allocations would be rationalized on their alleged contribution to the welfare of the children. The school board is portrayed as a weak actor that wishes to maintain the existing tax burden and minimize conflict and otherwise plays an unimportant role, particularly in budget formulation. Levin asserts his model helps to explain the outcome and allocations under Title I Elementary and Secondary Education Act (ESEA).

There was a striking absence of any external political interest groups or community participation in post-SB 90 allocations. This suggests some basic impediments to interest group articulation, particularly among the large Chicano populations in these suburban districts.[16] It also suggests a limited utility for the political models as defined in this paper.

We found no tacit coalition between school administrators and teachers' organizations over salary increases. Administrators, however, did not resist strongly teacher requests for additional professional personnel, and to that extent Levin's model provides good predictions. Two of the school boards reached a *de facto* impasse with their teachers' organizations and imposed unilateral settlements.[17] Strike votes by teacher groups were subsequently defeated. Taxpayer groups and other nonschool organizations played no significant role in any of the five districts. Consequently, none of the unrestricted state aid substituted for local tax effort.[18]

The case studies are congruent with other research that stresses the dominance of education professionals in the school budget process and the lack of influence by school boards and the lay public.[19] Lacking staff, information, and linkages to the community, school board members find themselves reacting to the superintendent's agenda, which highlights expertise and routine as much as possible. Two-thirds of the board members and three-fourths of the superintendents do not think the board's role should be that of a representative of the public desires—they stress the trustee role.[20] Community group activity does escalate in an episodic fashion and is strongly associated with financial defeats, teacher firings, and superintendent turnover. There is a strong incentive for education authorities to buffer themselves against assault by "outside" groups. The at-large, nonpartisan election held in an off year with only a few school board members running is designed to minimize the link between community demands and school policy.

In view of this pattern of policy, school reformers are watching closely the developments under Florida's new school site governance plan.[21] The Florida plan provides lump sum budgets for each school principal rather than central allocation. The related parts of this program are:

1. An annual report of school performance.
2. The ability of the principal to have more autonomy from the central office in terms of budget, curriculum, personnel mixes, etc. At present principals seldom have, or use, the authority to make their school outstanding.
3. A parent advisory council (PAC) at each school, with one of its primary duties a recommendation on the retention of the principal. The PAC would also help provide criteria for selecting teachers and compile the school performance report.
4. Parent-choice clusters that provide clearly defined programmatic options for parents to choose from within the public schools.

Organizational Models

We will explore the utility of three different organizational models. The *first type* can be considered a version of classical bureaucratic theory. Local decisions about spending unrestricted state school aid would have two main characteristics. They would be value-free (neutral) and rational. This would be neutral with respect to the conflicting interests in society and in the sense that the value premises are treated as given. The proof of the neutrality is that decisions can be subsumed under general objective decision rules. It is these rules (often in a legal code or administrative procedures handbook) that determine the decisions. In the bureaucratic's model pure form, political pressure and personnel preference have no impact. The decisions would also be rational in a particular sense; *e.g.*, they are intended to realize some goals. The goals, however, are derived from application of rules to concrete cases. This model is most often found in three theoretical traditions:[22]

1. Theories of jurisprudence that assume that judges use the law to fit it to specific cases
2. Theories of bureaucracy that posit that organizations execute policy merely by following some sort of formal rule book or regulation book
3. Theories of governance which presume that policies and administration are separate and the administration simply implements clear policies.

In its purest form the judge is sometimes conceived as an automaton who does not add or subtract any value items.

Clearly, this theory has some applicability to a situation of a local school district budget with its legally required built-in cost increases. Teacher retirement benefits by state law are based on salary schedules. Schools must stay open by state law so many days and offer certain courses. But all of the school districts, even the poorest ones, complied with most of these legal bureaucratic rules *before* SB 90. Consequently, such automatic decisions determined a minor proportion of SB 90 spending in the five districts.

A type of modern organizational model can be derived from the work of Cyert and March. Their writing illuminates three main sets of variables that are particularly relevant to SB 90 response.[23]

1. Which set of alternatives do local school districts consider?
2. What do they perceive the consequences of different alternatives to be?
3. Which goals does the school district seek to realize?

Economic theory stresses that the decision maker considers all feasible alternatives. Organizational process models posit that only *some* alternatives are considered, and which set of possible alternatives under consideration is crucial for explaining school district choice. For example, earlier consideration of similar budget choices may have made a set of alternatives. Restoration of 1970–71 decreases is a logical alternative even though these programs might not maximize cost effectiveness. The concept of pent-up demand applies here also. So does a school "organization's memory" restrict the alternatives considered.

If none of the *given alternatives* are considered good enough, school decision makers will search for new and better ones. Cyert and March assume three characteristics of organizational search: it is motivated, it is simple-minded, and it is biased. A plausible motivation for search is obvious in this study because of the large infusion of new resources.[24]

Simple-minded search follows two rules: (1) search in the neighborhood of the symptom; and (2) search in the neighborhood of the current alternative. Consequently, we would not expect dramatic departures from past educational approaches. Class size cuts, replenishing reserves, restoring services cut, and urgent maintenance projects would be prime expenditure candidates. Other simple-minded search rules would be to allocate enough to each expenditure category so that it maintains its historical budget share. Still another would be to move toward the Los Angeles County average in salaries, class size, and other traditional measures of school input quality. But this simple-minded and organizational routine approach may be overwhelmed by the amount of unrestricted money available from SB 90. Consequently, new alternatives may be sought. But Cyert and March stress that particular parts of the organization responsible for budget search are important.

Decision-making units are seen as coalitions where the different parts of the coalitions have different goals. The way this goal conflict is resolved has important consequences for what choices are made. Decision makers may avoid conflict by sequential attention to goals; *e.g.,* first one goal is attended to and then another. Regardless of the outcome of this coalition and bargaining, the various units of the organization are viewed as purposive. They act to accomplish goals and use goals as a function to evaluate consequences of alternatives. In order to predict budget outcomes under SB 90, one must understand the social structure of the organization, *e.g.,* the division into interest groups that hold different values.[25] Second, one would pay particular attention to interest articulation, or the process by which groups exert pressure on budget decision makers in order to fund their special interests.

The social science models that best predict the expenditure patterns are derived from modern organization theory of Cyert and March. In particular, their concepts of organizational search and the organization as a coalition were the most useful in explaining school district response. Budget decisions were hardly bureaucratic orders. They were negotiated compromises among competing organizational subgroups. In most of the cases the superintendent finds himself jockeying among interest groups and building viable compromises among powerful intraorganizational blocs. In all but one of the five cases, the superintendent was able to control the school board's views on the proper amount of the teacher salary increase. But most organization subunits also received some money. For example, the business office received increased maintenance and more custodians. The instructional division received special reading programs, psychological services, and instructional materials. The vocational education and handicapped pupil divisions also received program increases.

A more recent type of organizational theory is called "organized anarchies" or a "garbage can" model of organizational choice.

Cohen *et al.* stress that some organizations (like LEAs) are characterized by inconsistent and ill-defined goals, unclear technology about what inputs lead to specific outputs, and fluid participants who vary in the amount of time and effort they devote to different domains.[26] Cohen *et al.* have described those organizations and decision situations where the prerequisites of rational choice are not satisfied as "organized anarchies."

Weiner then predicts the response of urban school districts to SB 90 in this way:[27] Within a rational economic model of organizational choice it is assumed that choice opportunities lead first to the generation of decision alternatives, then to an examination of their consequences, then to an evaluation of those consequences in terms of objectives, and, finally, to a decision. The meaning of the choice is imagined to be fixed from the outset.

Within an organized anarchy the meaning of a choice varies over time, as the problems, solutions, and decision makers associated with the choice come and go. Decisions emerge from a complicated interplay among problems, the deployment of personnel, the production of solutions, and the nature of the alternative choice opportunities.

Thus decision opportunities are ambiguous stimuli. The choice opportunity may be viewed as an empty vessel, or a garbage can, into which various kinds of problems and solutions are dumped by participants as they are generated.

According to Cohen, March, and Olsen, despite the dictum that you cannot find the answer until the question has been well formulated, in organized anarchies you often do not know what the question is until a solution discovers or creates it. Unlike rational models of choice, where choices and problems are assumed to be specified in advance, where all alternative solutions are assumed to be evoked by the existence of the choice and its associated problems, and where adequate participant energy to make a choice is assumed to be present, a theory of organized anarchies views the flows of problems, solutions, participation, and choices to be variable and relatively independent of one another.

The garbage can model is oriented to decision process rather than to predicting categories of expenditure outcomes. SB 90 expenditure patterns would primarily be determined by who has time to participate in decisions, what the other demands are for the time of organizational participants, current "hot" problems, and external solutions promoted when money is available (like career education by the U.S. Office of Education). The theory stresses that future or long-range concerns are of minimal importance. At this stage, the garbage can model is more a reflection of doubts about the usefulness of current decision theories than a precise model.

STATISTICAL RESULTS

One of the strategies for anticipating the use of new general aid is projection from the past patterns of budget allocation. Our task, then, is to uncover regularities in the relationship between total expenditure per pupil and the per pupil expenditures in standard budget accounts. If expenditure categories vary systematically with total expenditure in the past, we can construct statistical predictions for a period after school finance reform. Since the audited expenditures for the 1973-74 school year are not complete, this paper must rely on data for the years prior to implementation of SB 90.

The model used to relate total expenditure to budget expenditures is a simple linear regression in the form

$$BE_i = a_o + bTE \qquad (1)$$

where

BE = budget expenditures in the ith account

TE = total expenditures

The literature of school budgeting offers little from which to draw hypotheses about this relationship. While students of public budgeting, especially in the "organization process" school, have been prolific, most of their work has a single organization focus. Indeed, analysis of more than one school budget at a time is rare. In most organization process studies it is found that stability of budgets from year to year is the hallmark of public budgeting.

Cross-Section Study

Across a variety of districts, our research uncovered the following statistical relationships (all analysis is on a per pupil basis):

Total expenditure is highly correlated with most major accounts in school budgets. Basic accounts, defined here as those with high correlations with total expenditure, account for over 85 percent of the total expenditure in districts (see Table 7-2). Expenditures under these accounts rise when total expenditures rise. Idiosyncratic accounts are defined as those with low correlations to total expenditure. Expenditure levels under these accounts respond to other factors; *e.g.*, the level of transportation expenditures is influenced more by geography than by total expenditure.

Given the strength of these correlations, we *would not* expect the percentage of expenditures in basic accounts to be linearly related to total expenditure; *i.e.*, if

$$\frac{BE_i}{TE} = a_o + bTE \qquad (2)$$

it would imply that

$$BE_i = a_o TE + b(TE^2)$$

and therefore the percentage relationship to total expenditure is a form of quadratic and would not be expected to have a strong linear correlation. A visual inspection of scattergrams of total expenditure and budget allocation percentages, however, did not suggest a curvilinear relationship. Although we could not find a basis for a systematic relationship between total expenditure and allocation percentages, it is noteworthy that the range of percentages for many accounts is small. Table 7-3 lists the mean and the standard deviation for budget variables in different years. For certain accounts—administration, other certified salaries, teachers' salaries, and operations—the standard deviation is less than one-fifth of the mean. This low dispersion itself may indicate budget allocation patterns which are stable *despite* variations in total expenditure.

The high correlation between total expenditure and the amounts spent in basic accounts and the relatively stable expenditure shares in the basic accounts suggest simple predictive models. These models yield a general statement for the marginal use of total expenditure in particular accounts. The regression coefficients (b) in Table 7-4 describe the portion of each new dollar of total expenditure which can be expected to be allocated to each of the accounts. The higher the variation explained (R^2), the more accurate and reliable the use of this linear model. Such a model may be used to estimate expenditures in a given account, provided the total expenditure of a specific district is available.

The linear correlation between percent spent on teachers' salaries and total

TABLE 7-2. *Basic and Idiosyncratic Accounts 1971–72, Unified School Districts in Los Angeles County (N = 42)*

			Basic Accounts					
Correlation to Total Expenditure	*Adm.*	*Prins. & Supv.*	*Tchrs.*	*Other Cert.*	*Other Exp. Instr.*	*Health*	*Operation of Plant*	*Maint.*
Amount of Total Exp.	.81	.70	.93	.78	.72	.72	.92	.70
Percent of Total Exp.	.17	-.20	-.53	.28	.09	.39	.16	.34

	Idiosyncratic Accounts				
Correlation to Total Expenditure	*Aides*	*Texts*	*Other Books*	*Transportation*	*Community Services*
Amount of Total Exp.	-.08	.42	.30	.23	.50
Percent of Total Exp.	-.25	.10	-.15	.03	.21

TABLE 7-3. *Absolute and Percentage Variables' Means and Standard Deviations for Base Year and Comparison Years*

	Mean Expenditure per ADA			Mean Percent of Current Expense		
	1967-68	1971-72	1972-73	1967-68	1971-72	1972-73
Administration	23.8	30.7[1]	32.5[1]	3.60[1]	3.45[1]	3.42[1]
	6.7	8.3	8.1	0.68	0.55	0.55
Prins. and Supv.	36.8[1]	47.8	49.5[1]	5.63[1]	5.42[1]	5.25[1]
	7.3	10.1	9.2	0.73	0.77	0.67
Teachers' Sals.	363.8[1]	487.2[1]	509.5[1]	55.50[2]	55.30[1]	53.86[1]
	57.6	83.7	85.7	2.30	2.90	2.92
Other Certified	25.9[1]	35.3	38.3	3.91[1]	3.95[1]	4.00[1]
	6.8	11.2	11.2	0.73	0.77	0.73
Other Expenses of Instr.	22.0	27.9	29.7	3.33	3.14	3.12[1]
	7.5	8.8	8.0	0.74	0.66	0.53
Health Svcs.	6.5	7.0	7.0	0.99	0.77	0.71
	2.5	3.6	3.8	0.33	0.32	0.31
Operations	56.8[1]	74.4	79.0	8.67[2]	8.38[2]	
	9.9	17.4	17.0	0.80	0.76	
Maintenance	25.2	33.3	35.5	3.83	3.69	3.69
	7.6	14.8	13.0	0.95	1.23	0.97
Instr. Aides		13.6			1.6	
		9.2			1.1	

	Col 1	Col 2	Col 3	Col 4	Col 5	Col 6
Class. Sals. Instr.	30.6		58.7	4.66[1]		6.20
	7.3		16.2	0.80		1.40
Textbooks	2.3	2.3	2.3	0.34	0.26	0.23
	1.2	1.3	1.5	0.15	0.13	0.14
Other Books	3.7	2.8	2.9	0.56	0.32	0.48
	1.9	1.2	1.9	0.27	0.13	0.11
Transportation	9.9	12.6	13.3	1.50	1.40	1.40
	7.7	8.9	9.3	1.10	0.84	0.84
Community Svcs.	12.7	16.8	17.4	1.90	1.87	1.80
	6.6	9.0	9.3	0.99	0.89	0.82

[1] Mean is five times greater than standard deviation.
[2] Mean is ten times greater than standard deviation.

153

TABLE 7-4. *Budget Variables and Total Expenditure Simple Regression 1971–72 Data, Los Angeles County Unifieds (N = 42)*

Budget Account Expenditure– Dependent Variable	Constant	Coefficient of TE(b)	Standard Error of Estimate	Significance Prob. s ≠ b > .975	Standard Error of b	R^2
Administration	-2.65	.036	4.84	Yes	.004	.67
Total Instruction	116.55	.582	31.99	Yes	.026	.92
Prins. and Supv. Sals.	12.78	.038	7.27	Yes	.006	.49
Teachers' Salaries	106.14	.412	30.64	Yes	.025	.86
Other Certified	-7.30	.046	7.06	Yes	.006	.61
Aides	17.23	-.003	9.24	Yes	.008	.01
Textbooks	-.42	.003	1.21	Yes	.001	.17
Other Books	1.04	.002	1.14	Yes	.001	.09
Other Expenses of Instr.	-3.15	.034	6.08	Yes	.005	.53
Health Services	-5.76	.014	2.50	Yes	.002	.53
Transportation	2.39	.011	8.84	No	.007	.05
Operations	-2.62	.083	6.75	Yes	.006	.85
Maintenance	-17.04	.054	10.73	Yes	.009	.49
Community Services	-5.54	.024	7.93	Yes	.007	.25

expenditures is negative in the three years we analyzed. This suggests possible tradeoffs between the proportion for teachers and other accounts within an expanding budget. *As the absolute amount spent on teachers increases, the proportion for this account has a tendency to decrease, allowing other accounts to increase in proportion of total expenditure.*

Since teachers' salaries do not command an increasing share of an expanding budget, opportunity arises for particular attendance to needs in other accounts such as instructional materials and maintenance. Moreover, we found that both teacher salary levels—maximum and minimum—and class size were related to total expenditure. As total expenditure rises, class size shrinks and salary levels are raised. But as a companion study of all California LEAs by the Rand Corporation concluded, teacher dollars increase with total dollars but at a slower rate—51.6 percent of the budget at $800 per pupil expenditure; falling to 43.7 percent at $2,000.[28] Moreover, as poor districts receive more state aid, most of the teacher expenditures are allocated for added instructional personnel rather than for salaries of existing teachers (or longevity increases).

This quantitative study will continue longitudinally. By comparison of the results from this 1971-72 statistical analysis with those for different years—including 1973-74, the year after the school finance reform—the conclusions reached here might be reinforced. Such future work on post-reform expenditure patterns is necessary to reestimate these results in the absence of the risky assumption used here that LEAs will spend windfalls from the state in the same manner that they spend locally raised tax dollars. Such an assumption is similar to assuming that an auto worker will buy the same things with his Irish sweepstakes ticket as with his overtime earnings.

CASE STUDIES

Our five case studies have revealed a mixture of rich variety with some central tendencies. For example, the strength of teachers' organizations ranged from a knowledgable executve secretary for one locale to another locale which had little knowledge of SB 90 budget increases. As for the major policy issue stressed in this paper, the case study results are congruent with the statistical predictions. Most of the new money was used for additional instructional personnel, including reductions in pupil/teacher ratios, math specialists, career education, and so on. Salary increases for existing teachers were in the 5 to 7 percent range, which is not unduly high considering teachers' wages were held down in prior years by the Cost of Living Council.

While minor amounts were spent for plant and maintenance, new instructional materials, and replenishing of depleted reserves, most of the subunits of the school organization received some money. Personnel costs absorbed 80 to 85 percent of the new money in one district and 69 percent in another. However, in different districts, there were different allocations of this added personnel cost. In one, the major stress was on more curriculum specialists (including bilingual), department chairman, and assistant principals; in another, principals were given lump sum budget allocations to spend for anything they deemed most important; a third restored sixth period in high school, added more aides, and expanded vocational education. Consequently, when one gets below the aggregate budget accounts used in the state reporting forms, there are significant program differences.

CONCLUSIONS

These results provide some insight into the issue of whether school finance reforms designed to improve equity will also improve the quality of services. From the reformer's viewpoint, not all the increased state aid will be consumed in price or salary increases (especially personnel compensation) for the same services. Consequently, Moynihan's argument does seem overstated. Indeed, if past expenditure patterns continue, teachers' salaries will command a lower percentage of state aid in the post-finance reform period.

But critics can charge that this finding represents only a temporary phenomenon, and that once facilities maintenance is restored and programmatic pent-up demands are satisfied, salary increases will accelerate. Moreover, they will stress the organization process models that appear to explain that the decision-making process in low-wealth districts gives little hope for significant pupil progress. Organization process decision models will merely result in old and discredited education programs including reduced class size, special personnel, curriculum experts, and more traditional textbooks. This outcome will provide little solace for educational economists who doubt the effectiveness of "more of the same." Neither the rationality of economic analysis nor the demands of parents (or other groups outside the organization) are likely to have much influence on the spending of unrestricted state aid.

Organizational theorists argue that one way to break routines and standard operating procedures is to "shock" the system. For example, state policy makers could provide huge sums of grant money which would attract more attention by all actors to the resource allocation process, or the school site governance plan outlined could be implemented to try to stimulate decision-making participation by parents and nonbureaucratic forces.

NOTES

1. For an analysis of the Rodriquez case in the perspective of school finance reform, see Joel S. Berke, *Answers to Educational Inequity* (Berkeley, Calif.: McCutchn Publishing Corp., 1975.

2. Daniel P. Moynihan, "Equalizing Education: In Whose Benefit?" *Public Interest,* 29 (Fall 1972), p. 71.

3. Harvey A. Averch *et al., How Effective is Schooling?* (Santa Monica, Calif.: Rand Corporation, 1972), pp. XII and XIII.

4. Moynihan, *op. cit.,* p. 75. Moynihan assumes salary increases are valueless. Higher salaries, however, could improve employee morale or attract better-quality people to teaching in low-income areas.

5. *Ibid.,* p. 76.

6. For conflicting views, see Christopher Jencks *et al., Inequality* (New York: Basic Books, 1972), and James Guthrie *et al., Schools and Inequality* (Cambridge, Mass.: M.I.T. Press, 1971).

7. See, for example, Charles Benson *et al., Final Report to the Senate Select Committee on School District Finance,* June 12, 1972, pp. 29–37.

8. James R. Glenn, Jr., "An Exercise in Modeling," unpublished manuscript, Stanford University, 1972.

9. For an example of this model, see Graham Allison, *Essence of Decision* (Boston: Little, Brown, 1971), pp. 10-39. See also Charles Schultze, *The Economics and Politics of Public Spending* (Washington: Brookings, 1971).

10. Jesse Burkhead, "Economics against Education," *Teachers College Record,* 75, (December 1973), p. 198.

11. See, for example, Robert Aaron Gordon, *Business Fluctuations* (New York: Harper, 1952).

12. T. Dernburg, and D. McDougall, *Macro-economics: The Measurement, Analysis and Control of Aggregate Economic Activity* (New York: McGraw-Hill, 1960), pp. 76-79. For a discussion of Friedman's ideas, see Michael K. Evans, *Macroeconomic Activity: Theory, Forecasting, and Control* (New York: Harper & Row, 1969).

13. See Robert A. Dahl, *A Preface to Democratic Theory* (Chicago: University of Chicago Press, 1956); also Anthony Downs, *An Economic Theory of Democracy* (New York: Harper, 1957).

14. David B. Truman, *The Governmental Process* (New York: Knopf, 1956).

15. For a review of public school politics, see Frederick Wirt and Michael Kirst, *The Political Web of American Schools* (Boston: Little, Brown, 1972).

16. For a discussion of school governance and interest groups, see *ibid.*

17. California does not have a collective-bargaining law.

18. As noted before, another provision of SB 90 provided direct and indirect property tax relief to homeowners and renters.

19. See Wirt and Kirst, *op. cit.*

20. See Harmon Ziegler and M. Kent Jennings, *Governing American Education* (Scituate, Mass.: Duxbury Press, forthcoming).

21. For an elaboration of this plan, see Walter I. Garms and Michael Kirst, *Improving Education in Florida* (Tallahassee: Office of the Governor, 1973).

22. See Max Weber, *Economy and Society* (New York: Bedminister Press, 1968), and J. W. Peltason, "Judicial Process," in *International Encyclopedia of the Social Sciences* (New York: Macmillan, 1968), VIII.

23. See R. M. Cyert and J. G. March, *A Behavioral Theory of the Firm* (Englewood Cliffs, N.J.: Prentice Hall, 1963). Allison's Model II in *Essence of Decision* integrates a number of the books and articles on organizational theory (pp. 67–97). For an interesting application to education, see Jerome Murphy, "Title V of ESEA," in *Harvard Education Review,* 43 (August 1973), pp. 362–85.

24. Based on survey by Arthur Alexander, Rand Corporation, reported in interview with M. W. Kirst. The increase in inflation rates in 1973–74 may make even a 15 percent increase a simple cost-increase-type decision.

25. J. Victor Baldridge, *Power and Conflict in a University* (New York: Wiley, 1971).

26. Michael D. Cohen, James G. March, and Johan P. Olsen, "A Garbage Can Model of Organizational Choice," *Administrative Science Quarterly,* 1972.

27. Stephen S. Weiner, "Educational Decisions in an Organized Anarchy," unpublished Ph.D. dissertation, Stanford University, 1972.

28. Arthur Alexander, "Issues in State and Local School Finance," paper presented at the Educational Testing Service, Princeton, N.J., Feb. 1, 1974.

Comment: Reforming Education Finance

Robert E. Firestine

There are two concerns in this comment. The first is a critique of and commentary upon certain parts of the Kirst paper and a suggestion of alternative frameworks for the empirical problem that he addresses. The second relates to a broad concern with both the form and the substance of some of the recent efforts being carried out under the general banner of school finance reform.

Despite the title of Professor Kirst's paper, I believe that this provocative report would be much more accurately described as an "inquiry into the nature of local fiscal response to changes in the state aid instrument in California." I fully subscribe to his contention that the most meaningful and comprehensive approach to this problem must include a complete assessment of the possible intellectual contributions of a variety of disciplines. He has chosen to discuss what are probably the major fields that might aid our understanding (and, therefore, our prediction) of this phenomenon. These are economic analysis, political decision making, and organizational behavior theory. While by setting out these disciplines Professor Kirst signifies the critical multiple dimensions of local government behavior at the margin, it seems that in his subsequent discussion he does not clearly express a crucial implication of his own analytic framework. This is that the fullest application of his cross-disciplinary research would suggest an approach which would select the most promising aspects of *each* theory (economic, political, and organizational, to follow his scheme) and weld them together into a behavioral model (or models) which would incorporate the essential *interactions* of these major analytic disciplines. This, of course, is challenging and difficult work, and I do not mean to take him to task for not having given us a full-blown general equilibrium model of local governmental behavior. Nonetheless, to have couched his presentation in terms of virtually alternative, "competing" models is not, I feel, in the better interests of producing good empirical estimates or of advancing the methodological state of the art.

Specifically, I note that the analysis is presented purely in terms of changes in the subbudgetary shares of local educational spending: the shifting of school district expenditure components as a result of modifications in the "delivery mechanism" of state aid. This is certainly a very important concern under such circumstances, but I believe that a more elemental problem is the prediction of local choice between taxing and spending in light of altered "price" or (synthetic) local "wealth" characteristics facing districts in the wake of SB 90. Abstracting from the California experience, some of our recent work in this area

159

suggests that variations in this "tax-expenditure substitution rate" across different types of school districts can have substantial fiscal consequences for the state under various levels of state aid revision schemes.[1] Thus, while the problem of differential effects upon local educational expenditure components is indeed pertinent, of at least equal concern should be an examination of the variable incidence of tax-expenditure substitution among the school districts of a state. Taken together, these two phenomena seem to comprise the economic manifestations of the operation of "local choice" as it may be available to a school district under these circumstances. Given this outline of the nature of such local district fiscal responses, we next turn to some economic approaches by which such responses might be predicted empirically.

My remarks on Kirst's economic considerations are aimed at establishing two ends of a continuum within which a number of economic models might usefully be applied to the question of local district response. Once having defined the extremes of this continuum, we shall then outline a few simple empirical approaches to this problem. This so-called continuum may be defined within the standard concepts of normative and positive analysis. In this type of normative analysis, we might think of the researcher as working to adapt an appropriate and generally accepted theory of the problem at hand. Such attempts to specify various forms of a "community preference function" have indeed appeared recently, and have been generally based on the microanalytic techniques of the "new" welfare economics. Notable among these is the work of David Stern, W. Norton Grubb, and Stephen Barro.[2] It is in the derivation of this community preference function that the interdisciplinary premise of this work should be (but seldom is) most intimately joined. Specifically, who *is* the "community" whose preferences are to be analyzed? Kirst's cogent references to Levin's paper suggest a number of competing interest groups—each seeking to maximize its own separate utility function. Depending on the interest group, the economic analyses might usefully be combined here with either the political or the organizational models outlined by Kirst. Thus far we have only scratched the surface of the possibilities that may be contained in such considerations.

At the opposite extreme is the positive type of policy analysis, wherein the aim is essentially to derive or construct a viable theory (in the absence of normative doctrine) from a close scrutiny of the available (empirical) evidence. In the case of predicting the impact of SB 90 by this approach, one might look at other states in which school finance reforms had occurred and attempt to impose any applicable findings to the California situation. With the complexities of the California law, a number of relatively diverse reform plans from several different states might have to be examined in order to build up a (synthetic) structure that was roughly analogous to the new California law. For such a purpose, only some portions of the reforms in other states might be relevant, and an assessment of their particular effects might prove quite challenging in some instances. Such efforts, nonetheless, should at least be considered.

There are at least two additional econometric approaches to the estimation of local district fiscal response which lie somewhere between those two extremes on the continuum of techniques to deal with the problem. The first is a simple expenditure determinants analysis, derived from the rather extensive literature on this topic, and the second is a so-called time-trend analysis, using longitudinal data. Let us look briefly at each of these procedures.

AN EXPENDITURE "DETERMINANTS" APPROACH[3]

The procedure is to develop and test several cross-sectional regression models of school district expenditures as "determined" by local school district socio-economic characteristics.[4] In one of many approaches to this task, a simultaneous-equation system might be developed in which per pupil revenues from local sources (L) and state aid (S) would be endogenous, or determined by the remaining variables in the model (the exogenous variables). Total expenditures per pupil (E) would then be a linear function of local revenues (L), state aid (S), and federal aid (F) or

$$E \equiv \hat{L} + \hat{S} + F \tag{1}$$

Though several equations would be examined, the following might be used to estimate L:

$$\hat{L} = f(V, Y, Ed, Oc, R, P) \tag{2}$$

where

$\hat{L}$ = estimated local revenues per pupil

V = local equalized property valuation per pupil

Y = median family income

Ed = percentage of persons 25 years old and over who have completed high school (or college)

Oc = percentage of employed persons 16 years old and over who are employed in professional, technical, or managerial occupations

R = percentage of district residents residing in rural areas

P = percentage of elementary and high school students enrolled in non-public schools

As a test of the model, the best equation for $\hat{L}$ (which yields those values of $\hat{L}$ that most closely approximate the actual L) would be used to estimate E by using L, F, and the actual value of state aid (S). After satisfactory results are obtained, estimates of $\hat{S}$ will be used in place of actual S—estimates which have been derived from potential alternative state aid formulas which might incorporate a variety of equalizing mechanisms. Of course, many variations of this model are possible, including ordinary least-squares single-equation schemes with the use of E rather than L as the principal dependent variable.

"TIME TREND" ANALYSIS

This method constitutes an examination of local district response from an *ex post* perspective, for it would make use of actual tax-expenditure choices which have occurred in response to *enacted* state aid modifications. A series of longitudinal observations will be made of local fiscal patterns as they existed before the change in the law (*ex ante*). Probably relying on pooled time-series and cross-sectional data, predictions made from the *ex ante* data would be compared to the *ex post* per pupil expenditure response of individual districts. The differences between the actual and the predicted responses—the residuals—would then be regressed upon numerous district socioeconomic characteristics in an attempt to derive a predictive local district response model.

The recent Kansas school finance reform law may afford a good opportunity to take an across-the-board, after-the-fact look at the initial results of a changed state aid law which permits some degree of local fiscal choice. This is fortuitous, for Kansas has also collected reliable information for the last several years on levels of family income *by school district*. With this income measure, the available annual data on per pupil property wealth in each district, and perhaps the annual unemployment rate in the county containing each district, a simple model could be built to predict the level of per pupil expenditures which would have obtained in each district had no change taken place in the state aid statute. The predicted value may then be compared to the actual value, with the residual (the difference between the actual and the predicted) being attributable to the imposition of the new law. This residual may then be regressed on a number of socioeconomic variables so as to define a predictive empirical model of local district response based solidly on district socioeconomic characteristics.

The simple initial model of expenditures might take any one of several forms. The dependent variable could be the level of per pupil spending in the year to be predicted (E_t), but it might also be expressed as a change from that of the previous year ($E_t - E_{t-1}$, or ΔE). In the former version, the expenditure equation would take the form

$$E_t = f(E_{t-1}, Y, V, UN, d, T) \tag{3}$$

where

E_t = per pupil expenditures in year t (predicted)

E_{t-1} = per pupil expenditures in the previous year (known)

Y = the annual income measure

V = per pupil equalized property valuation

Un = the year's average unemployment rate in the county containing each individual district

d = a dummy variable for operation of the new aid program (0 or 1): a "shift" dummy

T = a dummy variable for each successive year in the analyses, beginning with $T = 1$: a "slope" dummy

The data would be pooled for all districts in the state (or, perhaps, for all districts in our ELSEGIS sample), with the time series going at least as far back in time as the income (Y) data are available. If other possible relevant variables were discovered to exist annually for school districts, they would, of course, be included. Also, a number of devices might be employed in this equation, including the purging of the influence of, say, valuation on income (if it should prove to be highly multicollinear) by the "residualization" technique, which extracts from V that portion of its variation which is not correlated with Y. This uncorrelated, residual measure, RV (as derived from the simple regression

$$V = a + bY + u = a + bY + RV \qquad (4)$$

where the correlation between Y and RV is thus zero), is then included in the equation for E_t in place of V itself. The remainder of the exercise (regressing the residual of $E_t - \hat{E}_t$ on the "usual" hypothesized explanatory variables) should be relatively straightforward.

Obviously, those suggestions by no means exhaust the possibilities of dealing analytically with the prediction of local school district response to changes in state aid laws where some local fiscal choice is permitted. They are included here as simple examples of how one might derive such estimates by relatively straightforward empirical means. Analytically, they stand as expressions of a related, but alternative, concern to the budgetary components questions raised by Professor Kirst.

REMARKS ON EQUITY AND THE STATE OF THE SCHOOL FINANCE REFORM MOVEMENT

An issue that bears a considerable relation to the general topic is service quality versus fiscal equity in school finance reform. Specifically, I am troubled by the general discussion of equity in the present school finance reform movement. There seems to be a fundamental misconception which is endemic to both the rhetoric and, in part, the litigation of current school finance reform.

The confusion is over the appropriate treatment of *educational* equity versus *fiscal* equity as a legitimate object of reform. Educational equity relates to the elusive definition of the phrase "equality of educational opportunity." Such "equality" may be conceived in terms of equal (or compensatorily unequal) educational *inputs* (pupil/teacher ratios, teacher "quality," teacher salary, etc.) or of equal (or perhaps even compensatorily unequal) educational *outputs* (achievement test scores at graduation, or even equal lifetime earnings.

Fiscal equity in its present context refers to an attempt to redress the disparities that exist within a given state whereby property-rich districts can raise large amounts of revenue per pupil with a low tax rate and, at the same time, property-poor districts are able to raise much less revenue per pupil with even much higher tax rates. There are a number of controversies evolving from each of these very different perspectives of equity, but I believe that one fundamental distinction can nevertheless be made: the discussion over fiscal equity is merely how to achieve (or approach) it in the most politically acceptable way, while the controversy over educational equity is still even how to define it. Both are healthy debates to which the social sciences have and will continue to contribute much. At this juncture, however, it does not appear promising that we will soon arrive at any generally acceptable understanding of what educational equity really is. This is true for the very reason Kirst has already observed: we have no good perception of the education production function. That is, we just do not know very much about controlling our educational output by the manipulation of our educational inputs. This is especially and painfully the case for the education process within our nation's troubled inner cities and for those of our children who are economically and culturally disadvantaged and physically and emotionally handicapped.

For pupils in these circumstances, it may well be correct to assert that additional dollars of expenditure will reduce or "solve" the educational problems, but a growing number of scholars *and* laymen are coming to realize that additional dollars alone are not enough. What may also be needed, then, is a modification in the production process for education. Such modification may take the relatively simple form of school site budgeting to provide greater local choice, or it may require a much more drastic reworking of some of the methods with which disadvantaged and special pupils (including the gifted) are taught.

We must firmly distinguish between the possibilities of achieving *educational* versus *fiscal* equity through the present-day school finance reform movement. We surely have the tools to enable us to approximate *fiscal* equity. Contrarily, we know all too little about making a substantial move toward *educational* equity. In light of this, it is most disturbing to hear attorneys who are prominent in the school finance reform movement assert that educational equity—and *not* fiscal equity—must be the *cause célèbre* in presenting their cases before the courts. To some extent, at least, this appears to be the current mood in legal circles, despite the widespread (though not quite universal) evidence from the social science and educational research.

My point, therefore, is a simple one. If school finance reform is to be "sold" to the courts and then to the state legislatures and the public at large, as a means of achieving educational equity (with fiscal equity as a sort of by-product), then the product will have been mistakenly and disastrously oversold. We will never deliver more than we *can* deliver, and fiscal equity is the only non-perishable commodity presently in the school finance reformer's bag of wares. To attempt to promote school finance reform on the promise of educational equity will be, I believe, to reenact the mistake of the "Great Society," wherein hopes were aroused for needs to be fulfilled before the methods and the means to do so were fully appraised.

NOTES

1. See Robert E. Firestine, John N. Carvellas, and Anthony B. LaMacchia, *Analytical Tools for School Finance Aid Simulations* (Syracuse, N.Y.: Syracuse University Research Corporation, October 1973), pp. 5-11, 18-22, 28-33, 36-39.

2. David Stern, "Effects of Alternative State Aid Formulas on the Distribution of Public School Expenditures in Massachusetts," *Review of Economics and Statistics*, IV, 1 (February 1973), pp. 91-97; W. Norton Grubb, *"Intergovernmental Aid and Resource Disparities: School Finance in Massachusetts,"* preliminary dissertation draft, Harvard University, August 1973; Stephen M. Barro, "Theoretical Models of School District Expenditure Determination and the Impact of Grants-in-Aid," Paper No. R–867–FF, Rand Corporation, (Santa Monica, Calif.: February 1972); Barro, "The Impact of Grants-in-Aid on State and Local Education Expenditures," Paper No. 4385, (Santa Monica, Calif.: Rand Corporation, 1970); and Stephen M. Barro, "An Econometric Study of Public School Expenditure Variation across States," Paper No. 4934, (Santa Monica, Calif.: Rand Corporation, 1972).

3. This procedure is now being explored in a doctoral dissertation in economics at Syracuse University by John N. Carvellas, a research assistant with SURC's Educational Finance and Governance Center. Carvellas's approach is considerably more comprehensive than that outlined here, which is developed primarily from an unpublished draft by W. Norton Grubb and Stephen Michelson, "Public School Finance in a Post-Serrano World," mimeograph, Apr. 25, 1973.

4. A data tape containing 1969-70 school finance statistics from the ELSEGIS IIIB (Elementary and Secondary Education General Information) Survey merged with 1970 U.S. Census data on school district socioeconomic characteristics has been prepared for a number of states. See Robert Firestine, John Carvellas, and Anthony LaMacchia, *A Data Capability for School Finance Aid Simulations* (Syracuse, N.Y.: Syracuse University Research Corporation, October 1973).

8. Revenue Sharing: New Federalism or New Conservatism?

Jesse Burkhead

We are now engaged in restructuring the existing patterns of fiscal federalism. The theme of this paper is that a new pattern should embrace a strengthened and revised form of general revenue sharing, certain types of block grants, and the retention of some kinds of categorical grants. These three elements must somehow be made to work in concert. The federal government should not retreat and withdraw from the cities. We should restore the possibility for developing a national urban policy. None of this is easy, and it will not be done in the next year or two.*

THE CHANGING SCENE IN FEDERALISM

It was just 10 years ago that a task force headed by Joseph Pechman of the Brookings Institution reported to President Johnson on a proposal for sharing federal revenue with the states—a proposal that came to be known as the Heller-Pechman plan. Those were halcyon days on the fiscal scene. Tax reduction as a means for stimulating the economy had been accepted by the Congress and the business community, and the 1964–65 revenue reduction measures were already working. The GNP was rising; prices were reasonably stable; growth rates had been restored; and we were confidently anticipating an annual increase in federal revenue of $7 billion—the fiscal dividend. This would be shared with state and local governments, accommodate a normal expansion in federal programs, and leave something for further tax reduction.

We were all Keynesians at that time, and indeed John Maynard Keynes's picture was on the cover of *Time* magazine on December 31, 1965. The prestige of economists and economics was so high that the Nobel Committee established

*Portions of this paper were presented at the December 1973 Annual Congress of Cities, sponsored by the National League of Cities.

an Economics Award. In those years the salaries of economists exceeded even the salaries of physicists.

But it hasn't turned out quite as expected. The expansion of the Vietnam War absorbed a good part of the fiscal dividend. Then there were additional federal tax reductions in 1969 and 1971. Even with the increases in social security taxes the federal tax structure lost $27 billion of revenue potential from 1963 to 1973, according to Brookings estimates.[1] Accompanying the tax reduction, Great Society programs were enacted, and while many were underfunded, expenditures in some areas rose sharply. Federal expenditures on community development and housing increased from $288 million to $4.1 billion between 1965 and 1973; education and manpower increased from $2.3 billion to $10.2 billion; health, excluding Medicare but including Medicaid, increased from $1.7 billion to $18.4 billion.[2] The major fiscal characteristic of most of these programs is that they were categorical grants. Depending on how the titles and subtitles are counted, the number of federal grant programs increased from about 400 to 1,000 between 1964 and 1970—well into the Nixon administration.

During the years from 1964 to 1970 new actors appeared on the scene—actors that have had an impact on the fiscal dimensions of federalism. The civil rights movement directed attention to inner city problems, as did the summer riots from 1964 through 1967. Many of the new programs encouraged low-income families to assess their eligibility for social welfare programs, so that OEO, Medicaid, and AFDC all interacted with each other, and a new tactic—the politics of confrontation—emerged to support the demands for social welfare expenditures. Increased expenditures on education and the rapid growth of public employee unionization added to the pressures. At the same time, a new dimension in federalism emerged as demands for community control and neighborhood government became significant as an expression of antagonism to centralized bureaucracy.

The state-local fiscal dimensions of this concatenation of events are startling. During the 1950s state-local expenditures increased rapidly—from $22 billion to $50 billion. But from 1960 to fiscal 1974 state-local expenditures increased from $48 billion to more than $200 billion—a 400 percent increase in current dollars, and an increase of from 10 to 15 percent of the GNP.[3] Most evidently, such growth rates could not be maintained, particularly when the national economy came to be plagued after 1971 with low growth rates, increased unemployment, and inflation.

NEW FEDERALISM

The Nixon administration's "New Federalism" was the product of this complex set of forces. It had administrative dimensions and fiscal dimensions. It shifted, in a modest way, the centers of decision authority in the federal system. It contained about equal portions of realism, romanticism, and rhetoric.

It may be viewed not as New Federalism but as New Conservatism, reflecting a resurgence of traditional middle-class American antagonism against the poor and minority groups. It was at first accompanied by impoundments of federal funds for social programs, of sharp cutbacks in categorical grants that had helped the inner city, by moratoria on neighborhood renewal and low-income housing projects. And, while some of these antipoor attitudes started to build up as early as 1968, some of them solidified very rapidly. In the fall of 1972 Congress was still debating the Family Assistance Plan, which would have been an important step toward the nationalization of welfare. Since that time welfare reform has become a very dead issue, and almost every month some governor, some county welfare executive, and even some mayors will anounce with pride that welfare rolls have been reduced and the chiselers and the cheats have been removed from the rolls.[4]

We have also been told that many of the social programs of the 1960s "didn't work," but sober reflection should convince almost anyone that some were never tried.[5] The combined annual expenditure of OEO and Model Cities, for example, never amounted to more than $2.5 billion in a trillion-dollar economy. Those who had hoped, during 1964-68, that poverty could be eradicated from American society within a decade must revise their projections.

The New Federalism has been accompanied by a great deal of rhetoric about returning government to the people, about strengthening the innovative capacities of city halls, and about reducing the evils of overcentralization. The irony here, as we now understand from Watergate, is that in the Nixon administration this rhetoric was accompanied by the greatest centralization of power within the federal executive office in peacetime history. The further irony is that the New Federalism is a great backward step from the efforts of the late 1960s to devise a national urban policy. The New Federalism suggests that a better way to deal with national urban problems is by means of thousands of uncoordinated local urban policies. A policy—general revenue sharing—was adopted to deal with administrative and fiscal problems without any thought of its substantive impacts.

But the New Federalism must also be viewed as a legitimate response to what had become—if the 1969 and 1971 tax reductions were inevitable, and if national defense expenditures are not to be curtailed—a federal expenditure pattern that could not be sustained. The New Federalism was also a legitimate response to an unplanned and cumbersome pattern—not a system—of categorical grants. One had only to look at intergovernmental relations in the manpower field to appreciate the nature of this chaos. The antagonisms of local government officials to the paper work necessary for grant applications, the inconstant review procedures established by federal departments and agencies, and unrealistic auditing—these antagonisms were and are most legitimate.

The New Federalism is also a legitimate recognition that the taxable capacity of the 50 states is equal to the taxable capacity of the national government.

What limits state-local tax effort is not the absence of capacity, but institutional and attitudinal constraints, often grounded on a concern to maintain competitive advantage. The New Federalism may be viewed as an effort to encourage the "willingness" of state-local jurisdictions to tap the resources that they have within their boundaries.[6]

The reality of the New Federalism now consists of general revenue sharing (GRS) and special revenue sharing for law enforcement, rural development, manpower, and community development. The two additional areas that were proposed several times by the Nixon administration for special revenue sharing— education and transportation—have thus far failed to win Congressional approval. A program for assisting state and local governments in their managerial capabilities, labeled the Responsive Governments Act, which was proposed in January 1974, has also encountered Congressional inaction.[7]

General revenue sharing is a most complex affair. The statute violates the first rule of policy making, which is that there should be at least as many tools as there are objectives. GRS attempts to accomplish far too much with a single piece of legislation. Consequently, there are a great many side effects that surely were not intended.

Only the major proivsions of GRS will be set forth here:

1. The amounts appropriated were $5.6 billion for the first full year; this increases to $6.3 billion in the last full year (1976) covered by the statute.
2. The states receive one-third of the shares; local governments receive two-thirds.
3. Because the House and Senate could not agree on a single formula, there are two formulas, and states may choose the more generous one. The Senate formula, utilized by 31 states, has three factors: population, tax effort, and inverse relative per capita income. The House formula, used by 19 states, has the same factors in its formula, but adds two additional ones: urbanized population and income tax collections. The Senate formula is multiplicative. The House formula is additive.
4. Once the state share is determined, the two-thirds pass-through to local governments is on a county basis. The formula here is population, tax effort, and inverse income levels.
5. The county government and municipalities within the county receive their shares on the basis of "adjusted revenues," that is, general taxes defined to exclude taxes for education, fines and fees, and special district levies.
6. Except for local education and housing, there are relatively few restrictions on the states or local governments on the purposes for which revenue sharing funds may be spent.
7. Each jurisdiction must file "Planned Use" and "Actual Use" reports with the Treasury Office of Revenue Sharing. It may be noted that this is an almost meaningless requirement, since budget officers are adept at bring-

ing the "Use" reports into line with statutory requirements regardless of how, in fact, the funds are allocated.

A brief examination of some of the intended and unintended effects of GRS is appropriate.

GRS expresses the clear intent of the Congress to effect a modest jurisdictional redistribution of resources among states. The House formula is stronger on this point than the Senate formula. The 19 states that use the House formula are, not surprisingly, the more populous urban states.

There is also a modest intrastate jurisdictional redistribution to the county level, but not to the municipal level. The Congress is apparently concerned with intrastate jurisdictional equity—up to a point.

The Congress has also built into GRS an incentive to (1) tax more heavily at the state-local level, and (2) utilize state income taxes. The incentive (some would call it coercion) is mild and may well be offset in any state or local jurisdiction by taxpayer resistance. Nevertheless, for state-local jurisdictions that do tax more heavily, GRS changes the relative price of state-local public goods, making them less expensive relative to private goods.[8]

The important incentive that was probably unintentional on the part of the Congress is in the GRS treatment of nongeneral revenue. An increase in special district fees and charges will not increase a state-local share or a local share within a state. This may contribute to a modest shift, over time, from fees and charge finance to locally raised taxes.[9] And this shift may be unfortunate at a time when local governments are hard-pressed for general revenue from their own resources and when adverse environmental impacts can sometimes be reduced by water and sewage charges.

Table 8-1 helps to keep GRS in fiscal perspective. The $6.1 billion is about 12 percent of federal grants to state and local governments. This is less than the aggregates of each of four other categorical grant functions. Federal grants are expected to be 22.4 percent of state-local expenditures in fiscal 1975. The grants are about 3 percent of GNP.

Space does not permit an examination of the special revenue sharing that is now operative. It should be stressed, however, that manpower, rural development, and community development (the Housing Act of 1974) all embody significant jurisdictional redistribution. The poor jurisdictions get more. Fifteen years ago it was difficult to find any federal grants, with the exception of Hill-Burton hospital grants, that had equalizing features.

Whether special revenue sharing will return "power to the people," "improve local capacities for resource allocation," or bring "a better match between needs and resources" at the local level must still remain very much in doubt. There is nothing in special revenue sharing to prevent the Department of Labor, the Department of Agriculture, or the Department of Housing and Urban Development from piling regulation on top of regulation to thwart whatever local initiatives might develop under special revenue sharing. And there is nothing in the Housing

TABLE 8-1. *Federal Aid to State and Local Governments, Fiscal Year 1975 Estimates (in million dollars)*

National Defense	53.4
International	8.5
Agriculture	860.2
Natural Resources	4,153.3
Commerce and Transportation	6,507.7
Community Development	3,941.5
Education and Manpower	6,859.2
Health	8,544.9
Income Security	13,098.4
Veterans	46.1
General Government	1,491.5
Revenue Sharing	6,173.8
Total	51,731.5

Source: *Special Analyses, Budget of the United States Government, Fiscal Year 1975* (Washington: Government Printing Office, 1974), pp. 214–7.

Act of 1974 to prevent mayors from diverting resources from poor neighborhoods to middle- and upper-income neighborhoods. It is difficult to avoid the reassertion of central authority.

A SYSTEM OF GRANTS

Fiscal federalism should include general revenue sharing, block grants, *and* categoricals. Before turning to some observations on how this tripartite system might work, it would be instructive to briefly review the economic rationale for grants in a federal system and what may or may not have been learned in recent years about the response patterns to different types of grants-in-aid.

It should be stressed at the outset of an academic view of federalism that every government in the world, with the possible exception of Singapore, has federal characteristics. Even those governments that are customarily regarded as primarily unitary in nature, such as England and France, have delegated substantial authority over tax and expenditure decisions to local units. So we are all either federalists or Singaporeans.

In conventional economic theory there is a reasonably acceptable rationale for federalism. The national government must, of course, have responsibility for economic stabilization and for general policies on taxes and transfer payments that alter the distribution of income. But where a subset can be defined—perhaps a region, a state, a substate region, or an SMSA or a city—where tastes and preferences for public services are reasonably homogeneous, then, on the basis of rather formal criteria of economic welfare, this reasonably homogeneous subset should have responsibility for selecting its own mix of public and private goods. Decision making by this homogeneous subset will contribute to allocational efficiency. The transfer of decision authority to the subset will be a movement toward Pareto optimality.[10]

Conventional economic theory also suggests that in defining the spatial dimensions for the appropriate subset, attention must be paid to economies of scale. In the provision of local public goods and services it is important to capture such where they exist. Unfortunately, the empirical research that is available suggests that scale economies are neither uniform among local government functions nor uniform among jurisdictions.[11] It is most difficult to move from the conceptual generalizations to empirical findings that are helpful in delineating the appropriate area for local government goods and service delivery.

In the real world the local jurisdiction, left to its own initiative, makes expenditure and tax decisions that have consequences, and they may be good or bad, on other jurisdictions. In short, local decisions generate externalities. With economic growth and urbanization society becomes more interdependent, and the volume of externalities increases. At some point this becomes visible to the citizenry, interest groups, and program managers in bureaucracies. The externality becomes a political issue, and the previous concept of what is in the national interest or of what may be left in state or local hands is redefined. Over time, perceptions of what is national and what is local necessarily change.

The grant-in-aid thus becomes the great device for fiscal accommodation in a federal system. The "national benefit" portion of any program should, ideally, be supported by the national government, the "state benefit" portion by the states, and the "local benefit" portion by local governments. This is quite satisfactory from a conceptual standpoint, but unfortunately the operational content in this proposition is minimal. It is not possible to measure with any accuracy the proportions of national, state, and local benefit; they surely vary not only among programs but also within complex programs such as health or urban transportation.

The national-state-local benefit approach to grants also encounters difficulty because of fiscal disparities, as it carries with it the implication that the jurisdiction that enjoys the benefit should also be the jurisdiction that imposes the taxes to pay for such benefits. Unfortunately, the fiscal disparities among states, among substate regions, and between the central city and outside central city make fiscal concerns equal in significance to the appropriate attribution of benefits. This is the current situation in elementary and secondary education. The fiscal disparities among school districts within a state have generated strong pressure for state fiscal assumption, and over the next decade it is inevitable that a large number of states will move in this direction.

Jurisdictional externalities are thus at the center of the difficulties with federalism. Fiscal disparities, the practice of fiscal mercantilism, and exclusionary land-use regulations are either a reflection of jurisdictional externalities or represent the local welfare-maximizing efforts of jurisdictions (usually suburban) that are in a position to spill out their costs and spill in some benefits.

The counterpart concern of political scientists is local government fragmentation, particularly in urban areas.[12] Such fragmentation perpetuates the possibility of jurisdictional externalities and prevents the capture of economies of scale if they exist. And this is one of the serious liabilities of general revenue sharing. It has undoubtedly frozen the structure of local, fragmented government for the foreseeable future.[13]

If the existing patterns of local government fragmentation and consequent externalities are accepted as continuing reality, it follows that grants-in-aid should contribute to the equalization of fiscal resources among jurisdictions. Thus grant patterns should be redistributive—jurisdictions that are poor relative to their needs should get more. The fact that "poverty" and "needs" are difficult to define with precision should not preclude public policies that can move in this direction.

The economists' generalized concepts in terms of benefits, externalities, disparities, economies of scale, and jurisdictional equity are very often limited in their application, but are at least addressed to the appropriate issues in a system of fiscal federalism. To turn from these normative prescriptions to the positive research that economists and political scientists have done is to discover that a few, but only a few, useful generalizations have emerged.

Much of this research has been concerned with grant-in-aid impacts and response patterns. Conceptualization of impacts and responses is reasonably adequate.[14] The difference between income effects and substitution effects can be specified. For response patterns grants-in-aid may be *neutral*—that is, the grantee government spends additionally on a program the incremental amount of the grant. The grant response may be *stimulative*—more is spent in total than the amount of the grant, and the recipient government taxes additionally for program support from its own resources. The third response pattern is *substitutive*—the grantee may substitute the grant moneys for its own tax resources, thus reducing local tax rates. Or it may shift expenditures to support a nonaided program. A grant for health, particularly over a period of years, may actually end up as additional expenditure on streets and roads if a local government prefers streets and roads to health. This very real possibility diminishes the force of the argument that grants, particularly federal-local categoricals, are a serious distortion of local preferences. Budget officers and mayors possess great ingenuity in reshuffling the budget over time to accord with both local preferences for tax payments and that mix of budget expenditures that is deemed appropriate for the community.

Out of the large body of empirical work that has been done on grant-in-aid response patterns in the past decade a few generalizations have emerged.[15] First, categorical grants appear to be more stimulative than block grants. Second, block grants initially appear to stay within the block. The partial consolidation of health grants in 1966 seems to have led to some shifting among health program categories, but to less substitution of other programs for health programs. Third, general revenue sharing—the most significant of block grants—appears to be most likely to elicit a tax reduction response which, for 1972 and 1973, probably amounted to from 20 to 40 percent of state and local shares.[16] Fourth, in the field of education grants, which has probably been the most closely examined, the stimulative effects of the grant are much stronger in the suburbs, where preferences for education run high, than in the central city, where program needs in areas other than education will frequently divert resources to non-education local government service provision.

The attempts to untangle the response patterns to general revenue sharing will occupy the attention of students of public finance for some time to come. Long-range and large-scale efforts to monitor the outcomes are already well established, as in the Brookings Institution, and it is safe to predict that several dozen doctoral dissertations will be written on this subject in the universities. Those who engage in this kind of research will be able to describe what governments receive how much, and this information will be classified and reclassified by population size, region, and type of government, with appropriate cross sections and time series. But researchers will never be able to determine what general revenue sharing funds are used for, or whether general revenue sharing did, in fact, bring tax reduction or discourage special district financing. Analytic tools are not adequate to answer such questions.

On the basis of the first two-year experience little has been learned that permits a projection of response patterns over the next three years or response patterns if general revenue sharing should continue to be funded over the decade. It appears likely that the states utilized a good part of their one-third for the support of elementary and secondary education by way of state aid. Some states, by virtue of revenue sharing and an inflation that has helped their tax receipts, had surpluses in 1973. These surpluses, however, appear to have largely evaporated in 1974.[17] The large cities appear to have devoted the first two-year funds to meet their crucial operating and maintenance expenditure pressures; smaller cities apparently invested their proceeds in capital equipment. Many jurisdictions, under current pressures for property tax reduction, either held the line or reduced levies on property. But this limited experience, as suggested above, provides little guidance as to what will happen in the future, particularly in light of the uncertainty about the impact of special revenue sharing and uncertainty about the state of the economy.

REVISIONISM

The possibilities for rational restructuring of intergovernmental transfers will be determined, first of all, by what happens to the national economy and hence to federal revenue. If inflation can be contained within more reasonable limits and if unemployment can be brought closer to the magic number of 4 percent, and if the petroleum shortage does not curtail both employment and income, and if the military budget can somehow be stabilized, then the federal fiscal picture will ease sufficiently to permit a restructuring of grants-in-aid with some new money. These are all very big "ifs," and it would be most foolish to imagine that there will be an easy return to the happy fiscal scene of 1964–65.

Nevertheless, let it be assumed that there is a bit more federal fiscal freedom than is now the case or is believed to be the case by the federal establishment. In these happy circumstances there are three sets of policies to be worked out in a coordinated way. These would embrace general revenue sharing, block grants, *and* categoricals.

General revenue sharing would be retained and expanded. The amount of appropriations should certainly be tied, as was originally proposed by Heller-Pechman, and also by the Nixon administration, to the personal income tax base. This would protect states and local governments from the erosion of federal dollars through inflation and provide the flexible and expanding source of revenue that was the original intent of GRS. As the statute now stands, states and local governments will get fewer dollars in real terms in 1976 than they are now receiving. The linkage with the personal income tax base should be set at a rate that would start off in 1977 with about $10 billion of general revenue sharing. This would not appear to be an unrealistic number.

There are other ways to tidy up the statute. The 7.7 percent undercount of the black population in the 1970 census is an obvious inequity, as it works against large central cities. To overcome the present mismatch between governmental responsibility and the receipt of revenue sharing funds, it might be provided that unless a local government unit has responsibility for taxation of at least $10 per capita, its share should revert to the pool of funds for local distribution within a state. This reform, at least, would eliminate payments to New England counties and Middle Western townships that are governmentally insignificant. Conversely, the 145 percent ceiling limitation should certainly be removed. This works against the larger cities that have consolidated government structures, such as New York City, Philadelphia, and Denver.

Another attractive possibility is to reduce the states' share from one-third to one-fourth and to channel the saved funds to the larger cities. The continued failure to recognize the importance of large cities, both in terms of their needs and in terms of the external benefits that they provide to their regions and to the nation, is little short of disgraceful. In a reasonably well-articulated system of intergovernmental transfers the needs of the large cities would certainly have high priority. Similarly, there appears to be no good reason to retain state authority to revise the local distribution formula. As long as so many state governors and state legislatures are immune to a concern for the welfare of cities, they cannot be trusted to come up with a more equitable formula.

The second set of policies must be directed toward grant consolidation. This can take two forms—Congressional action on the remaining areas proposed for special revenue sharing—transportation and education—and/or the extension of authority to the President to initiate the consolidations.

Thus far the Congress has rejected the approach to educational grant consolidation that was proposed in the Better Schools Act and has thus far not seriously examined special revenue sharing for transportation. The new legislation for mass transit that was adopted in December 1974 will not facilitate this approach to grant consolidation. It will, in fact, complicate the possibilities for special revenue sharing for transportation.

It might be a good idea to pause for a few years in both education and transportation until the administrative and program experiences with special revenue sharing for manpower and community development have been examined and tested. It should be possible to learn something from the experiences of many governments, including the federal government, with program budgeting. The mistake that has been repeated time and again is to insist that program budgeting should be government-wide at the outset. Then it bogs down. It should be possible to introduce program budgeting, in any government, department by department, and build on experience. It is also possible that experiences with special revenue sharing in manpower and community development will provide a basis for appropriate legislation for education and transportation.

The second route—Presidential authority—raises once again the dangers of overcentralization in the Executive Office. But given the interplay of interest groups on Congressional subcommittees, there appears to be no way to consolidate grants except by extending authority to the President to do so, subject, of course, to Congressional authority to veto the Presidential action. Thus far special revenue sharing has reduced the number of grant programs by about 50, leaving perhaps 950 categorical grants. Opinions will differ widely on the program areas that are the best candidates for consolidation, and no attempts at generalization will be made here.

To prescribe an appropriate role for the categoricals is the most difficult of all. The resolution adopted at the 1973 conference of the International City Management Association points in the right direction. After expressing major support for block grants, ICMA went on to assert:

> . . . categorical grants are desirable when national priorities are at stake and state, local and private funding is scarce or unavailable. Or when the problems or matters being addressed occur only in a relatively small number of communities or when the political risks are too high for more responsive local or state government to bear.

The last sentence of this resolution is crucial—"when the political risks are too high. . . ." As noted above, the contemporary middle-class revolt against the poor is a political fact of life. Mayors are under the greatest of pressure to divert resources from the inner city to middle-class neighborhoods on the very plausible ground that the middle class must be favored to retard its exodus to the suburbs. Mayors cannot run against the tide, but they can still do a great deal for the inner city, not only by continuing to mention the problems from time to time but also by pressing for federal categorical dollars for the poor. And this means food stamps, school lunches, child care, and another half-dozen poverty-directed programs. Unless and until a reasonably adequate income maintenance program is adopted, the subsidies in kind will continue to be very important in improving the real income position of the poor. The justification for continuing propoor categoricals is not administrative efficiency or efficiency in terms of resource allocation. The justification is equity.

Restructuring fiscal federalism to embrace a coordinated system of general revenue sharing, block grants, and categoricals is not an easy task. The costs of agreement have run high and will continue to run high.

NOTES

1. Charles L. Schultze *et al. Setting National Priorities: The 1973 Budget* (Washington: Brookings, 1972), pp. 402–405.

2. Data from *The Budget of the United States Government, Fiscal Year 1975* (Washington: Government Printing Office, 1974) p. 326.

3. In 1972 the Metropolitan Studies Program, Maxwell School, Syracuse University, conducted a study of local government expenditures in New York State for the Temporary Commission on the Powers of Local Government (the Wagner Commission). As a part of the study, local government expenditure growth rates and personal income growth rates were projected from the 1965–70 experience. Carrying linear projections to an extreme, it may be concluded that by Jan. 10 in the year 2010, all personal income in New York State would be exhausted by local government expenditure. There would be no remaining resources for the federal government, the state government, or personal consumption expenditure.

4. The growth of some of the pro-poor categorical grants, such as food stamps, supplemental security income, and social security payments, will make the integration of income maintenance with the categoricals even more complicated than was the case in 1972. An analysis of the crosscurrents in federal legislation and administrative behavior that simultaneously move against the poor in one area and toward the poor in another lies far outside the scope of this paper. Why have we had more food stamps and less in funds for child care, for example?

5. The classic statement of the "didn't work" criticism has reappeared in Edward C. Banfield, *The Unheavenly City Revisited* (Boston: Little, Brown, 1974).

6. For further examination of the "willingness" issue see Jesse Burkhead and Jerry Miner, *Public Expenditure* (Chicago: Aldine-Atherton, 1971), pp. 280–81.

7. The literature on general revenue sharing is abundant. A good survey of the issues is contained in Edward R. Fried *et al., Setting National Priorities: The 1974 Budget* (Washington: Brookings, 1973), pp. 266–89. For an examination of both administrative and fiscal issues and a specific study of the Rural Development Act of 1972, see American Society for Public Administration, *The Administration of the New Federalism: Objectives and Issues* (Washington: ASPA, September 1973). See also Robert W. Rafuse, Jr., ed., *Proceedings of the Conference on Revenue Sharing Research* (Washington: National Planning Association, 1974).

8. At the local level, noneducation public goods would be less expensive relative to private goods plus public education.

9. Fried *et al., op. cit.,* p. 283.

10. See Wallace E. Oates, *Fiscal Federalism* (New York: Harcourt Brace Jovanovich, 1972), pp. 3–53.

11. Werner Z. Hirsch, *The Economics of State and Local Government* (New York: McGraw-Hill, 1970), pp. 176–84; Donald Phares, "Assignment of Functions: An Economic Framework," in Advisory Commission on Intergovernmental Relations, *Governmental Functions and Processes* (Washington: Government Printing Office, 1974), pp. 119–41.

12. See, for example, Committee for Economic Development, *Reshaping Government in Metropolitan Areas* (New York: CED, 1970).

13. One of the dozens of general revenue sharing bills introduced in the Congress during the years prior to 1972 was proposed by Senator Hubert Humphrey and Congressman Henry Ruess. This proposal, if adopted, would have required the states to develop plans for local government reorganization as a condition for participation in revenue sharing proceeds. It was not seriously considered by either Ways and Means or Senate Finance Committees.

    For a discussion of the implications of this freezing of governmental structure, see A. K. Campbell and Judith Dollenmayer "Governance in the Metropolitan Society" in Amos H. Hawley and Vincent P. Rock (eds.) *Metropolitan America in Contemporary Perspective* (New York: Halsted Press Division of John Wiley and Sons, 1975), pp. 355–83.

14. See, for example, Oates, *op. cit.,* pp. 65–118; Alan Williams, *Public Finance and Budgetary Policy* (London: Allen & Unwin, 1963), pp. 171–80; and George F. Break, *Intergovernmental Fiscal Relations in the United States* (Washington: Brookings, 1967), pp. 62–165.

15. See, for example, Seymour Sacks and Robert Harris, "The Determinants of State and Local Government Expenditures and Intergovernmental Flows of Funds," *National Tax Journal,* March 1964, pp. 75–85; and Alan K. Campbell and Seymour Sacks, *Metropolitan America* (New York: Free Press, 1967), chaps. 3–5.

16. Edward M. Gramlich and Harvey Galper, "State and Local Fiscal Behavior and Federal Grant Policy," *Brookings Papers on Economic Activity,* No. 1, (1973), pp. 15–58.

17. See "State and Local Fiscal Position," *Survey of Current Business,* November 1974, pp. 5–7.

Comment: Redefining the New Federalism

Norman Beckman

The paper by Jesse Burkhead develops an important thesis, namely the need for a strengthened three-part approach to intergovernmental fiscal relations: improved general revenue sharing, block grants, and categorical grants. His appraisal of "New Federalism" trends is somewhat pessimistic, pressing me to become an optimistic commentator. The overall trend in grants-in-aid has not been cut back, but rather has increased to some $52 billion in fiscal year 1975. The largest increases within this total are not particularly biased against poor or minority groups, but are, rather, made up of personal beneficiary programs—social security; unemployment payments; veterans' benefits; welfare for the aged, blind, and disabled; and food stamps. In short, the grant-in-aid system, as we know it, is not particularly responsive to rapid changes in Executive Branch ideology. It is impossible to unwind the system. At best, Presidents can, in judo-like fashion, use the momentum of the system to slightly change its direction. Impoundments of federal funds to the point where programs are imperiled may well have been eliminated by a passage of the Congressional Budget and Impoundment Control Act.

The grant-in-aid work continues to be dynamic. Welfare reform is *not* "a very dead issue." New block grant proposals for income maintenance are currently being developed in the Congress and by the administration. Separate aids for low- and moderate-income families in such program areas as housing, food stamps, welfare, and Medicaid are providing a budgetary and political base for the replacement of these activities by a comprehensive family assistance program.

Professor Burkhead's reference to current backward steps, from the efforts of the 1960s to devise a national urban policy, might be debated. It is true that much of the assistance, the new communities program, and the Congressional declaration on national urban growth policy in the 1970 Housing and Urban Development Act were individual efforts to deal with urban problems but they were done in the context of an overall policy. The current administration's thrust to decentralize, though revenue sharing, thereby giving greater discretion to state and local officials, is a change in direction. Neither approach can be characterized as a significant movement toward a coordinated national urban policy.

"New Federalism" does have more to point to than simply general revenue sharing and 10 regional councils. Both these activities and others that might be cited are essentially nonpartisan in nature. These include the Intergovernmental

179

Personnel Act; the decentralization of authority in administration of over 90 grant programs; the growth in "701" comprehensive planning assistance grants (including support for improving the management capability of state and local governments); the A-95 review and comment procedures at the state and regional level; integrated grant administration; several special revenue sharing proposals and enactments; the reduced processing time of federal applications; and public service employment.

The critique given in this paper to the existing general revenue sharing program is especially incisive. The first results of the ongoing Brookings Institution evaluation of revenue sharing confirms the need for greater equity in the allocation of funds. The majority of the states reported surpluses in 1973. The reverse of this is true for our larger central cities. All of this argues for improvement in the distribution arrangements when amendments to revenue sharing are considered. Given the range of reforms to general revenue sharing offered in Burkhead's paper, it may be useful to summarize the range of criticisms of the program to date. In a number of cases, legislative proposals have been introduced to deal with one or more of the specific criticisms.

- There is no federal surplus available to share with state and local units of government for revenue sharing purposes.
- There is some question whether state and local governments still have as pressing a financial need as when general revenue sharing was first recommended, and whether there is, therefore, any justification for continuing this program beyond its expiration date of December 31, 1976.
- Critics argue that without strict federal supervision and control state and local governments are not using the shared revenues for the most urgent needs of their citizens.
- It is contended by some that general revenue sharing, rather than representing new money from the federal government to states and localities as was promised by the Nixon administration when its proposals were being considered, actually has supplanted, rather than supplemented, categorical aid programs.
- It is asserted that federal revenue sharing violates an important principle of good governments—that the authority to collect taxes should not be separate from the authority to spend these revenues.
- It is argued that the Office of Revenue Sharing does not have an adequate staff to effectively monitor use of general revenue sharing funds by state and local governments and, in particular, to determine whether the antidiscrimination provision incorporated in the State and Local Fiscal Assistance Act of 1972 has been violated.
- Complaints have been voiced about the formulas contained in the general revenue sharing law which govern the amount distributed to nearly 39,000 state and local governing units.
- Some cite the difficulty of getting accurate and up-to-date statistical data

from the Bureau of the Census upon which to base revenue sharing allocations.

- The complaint has been made that there is not enough citizen participation at the local level in the decision-making process.
- It is contended that the general revenue sharing legislation fails to promote a strong federal system of government.
- The complaint is made that there are too many federal "strings" or restrictions incorporated in the general revenue sharing legislation, particularly in view of the relatively small amount of money which is spread so thinly among nearly 39,000 state and local governing units.
- Some are critical that the general revenue sharing program is funded by means of permanent appropriations rather than via the normal appropriations process.
- There is criticism that the general revenue sharing program is limited to a five-year period, and hence creates some uncertainty among recipient governments about the future availability of this assistance.
- There is criticism that this program is not adequately funded by the federal government to meet the need of states and, in particular, that of our large cities.
- There is criticism of the fact that adjustments are made from time to time by the Office of Revenue Sharing in the amounts disbursed to state and local governments which may require some refunding of allotments or reduction in future allocations.
- There is criticism that only units of general government qualify for this assistance, while special districts such as school districts, special utility districts, sewerage districts, etc., are excluded from the benefits of this legislation.

These will provide the grist for congressional deliberations on extension of revenue sharing in 1976. Reform of intergovernmental fiscal relations in general and of the State and Local Fiscal Assistance Act of 1972 in particular is worthy of further studies—a task complex enough to employ all of the interdisciplinary skills of the Maxwell School.

Comment: The Distributional Impact of Revenue Sharing

Michael Wasylenko

The purpose of this comment is to point out some of the possible interstate, interjurisdictional, and interpersonal equity effects of revenue sharing. There are four provisions in the revenue sharing allocation formulas that may discourage redistribution of funds from wealthier to poorer families. The first is the rewarding of tax effort, which biases the distribution toward states with more income-elastic tax structures, and therefore probably against states where local governments bear the major revenue-raising responsibility.

The second is the pass-through provision; *i.e.,* one-third of the funds remain with the state government, and the remaining two-thirds are passed through to local units within the state. Fixing the same proportion to be passed through for all states does not take into account the substantially diverse fiscal responsibilities among states.

A third feature is the floor and ceiling provisions that require that every local government unit must receive at least 20 percent, but not more than 145 percent, of the statewide average local government revenue grant. This provision arbitrarily fixes a ceiling on the amount of diversity in fiscal need that will be accommodated.

Fourth, the allocation of funds among localities within a state includes a tax effort provision. This provides an inducement for localities to raise tax effort with regressive taxes in order to obtain more revenue sharing funds, which runs counter to improvement of interpersonal equity.

These provisions, together with the tax effort reward in the interstate distribution formulas,[1] combine to create various interstate, interjurisdictional, and interpersonal distributional impacts. Although the distributional impacts of these provisions are not easily separated—there is much overlap and simultaneity—they will be treated separately here for conceptual ease.

Consider first the issue of tax effort and the interstate distribution. Because the allocation formula includes a tax effort reward, states relying on relatively elastic taxes, such as income and sales taxes, will have a higher "built-in" increase in tax effort than will states where the more inelastic taxes dominate the revenue structure.[2] This result introduces a bias in favor of heavily state-government-financed fiscal systems, since the state governments which assume a relatively heavy fiscal responsibility would rely on the more elastic sales and income taxes, while states in which local governments bear the major portion of the fiscal responsibility will tend to rely more heavily on the inelastic property tax.

In sum, the allocation of revenue sharing funds would appear to penalize states where local governments bear the larger portion of fiscal responsibilities, with the penalty being particularly severe in a period of inflation. While such a bias may be desirable in the longer run in forcing less reliance on the property tax financing, in the short run it may divert revenue sharing funds away from needy local governments.

The tax effort feature, when combined with the pass-through provision, may create a dual bias against states where local governments bear a heavier fiscal responsibility within the state.[3] Arbitrarily fixing the pass-through requirements at one-third state and two-thirds local does not distinguish between states in which localities bear the major fiscal responsibility and those in which heavier use is made of state financing. The policy recommended here is not to eliminate tax effort rewards or the pass-through provisions, but to adjust the formulas to recognize the wide interstate variance in the division of fiscal responsibility between states and their local governments. One possibility might be to make the state and local shares flexible depending on state characteristics, *i.e.*, to allocate more than one-third to state governments having more than the median level of fiscal responsibility, and more than two-thirds to local governments where they bear more than the median level of fiscal responsibility within a state.

A third distributional issue concerns interjurisdictional and interpersonal disparities within states. The 20 and 145 percent floor and ceiling provisions on revenue sharing ensure that all localities obtain some funds, but serve to dampen the maximum redistributional impact of revenue sharing. The 145 percent ceiling may be defended as a guard against inequitable comparisons of intrastate tax effort—a factor which affects the intrastate distribution. Because central cities often have a large nonresidential property tax base, and to the extent that the property tax is shifted forward onto the prices of products consumed by residents of other areas, the central city is able to export substantial portions of its property tax. Under these conditions, the real tax effort of the central city is overstated. Hence the ceiling may serve to mitigate against the overstatement of the tax burden on city residents. Still, the ceiling is arbitrary, and the ability to export taxes does vary widely among cities. Perhaps a better alternative to the 145 percent ceiling is a separate revenue sharing amount for distribution among large central cities. Such a provision would substantially increase the equalization potential of the intrastate distribution of revenue sharing funds.

Interpersonal inequity may also be fostered by revenue sharing distribution formulas. The two-thirds local share is allocated among local governments using the Senate formula. If a locality relying heavily on the regressive property tax[4] attempts to increase its allocation share by raising taxes, then the effect is to increase the interpersonal inequity of the already regressive local tax system. The effect also operates on an interstate level if states with regressive tax structures raise their tax effort to increase revenue sharing funds.

These four effects do, at least in theory, have unfavorable equity effects. The magnitude of such effects is an empirical question, and one that has not yet been adequately studied.[5]

NOTES

1. There are two formulas (Senate and House) which the states may choose between according to which gives them more funds. The Senate formula is multiplicative, and the terms are state tax effort, state population, and state per capita income. The House formula is additive and includes these three terms as well as urbanization and extent of state use of an income tax. In 1973, 31 states used the Senate formula (59 percent of the population resides in these states), and 19 states used the House formula (41 percent of the population).

2. The elasticities of the income, sales, and property taxes range from 1.5 to 1.8, 0.9 to 1.05, and 0.7 to 1.1 respectively; see Advisory Commission Intergovernmental Relations, *State and Local Finances: Significant Features, 1967-1970* (Washington, November 1969), p. 64.

3. Of course, the reverse is also possible; *i.e.*, states in which relatively heavy financing responsibility is at the state level would be penalized by the fixed pass-through provision.

4. A "new view" challenges the traditional concept of a regressive property tax. See Peter M. Mieszkowski, "The Property Tax: An Excise Tax or a Profits Tax?" *Journal of Public Economics*, April 1972, pp. 73-97; and Dick Netzer, "The Incidence of the Property Tax Revisited," *National Tax Journal*, December 1973, pp. 515-35.

5. One notable exception is Charles J. Goetz, "Federal Block Grants and the Reactivity Problem," *Southern Economic Journal*, July 1967, pp. 160-5.

9. The Implications of Local Government Reform: Efficiency, Equity, Cost, and Administrative Dimensions

Roy W. Bahl and
Alan K. Campbell

The metropolitan fiscal problem is for most metropolitan areas severe. The imbalance between central city expenditure needs and public resources available to meet these needs and the disparity in service levels and tax burdens between cities and their suburbs are large and appear to be growing. Since the early warnings about an urban fiscal problem in the fifties, scholars have recognized that a major contributing factor is a fragmented assignment of financial responsibility (both intrametropolitan and state-local) which effectively prohibits an allocation of public resources according to service needs. In recent years the problem has been accentuated by cost pressures resulting from the success of public employee unions and inflation. There is little doubt that it will continue to worsen.

The response to this problem has been varied, and at one time or another initiative for change has been taken by all levels of government. Through the fifties, there was still some population growth, considerable construction activity, and a growth in service sector jobs in most central cities, and hence some income elasticity to the local property tax. Assessment improvements and discretionary rate changes helped to hide the gradually deteriorating fiscal position of many large cities. In the fifties and particularly in the sixties, local resources were augmented by a proliferation of federal and state aid programs and increased fund allocation under both.[1]

In the sixties, some central city governments diversified their tax structures and turned more heavily to local sales and income taxes in an effort to increase revenues. Moreover, there were a number of government reform measures designed to capture regional tax bases and to provide services on an area-wide basis, *e.g.*, the creation of special districts, some service consolidations, and a

185

baker's dozen metropolitan governments. A slowing of the rate of increase in local nonproperty tax revenues and restrictions on increased discretionary tax actions in the late sixties resulted in a trend toward increased state government involvement through direct assumption or increased aids.[2]

Federal revenue sharing picked up a fraction of the continuing shortfall of urban government resources in the early seventies. Still, cities continue to face severe financing constraints, which have been compounded by inflation-induced cost pressures. In very recent years city governments have resorted to increasing use of financial management "gimmicks" to improve their short-term cash flow position. The most prominent of these are the heavy use of short-term debt (*e.g.*, revenue anticipation notes) and the underfunding of retirement system programs. Most recently, having exhausted all other possibilities, city governments have been turning to their last resorts, reducing public programs, postponing capital expenditures, and finally laying off public employees.

If one accepts the thesis that public sector output is proportional to the amount of public employment, the seriousness of these last-resort actions is underscored.[3] The implication is an absolute deterioration of central city services and additional central city decline. Further reform is imperative—the issue is the direction which the new reforms will or should take. Whatever that might be, it must address the problem of central city decline by dealing with the twin issues of intrametropolitan fiscal disparities and the functional overburden of local governments.

The purpose of this paper is to pull together the conventional wisdom about four likely types of reform for the next decade: direct state government assumption, increased state and/or federal aids to local governments, the creation of metropolitan governments, and metropolitan decentralization or neighborhood government. In each case we are concerned with the effect which the reform would have as compared to the existing structure of urban government financing. Direct state government assumption refers to the state governments' assuming complete responsibility for financing certain functions; concurrent administrative centralization is not a necessary but nonetheless a highly likely ingredient in the state assumption alternative. Increased state aid means the enlarging of the size of the existing state-to-local grant system, with no changes in allocation formulas. Metropolitan government refers to any form of consolidating general-purpose local governments, and decentralization refers to the creation of neighborhood-level governments which have some discretion over expenditure composition and level.

Our concern is with five implications of such reforms: interjurisdictional and interpersonal *equity* effects, technical and economic *efficiency* effects, the long- and short-run *cost* effects, possibilities for *planning coordination,* and *political feasibility* for effective implementation. Our intent with respect to such evaluation is modest. We plan only to outline the basic issues, to survey current thinking on these issues in terms of the existing body of relevant literature, and to suggest what we see as major gaps in knowledge and future research needs.

Our approach to government reform differs from that taken in the excellent ACIR series on the proper assignment of functions[4] in that we are concerned with evaluating particular changes, whereas their interest is with how functions may be "best" assigned between levels of governments. Hence, while their conclusions include guidelines for optimal actions,[5] ours will relate to the possible effects of changing from one government form to another.

EFFICIENCY EFFECTS

Two kinds of efficiency effects are relevant in studying the implications of government reform: economic efficiency and technical efficiency. Economic efficiency is a market concept; in the private sector, an individual allocates his income efficiently if he divides his consumption between every pair of goods such that the ratio of their marginal utilities to him is exactly equal to their price ratio. When all individuals reach this position, the outcome is "Pareto-optimal"; any reallocation will make at least one person worse off in terms of an "efficiency" or "welfare" loss.[6]

There is an economic efficiency analogy for the local public sector which involves defining maximum efficiency as occurring when *each* individual allocates his income between public and private goods according to his relative preference for public goods and the relative price of public goods. However, because of the nonexclusion feature of public goods, such allocative efficiency is not generally possible. Every person is bound to accept the level of services offered by the government. Hence, if there are no externalities, the existence of a government always results in an efficiency loss, and the larger is the government and the more diverse are citizen preferences, the greater the loss.[7] Carried to its logical extreme, maximum efficiency in the no-externality case may be obtained where there is one local government for every different set of public-private preferences, *i.e.*, for every person. In the more realistic case where public good externalities do exist, this argument for small government breaks down, and larger units which can recognize and capture spillover effects may produce higher levels of welfare. In terms of the popular arguments for government reform, economic efficiency gains and/or losses are referred to as the gains and/or losses from increased and/or decreased local autonomy.

Technical efficiency, on the other hand, refers to the relationship between government costs per person and the number of people in the government jurisdiction. The popular notion is that per resident costs decline with an increase in the number of residents covered by the government jurisdiction, so that technical efficiency gains are a result of economies of scale. Certainly there is much intuitive appeal to the scale economy argument. When one larger government replaces many smaller governments, there are bound to be savings from the elimination of duplication of services, and with increased size may come a greater possibility for capital-labor substitution and, therefore, cost savings. On the other hand, many public functions are of the direct service type, characterized by high labor intensity, and it is difficult to see how increased size could result in cost savings from capital-labor substitution. And, of course, the antithesis of the elimination-of-service-duplication argument is that larger governments will result in larger and more costly bureaucracies. Finally, there is the possibility that there exist pecuniary diseconomies of scale *i.e.*, that as government size rises, so does public employee specialization and the strength of the public employee unions, so that wage rates are bid up to a higher level.

There is little agreement in the literature about the existence or nonexistence of scale economies in the provision of local public services. Since there is not a generally accepted proxy for public sector output, most positive findings of scale economies are based on statistical results which show a negative relationship between population size and per capita expenditures. There are great statistical and theoretical problems with interpreting such results as showing scale economies, and about as many studies find a negative relationship as find a positive one.[8] If there is any consensus, it is that unit costs probably do decline as population rises for utility-type, capital-intensive services.

The conventional thinking about the effect of urban government reform on these two kinds of efficiency is that as the number of residents of a jurisdiction is increased, there are technical efficiency *gains* and economic efficiency *losses*.[9] For example, in the case of the creation of a metropolitan government, there surely are welfare or local autonomy losses. These losses are greater where the area population is more heterogeneous and, therefore, where public good preferences are more diverse. On the other hand, the larger metropolitan government is more able to capture any scale economies which do exist. Where such technical gains are accomplished depends on the services consolidated. In fact, those services where scale economies probably do exist—water, transportation, electricity, gas and sewage plants—have been consolidated, and there is less reason to expect cost savings from the metropolitanization of the more labor-intensive municipal activities. In any case, cost reductions per se will almost never be observed in the event of metropolitan government; rather, any scale economy benefits will most likely show up as improved area-wide service levels.

From this literature, we conclude that movement to a metropolitan government structure from the present systems may reduce local autonomy and cause economic efficiency losses but will not likely result in substantial technical efficiency gains. Decentralization of service delivery, as in the creation of neighborhood governments, has the opposite effect—there are local autonomy or economic efficiency gains but possibly technical efficiency losses. Moreover, very small units of government may not have the financial resources necessary to overcome the indivisibility impediments to specialization and capital equipment use. Hence, service levels may suffer.

Whether the present system of fragmented government is better or worse than these alternatives on efficiency grounds is uncertain: in terms of economic efficiency it is worse than decentralized government but better than metropolitan government, and in terms of technical efficiency it is better than decentralized government but worse than metropolitan government. Happily, the only reform alternative is not to look for an "optimal size" government along a continuum which ranges from decentralized to metropolitan-sized units. A proposed compromise which partially deals with the apparent contradiction between technical and economic efficiency goals is two-tier government.[10] Under this scheme, "neighborhood" services—those where intrametropolitan preferences vary widely, where externalities are small, and where scale economies presumably are not present—are delivered at the neighborhood level. All other services are delivered at the metropolitan level. In terms of theoretical efficiency considerations, this system is optimal. In practice, the problem remains—which functions (or subfunctions) should be assigned to which level of government on efficiency grounds. In the last analysis, neither kind of efficiency effect has been adequately measured; hence evaluation of the efficiency implications must rest on theoretical reasoning, the specifics of the proposed reform, and the socioeconomic structure of the community.

Of the two reforms directly involving state government—financial assumption or increased state assistance—only financial assumption will have any potential impact on technical efficiency; both may effect economic efficiency. State financial assumption will capture economies of scale, to the extent they exist, if it is accompanied by statewide management of the activity assumed. This might be the case with such activities as transportation, pollution (water and air) control, and other capital-intensive activities.

In the case of economic efficiency, state financial assumption may prevent local maximization of benefits but increase the possibility of statewide maximization. Assume, for example, that full financial responsibility for the education function is assumed by the state government such that the level of education services provided (financed) in any given local area is determined at the state level. To the extent that local preferences for education services differ from state preferences (as translated by the state legislature), there will be a local area welfare loss. If, however, local education services generate a spillout effect—which the legislature can identify—variations in the level of local education services provided may be consistent with the maximum level of state welfare. In sum, whether there are economic efficiency effects associated with state assumption depends on whether public service preferences within the state differ and whether there are statewide externalities associated with the function under consideration which would make it beneficial for the state to manipulate the level at which the service is provided.

Whether the second type of state reform—state financial assistance—has an efficiency effect depends on the type of state aid. Three general kinds of state aid might be considered: unconditional grants, categorical grants, matching grants. An unconditional grant to a local government would have no effect on resource allocation—the community would view it as "extra" resources and would lower taxes or raise expenditures according to the income elasticity of demand for public goods. A categorical, nonmatching grant would likewise have no effect if local resources were completely fungible. However, a matching grant would effect resource allocation. By lowering the price of a unit of public goods, such a grant induces the community to substitute public for private goods because the former are now cheaper (a price or substitution effect) and to spend more in total because overall purchasing power is now greater (an income effect). Whenever a price effect exists, overall welfare is lower than that which would have resulted from an equal-yield nonmatching grant.[11] Again, such distortions may be justified, even guided, by knowledge of externalities.

A final note about the state aid option is that state aids may induce secondary effects. A dollar grant, for example, in the case of a capital function may call forth current maintenance or complimentary expenditures in the grant year and in the future. Similarly, the grant may occasion the initiation of a new program which must be maintained in the future; or a grant may stimulate public employee unions to bid up wage and fringe benefit demands which in turn become permanent obligations to the urban government. All of these reasons support the "high-powered money" thesis about state aids and imply that grants distort local resource allocation to a much greater extent than is usually thought. Justification for this thesis is the simple contention that communities will "do different things" with state grant funds than they will with funds they raised themselves.[12]

No consensus, and few conclusions, may be drawn from this discussion. Though there are two types of efficiency effect which must be considered, technical efficiency is likely to be less effected by either of the state-initiated reforms.

Only some general guidelines may be offered as to a choice between these two. Additional state assistance may be used to augment local resources, through a program of general-purpose grants, if minimum allocation disturbance is a major goal. In the presence of externalities, best efficiency effects may be achieved if service delivery for functions with significant intrametropolitan externalities is assigned to a metropolitan area-wide government and financing responsibility is transferred to the state. In such a case, state financing is better through direct assumption if intrastate preferences are relatively homogeneous and through a state matching grant program if preferences are heterogeneous.

EQUITY EFFECTS

Government structure or financing reforms may be offered as remedial actions for two metropolitan equity problems: (1) tax burden and service benefit disparities between similar families in different jurisdictions and (2) tax burden and service benefit variations among families in different income classes.[13]

Though these equity issues are related—both are concerned with how real income may be redistributed through the public budget—they are affected in different ways by different reforms; hence we treat them separately below.

Interjurisdictional Equity

The stereotype picture of the inequitable distribution of public sector activity in American metropolitan areas is one of poor central cities with low public service levels and high tax burdens, and wealthy suburbs where the reverse is the case.[14] The stereotype is very nearly true for most large metropolitan areas. Public sector output and therefore service levels cannot be compared across jurisdictions, but comparison of city-suburb fiscal disparities verifies the rich suburb-poor city impression. Largely through the work of Seymour Sacks, it has been shown that per capita education expenditures and per capita state education aids are higher outside than inside central cities, and that taxes raised per dollar of income are higher in central cities than in suburbs.[15] Per capita noneducation expenditures and noneducation aids are higher in central cities, reflecting in part the need for cities to service a particularly large poverty population and perhaps to meet the needs of a large suburban commuting population.

In order to evaluate the implications of alternative government reforms, we will argue normatively that reform should at least equalize per capita expenditures and impose equitable tax burdens. Each potential reform will be related to how it improves the present situation with respect to these norms.

The root of the metropolitan disparities problem is a fragmented government structure which separates taxable resource base from expenditure needs. Clearly the creation of metropolitan government, in eliminating jurisdictional boundaries, is capable of eliminating spending and tax burden disparities. Whether service levels are actually equalized depends on the mechanics of the consolidation. Typically, when jurisdictions are amalgamated, wages, benefits, and work rules tend toward equality, and whether service levels are equalized or not depends on whether and how service boundaries are redrawn. For example, in the case of consolidating fire services, there would ideally be a reassignment of firemen and equipment from suburban to central city areas, from richer to poorer central city areas.

Metropolitan decentralization, as a reform of the present system of fragmented government, would do little to improve equity, since it would involve decentralizing government within existing jurisdictional limits. In general, the decentralization argument, under any circumstances, has to do with economic efficiency gains (*i.e.*, more local autonomy) and not with service-level equity.

Increased state assistance may improve interjurisdictional equity if aid formulas are based on need. However, state aids have not been, historically, based on needs and have not tended to be distributed on an equalizing basis. A sharp distinction may be drawn between education and noneducation aids in this respect. Central cities in some states tend to receive less aid because the tax effort provision in the formulas relates only to education tax effort. In fact, overall tax effort is higher in core cities because of the level of noneducation services provided, a phenomenon referred to as municipal overburden. Finally, aid formulas do not always explicitly recognize the higher costs of providing education services to lower-income students.

The hope that increased amounts of state assistance will reduce fiscal disparities rests on the possibility that the formula for aid distribution will be revamped. Since there is little indication that the suburban dominance of state legislatures will lessen, the possibility of such restructuring would appear to be slim.[16]

The other kind of state intervention—direct financial assumption by the state government—may offer better possibilities for equalizing interjurisdictional disparities. State governments may equalize spending levels directly and bypass the legislative process of reforming aid distribution formulas. There are a priori reasons to believe that state assumption will tend to equalize statewide salary schedules, work rules, and performance standards. The impact on service levels, however, has not been carefully analyzed.

Interpersonal Equity

Because so little is known about the distribution of public expenditure benefits across income classes, analysis of the income-distributional effects of government reform is concentrated on the tax side. That is, in considering how various government reforms effect interpersonal equity, we question only what changes in tax structure will occur and how these changes will effect the tax burdens of families at various income levels.

The decentralization of government would not likely have any effect on the distribution of tax burdens, since decentralization plans rarely have provision for significant autonomous tax action by the neighborhood units. Similarly, the creation of metropolitan government, city-county consolidations, and the creation of area-wide special districts do not always result in major tax structure changes. However, by moving financial reliance for some or all urban services to an area-wide tax base, some amount of absolute property tax relief for central city residents may be gained—and if the property tax is regressive, such a move may transfer financing responsibility from lower-income city residents to higher-income suburban residents.

Either direct state assumption or increased state aids will have marked and favorable tax burden equity effects. It is argued that any increment in financing from state tax sources is preferable on equity grounds to an increment from local sources—primarily because the major state revenue sources, sales and income taxes, are more progressive than the local property tax. A recently completed set of case studies on the income-distributional effects of state assumption shows that there are considerable tax burden reductions for the low income in the event of direct state financing—particularly if the state makes heavy use of the personal income tax.[17]

The assumption that the total property tax is regressive has been challenged, and several prominent students of taxation now argue that the residential property tax is borne by owners of capital and therefore is proportional, perhaps mildly progressive. However, this thesis is based on a set of very limiting assumptions (*e.g.,* a nationwide uniform property tax) which have caused other scholars in the field to hold to the conventional thinkings of a regressive property tax.[18]

COST EFFECTS

While the equity and efficiency effects of government reform have been studied intensively—theoretically and empirically—the cost implications of government reforms have not been given adequate attention. Policy makers, on the other hand, are most concerned about cost effects. Somehow, they argue, centralization or decentralization reforms will lower the costs of government. In the paragraphs below, we attempt to ferret out the reasons for expectations of higher or lower costs from government reform and emphasize the difference between the long- and short-run cost effects. We argue that in the short run, *any* reform will tend to increase costs. In the long run, the picture is less clear.

What follows is a kind of differential incidence analysis in which we assess the cost implications of each reform by comparison with the existing system of fragmented government. Note that in some cases this change in government structure would mean elimination of those fiscal characteristics which already exert measurable cost pressure, *e.g.,* a state assistance program with a stimulative effect on local government expenditures.

Our concept of the short run is a one-to-two-year period, or a period long enough for the initial adjustments to be worked out.

State Financial Assumption

State financial assumption of urban responsibilities would have a number of effects on the level of and trend in total expenditures: (1) a shift to a more elastic and more flexible revenue base, (2) centralized control over the collective-bargaining process, (3) shifting public program innovation from the local to the state level, and (4) a "leveling up" of local government services and thereby an increase in total local expenditures. Only the last is primarily a short-term effect.

Revenue Base

Since state tax revenues (primarily sales and income taxes) are more income-elastic than local property taxes, state financial assumption results in a greater overall growth in state-local government resources available. National estimates show the income elasticity of personal income taxes to be between 1.5 and 1.8, sales taxes between 0.9 and 1.05, and local property taxes between 0.7 and 1.1.[19] It would seem to follow that, *cet. par.*, a shift to heavier reliance on state revenue sources would result in a higher long-term expenditure growth rate.

There is further support for the argument that a shift to state resources results in a greater growth in resources available. There is more flexibility at the state than at the local level to make discretionary revenue changes, *e.g.*, to alter the tax structure or to borrow. This is because legal restrictions are less binding on state than on local governments and because local tax changes can be more closely identified with particular elected officials than can state-level changes. The latter implies more willingness to make unpopular tax decisions at the state than at the local level. As a result, increased reliance on state revenues should raise the long-term expenditure growth rate.

A final argument for an upward bias on expenditures is that because of the broader and more productive state revenue base, a greater level of capital spending may result. States will be more willing to take on capital facilities construction and expansion because of the broader revenue base and because of their broader discretionary taxation and borrowing powers. Such capital expenditures have a multiplier effect on total expenditures because they require future maintenance costs, because they may occasion "complimentary" costs (*e.g.*, the construction of a new municipal stadium probably also requires changes in traffic control, street lighting, street widening, bus routing, etc.) and because capital projects usually mean an interest cost in addition to the project costs.[20] While these are untested hypotheses, they seem plausible on *a priori* grounds as reasons for an upward long-term pressure on expenditures.

Centralized Collective Bargaining

Complete state financial assumption of a function would centralize the collective-bargaining process. How this would effect the level of and the long-term growth in expenditures is mostly speculation, since research in the area is thin. On an intuitive basis, there are some reasons to expect *less* cost increment with centralized collective bargaining. State government generally has more of a research orientation than local government and therefore may come to the bargaining table more equipped to assess the long-term revenue implications of union demands. The less precarious cash position of state government may result in less willingness to give up large benefit increments in anticipation of underfunding retirement system programs. Finally, there would seem more possibility for a state than a local government to set a program of public sector wage and benefit increment "guidelines."

In sum, the centralization of collective bargaining would seem to be a factor which has a dampening effect, over the long run, on the level of expenditures.

Program Innovation

One could argue effectively that shifting complete financing responsibility to the state level would reduce local area program innovation. The elimination of such "lighthouse effects" would have two implications: the loss of possible increments in public service levels, and lower costs. The latter occur because innovative programs typically have a high start-up cost, their continuation is typically costly, and they may fail completely or be cut out because of financial constraints.

Expenditure Equalization

In the very short run, state assumption will result in total expenditure increase because of a "leveling-up" effect, *i.e.,* because of equalization of local expenditure disparities at a level near the highest existing level. For example, if the state assumed complete responsibility for a function, it is unlikely that wages, pensions, performance levels, etc., in various local governments would be allowed to remain unequal beyond estimated cost-of-living differentials. Moreover, it is likely that wage rates, pension benefits, work loads, etc., in the low-expenditure districts would tend to rise toward that in the high districts. Reductions in wage rates and benefit levels in the high-paying districts would not occur; employment-level reductions in these districts would be unlikely, as would work load and service performance reductions (*e.g.,* student/teacher ratios, quality of fire department equipment, widening of service district boundaries). Together, these factors would seem to suggest at least a short-term increase in costs.

The cost implications in the long run require analysis of whether, *cet. par.,* there is reason to expect an "equalized" system to result in greater expenditure growth than a locally autonomous system where disparities are allowed. The positive answer is drawn from a model which has the more progressive local units bidding for higher real wage rates, benefits, and service levels and "carrying" the less progressive units along. The negative answer is drawn from a model where the increments gained under a locally autonomous system would have been even greater.

Increased State Aids

There are at least three reasons why one would expect increased state aids to increase the level of expenditures in the long run: the shift to the more elastic state revenue base, the maintaining of local program innovation, and the stimulative effects of state grants. On the other hand, there are indications that current factors are causing state legislatures to vote decreasing budget shares for state assistance.

Increased state aids will result in long-term expenditure increase if state aids are "high-powered" funds, *i.e.,* if there is a stimulative effect associated with state grants-in-aid. There is empirical evidence that such an effect exists, *i.e.,* that on the average a $1 increase in state aid results in a more than $1 increase in expenditures.[21]

State aids to local governments as a percent of total general expenditures of state governments have declined in recent years: from 34.8 percent in 1962, to 29.5 in 1967, to 29.0 in 1972. There are a number of reasons for this trend, a prominent one being the possibility that federal revenue sharing is viewed as a substitute for higher state aids.

Metropolitan Consolidation and Decentralization

Probably most difficult to evaluate in terms of long-term cost implications are intrametropolitan structural reforms such as consolidations or decentralization. In the short run, certainly, either centralization or decentralization will result in a cost increment. In the case of a metropolitan consolidation, costs will rise in the short run because of a "leveling up" effect. In the case of decentralization, the administrative expense associated with the creation of another layer of government and the loss of scale economies lead to the expectation of higher cost.

In the long term, cost implications are not at all clear and remain unresearched. The two most important questions to be answered about the costs of decentralization and centralization at the local level are which form would produce higher state aid levels, and which would produce greater program innovation.

PLANNING DEVELOPMENT

The analysis up to this point has treated the current distribution of residence and economic activities as exogenously determined as a product of private market forces and public policies. However, especially in the case of urban development decisions, both private markets and public policies are influenced by the current local government system. Regulations in such areas as zoning, building codes, and highway and utility location are made by relatively small fragmented jurisdictions seeking their own advantage, and there is no reason to assume that the overall result of this decision system will "improve" the distribution of people and economic activities for the entire community.

One criterion for choosing "improved" distributions relates to the economic costs of development resulting from this system, as well as social costs and the costs resulting from spillovers. One result is the practice of what has become known as fiscal zoning.[22] The purpose of fiscal zoning is to promote land uses which will maximize revenues and minimize service costs. Such practices are clearly made possible by a fragmented decision system which creates a competitive environment in the public sector. Since the public decision system tends to ignore spillover costs and since the competitive environment makes it likely that private decision makers will ignore social costs, it can be argued that the present decision system tends to promote policies that are least desirable from a social point of view. The resulting development pattern is the current suburban spread combined with the inability of most central cities to maintain their economic viability.[23]

Whether a system which permits planning for the entire area of economic and social interdependence, normally the metropolitan area, would create a different distribution of people and economic activities is not easily determined. However, the experience with foreign metropolitan governments, particularly Toronto and London, suggests it might.[24] The current fragmented system makes it impossible for the interdependencies and resulting spillovers to be taken into account in metropolitan development. There is no guarantee that an effective regional government or regional planning system would alter current development patterns—political pressures against a regional focus might be too great—but regional institutions would permit at least the guiding of development.

There is strong evidence that different development patterns would vary economic, social, and personal costs for residents, businesses, and governments in metropolitan areas. The Real Estate Research Corporation, in a study done for the Council on Environmental Quality, the Department of Housing and Urban Development, and the Environmental Protection Agency, attempts to measure cost differences resulting from different development patterns.[25] Assuming developments which have the same population and consume the same amount of land but which provide different residential patterns, the study carefully calculates the different costs and finds that these costs can vary by as much as 50 percent depending on the type development undertaken. The range of development types considered is from the highest-cost community, which is the low-density sprawl which characterizes most suburban development today, to a high-density planned community which is composed of 40 percent high-rise apartments, 30 percent walk-up apartments, 20 percent town houses, and 10 percent clustered single-family homes. To give an example of these cost differences, investment costs for the high-density planned community would be 44 percent below those for the low-density sprawl community, and the high-density planned community would generate about 45 percent less air pollution than the low-density one. In the case of energy and water use, the planned high-density community would save up to 44 percent. In the case of personal costs, the report states:

> These are more difficult to estimate. In general, planning and increased density reduce the amount of time the family members spend traveling to work,

school, etc., and higher density developments typically take less of the resident's time to clean and maintain. There are likely to be fewer traffic accidents with better planning, but crime may increase with higher densities as will various psychic costs which are particularly dependent upon design and planning details.[26]

Either metropolitan government or state assumption of the planning function could make possible area-wide planning. However, the gains from such an area-wide approach are impossible to predict and depend on the decisions such a planning system would make. Nevertheless, a planning system for the area of interdependence could improve both equity and technical efficiency, and its contribution to economic efficiency would depend on the range of the type and size of communities which residents could choose. It seems likely that the variety could be as great as that provided by the current fragmented systems, and probably greater.

POLITICAL FEASIBILITY

In general, public decision making in the United States is incremental. Further, changes produced by public policy are as frequently unanticipated as anticipated. These two characteristics make it unlikely that major overall reform or change in the local governmental system, or even in the participation of state government in the delivery of public services, will be made in a short time period.[27] Rather, change is both gradual and the cumulative result of many decisions often designed to deal with very specific problems.[28] The cumulative result of this piecemeal action may or may not move in the direction of basic change in the governmental system. For example, federal policy since the end of World War II has encouraged dispersion and fragmented metropolitan development through housing and highway policies. It simultaneously, by encouraging planning on a region-wide basis, has made some contribution to creating a region-wide decision-making system.

The primary reason for this nonattention to the overall structure of decision making is the distribution of political power. Altering governmental boundaries at the local level, or the movement of functions from the local to higher levels, inevitably produces political losers. Not only do officeholders suffer a loss of power, and in some instances an actual loss of office, but those interest groups which surround every decision maker are fearful of the uncertainty of a system which moves decision-making power to other individuals or other jurisdictions. The result is that most major efforts of reform have failed. There are exceptions in that there have been a small number of city-county consolidations since the end of World War II. Of 36 city-county consolidations attempted, 10 have been successful, and 26 have failed.

Through analysis of the consolidative efforts Vincent Marando has been able to state a few generalizations about politics of local government reorganization.[29] These include:

1. The higher the city vote turnout relative to the turnout outside the city, the more likely reorganization is to succeed, and vice versa.
2. The nature of the political campaign for reorganization matters, in that grass-roots efforts are more likely than mass-media campaigns to produce a favorable vote.
3. The higher the degree of government fragmentation in the metropolitan area, the less favorable the chances of success.
4. The double-majority requirement that necessitates majorities in both the central city and the outlying jurisdiction is generally fatal to reorganization. If a single majority is stipulated, however, reorganization has a fighting chance.
5. If fiscal (*i.e.*, cost) factors are stressed in a campaign, it is unlikely that the reorganization proposal will be successful. The possibility of new services does not appear to outweigh citizens' anxiety over higher taxation for either city or county voters.
6. A decrease in the possibility of members of the black community winning office in the central cities as a result of organization has, on occasion, negatively affected the likelihood of reorganization.
7. The overall size of the voter turnout, the quality of the research standing behind the proposal, and "get out the vote" campaigns appear to have no effect on the success of reorganization proposals.

Ideological issues often come to play a role in political campaigns for reorganization and normally work against the passage of such proposals. The emergence of ideological issues usually results in the political parties' playing little role in reorganization campaigns. Parties, given their internal divisions and their emphasis on immediate rewards, tend to mute ideological issues. Normally, therefore, they do not participate in reorganization campaigns, and the result is a lessening of the usual moderating role which parties bring to political campaigns.

The greatest opposition to metropolitan reform originally came from the suburbs and the right wing of American politics. The political right long ago decided that the "metro" concept is part of a broad communist plot to weaken American democracy. One publication of this wing of American politics suggested that "perhaps the choice of the word 'metro' is not coincidental as the name for this type of regional government, since the underground railway which connects Moscow with its suburbs is called metro."[30] Recently, black voters have become critical of the concept of metro government. Many black community leaders see this new governmental form as a ruse to dilute black political power just when blacks are attaining significant political influence in a number of cities. Of interest on this point is the change in the black vote in Cleveland between early and later reorganization referenda. As their proportion of central city population grew and the possibility of capturing City Hall became a reality, a majority of blacks in favor of reorganization became a majority against it. There is, however, division within the black community on this issue, and an increasing number have swung around to a favorable attitude to metropolitan government primarily as a result of the fiscal crisis in which many central cities find themselves.[31]

The political feasibility of transferring functions of government from lower to higher levels has not been as carefully studied as the politics of local government reorganization. However, it is likely that it is and will become politically easier than reorganization. Since transfer does not alter local government boundaries, it does not present as great a threat to local government officeholders. Further, the fiscal problems of local governments in general, but particularly of large central cities, have created an environment favorable to reducing the financial obligation of such governments. There is, as a result, a much greater willingness on the part of local public officials to give up a portion of their power in order to maintain the economic viability of their jurisdiction. The willingness of the state to assume additional fiscal responsibility depends on the character of its own fiscal situation as well as the distribution in the state legislature of political power between city, suburban, and rural legislators. The process is likely to be a gradual one that is incremental, with the state perhaps first increasing aid and then, as that aid comes to represent a larger and larger proportion of the total financing of a function, to assume full responsibility for that function.

CONCLUDING REMARKS

It is difficult to generalize about the impact of basic shifts in the responsibilities of the units which make up the current state-local governmental system. The nature of the changes themselves will obviously influence that impact, but since the criteria by which such changes should be judged are not internally consistent, a change may serve one criteria while simultaneously being in conflict with another. In general, it can be argued that a movement to an area-wide governmental system at the local level has the potential for improving technical efficiency and equity while providing the opportunity for a more effective planning system. In contrast, such a change, unless it is carefully designed to include a two-tier system with considerable expenditure autonomy granted to the small-community tier, will decrease economic efficiency. On the whole, it is likely that the first result of a move to a region-wide government will be an increase in cost because of the "leveling up" of services to a quality or factor cost equivalent to that now provided by the jurisdictions providing the highest quality of services.

Many of the same generalizations can be made about state assumption, however, its outcome is in part dependent on whether it involves only the financing of the service, with its administration and mix of activities being determined at the local level, or means an assumption of financing, policy, and administration by the state government. State assumption, like region-wide government, provides opportunities for increasing technical efficiency and improving equity while reducing economic efficiency. Both metropolitan government and state assumption would provide the opportunity for planning decisions which could overcome their economic efficiency disadvantages by making use of decentralized local decision making.

Politically, changes will occur. They will be largely incremental and gradual and will likely move in inconsistent directions. The current fiscal problems of central cities will probably play a larger role in bringing about change than the use of the criteria outlined in this paper. More fiscal problems dictate the use of a broader tax base than current fragmentation permits; movement is therefore likely to be in the direction of regional institutions, state assumption, and increased federal aid.

NOTES

1. Between 1964 and 1970, the number of federal aid programs increased from 400 to 1,000, and total allocations grew from $10,141 million to $23,954 million.
2. Trends in state financial assumption are described in some detail by John Callahan and Ruth Bosek, "State Assumption of Urban Responsibilities: Exception to the Rule or Wave of the Future?" in this volume.
3. The thesis that local government employment is an appropriate proxy for local government output and the implications of this thesis are drawn out in Ronald Ehrenberg, "The Demand for State and Local Government Employees," *American Economic Review,* June 1973, pp. 366–79; and Roy Bahl and Richard Gustely, "Wage Rates, Employment Levels and State and Local Government Expenditures for Health and Education: An Analysis of Interstate Variations," in Selma J. Mushkin, ed., *Services to People: State and National Urban Strategies,* part II, *State Aids for Human Services in a Federal System* (Washington: Georgetown University, Public Services Laboratory, May 1974).
4. Advisory Commission on Intergovernmental Relations, *Substate Regionalism and the Federal System,* vol. IV, *Government Functions and Processes: Local and Areawide* (Washington, 1974), and Advisory Commission on Intergovernmental Relations, *Performance of Urban Functions: Local and Areawide* (Washington, 1963). Particularly the first of these contains an excellent bibliography of related research.
5. The guidelines resulting from the 1963 study, *Performance of Urban Functions,* are reproduced in Roy Bahl and Walter Vogt, "State and Regional Government Financing of Urban Public Services," in this volume.

6. A clear, nonmathematical treatment of consumer equilibrium is given in Charles Ferguson and Charles Maurice, *Economic Analysis* (Homewood, Ill.: Irwin, 1974).

7. This "decentralization" theorem is elaborated in Wallace E. Oates, *Fiscal Federalism* (New York: Harcourt Brace Jovanovich, 1972), chap. 2.

8. One of the more interesting of these statistical cost studies is Werner Hirsch's analysis of "horizontally and vertically integrated" urban public services, "Cost Functions of an Urban Government Service: Refuse Collection," *Review of Economics and Statistics,* February 1965, pp. 87–92.

9. Formal treatments of this issue are contained in Michael Koleda, "A Public Good Model of Governmental Consolidation," *Urban Studies,* June 1971, pp. 103–10; and Yorham Barzel, "Two Propositions on the Optimum Level of Producing Public Goods," *Public Choice,* Spring 1961, pp. 31–7.

10. For discussion of the two-tier concept see Committee for Economic Development, *Reshaping Government in Metropolitan Areas* (February 1970); and Kent Mathewson, ed., *The Regionalist Papers: Toward Metropolitan Unity* (Detroit: Metropolitan Fund, 1974).

11. A good detailed treatment of these effects, in a context of federal grants, is contained in Edward Gramlich, "The Effect of Federal Grants on State-Local Expenditures," in National Tax Association, *Proceedings of the Sixty-Second Annual Conference* (Boston, 1969), pp. 569–92.

12. This possibility is addressed in Michael Kirst, "Reforming Financing of Education: An Issue of Quality of Services or Fiscal Equity," in this volume.

13. A third important equity problem is that of variation in service levels and tax burdens among similar families in the same jurisdiction. Since this problem is not amenable to solution through jurisdictional change, it is not considered further here.

14. A statement of interjurisdictional disparities as a part of the urban fiscal problem is elaborated in Roy Bahl, "Public Policy and the Urban Fiscal Problem: Piecemeal vs. Aggregate Solutions," *Land Economics,* February 1970, pp. 41–50.

15. Advisory Commission on Intergovernmental Relations, *Fiscal Balance in the American Federal System,* vol. II, *Metropolitan Fiscal Disparities* (Washington, 1967); Advisory Commission on Intergovernmental Relations, *Metropolitan Disparities: A Second Reading,* Bulletin 70-1 (January 1970); John J. Callahan and Seymour Sacks, "Central City–Suburban Fiscal Disparity," *City Financial Emergencies* (Washington: ACIR, 1973) app. D; and Seymour Sacks, *et al, City Schools/Suburban Schools: A History of Fiscal Conflict* (Syracuse, N.Y.: Syracuse University Press, 1971).

16. An overview of the equity implications of general revenue sharing is presented in Jesse Burkhead's "Revenue Sharing: New Federalism or New Conservatism?" in this volume.

17. These Urban Observatory case studies are summarized in Roy Bahl and Walter Vogt, "State and Regional Government Financing of Urban Public Services," in this volume.

18. The new view is presented and challenged in "The Property Tax: Progressive

or Regressive?" in *American Economic Review: Papers and Proceedings of the Eighty-Sixth Annual Meeting* (May 1974), pp. 212-36.

19. Advisory Commission on Intergovernmental Relations, *State-Local Finances and Suggested Legislation,* 1971 ed., M-57 (Washington: ACIR, December 1970), p. 212.

20. However, for any given level of borrowing, states' interest costs will tend to be lower because their bond ratings tend to be higher—particularly when compared to large central cities.

21. See, for example, Seymour Sacks and Robert Harris, "The Determinants of State and Local Government Expenditures and Intergovernmental Flows of Funds," *National Tax Journal,* March 1964, pp. 75-85; and Gramlich, *op. cit.* For a similar analysis of the stimulative effects of federal revenue sharing, see Marvin Johnson, "A Discussion and Estimation of the Tax Effort Inducements of General Revenue Sharing," Occasional Paper 19, Metropolitan Studies Program, (Syracuse, N.Y.: Syracuse University, May 1975).

22. Seymour Sacks and Alan K. Campbell, "The Fiscal Zoning Game," *Municipal Finance,* 36, 4 (1964), pp. 140-9.

23. Alan K. Campbell and Seymour Sacks, "Administering the Spread City," *Public Administration Review,* September 1964, pp. 141-52.

24. D. L. Foley, *Governing the London Region* (Berkeley: University of California Press, 1972); Committee for Economic Development, *op. cit.,* pp. 70-82; and Greater London Group, *The Lessons of London Government Reform* (London: London School of Economic and Political Science, 1968).

25. Real Estate Research Corporation, *The Costs of Sprawl: Literature Review and Bibliography, Detailed Cost Analysis, and Executive Summary* (Washington: Government Printing Office, April 1974).

26. *Ibid., Executive Summary,* p. 5.

27. For a historical account of local government efforts in the United States see Alan K. Campbell and Guthrie S. Birkhead, "Municipal Reform Revisited: The 1970s Compared with the 1920s," in this volume.

28. The development and use of one important form of this problem-oriented approach to restructuring, the intergovernmental agreement, is covered in Joseph Zimmerman, "Metropolitan Governance: The Intergovernmental Dimension," and in Robert E. Merriam, "Multipurpose Districts, Modernized Local Governments, and a More Systematic Approach to Servicing Assignments: A Tripartite Strategy for Urban and Rural America," in this volume.

29. Vincent Marando, "The Politics of Metropolitan Reform," this volume.

30. *The Dan Bell Report* (Palm Beach, Fla., Feb. 21, 1958), p. 3.

31. See comments by Mayor Hatcher, of Gary, Ind., in League of Women Voter Education Fund, *Shaping the Metropolis* (Washington: League of Women Voters, 1972), p. 30; and Dale Rogers Marshall, "Metropolitan Government: Views of Minorities," in M. Lowden Wingo, ed., *The Governance of Metropolitan Regions: Minority Perspective* (Washington: Resources for the Future, 1972), p. 26-7.

Index